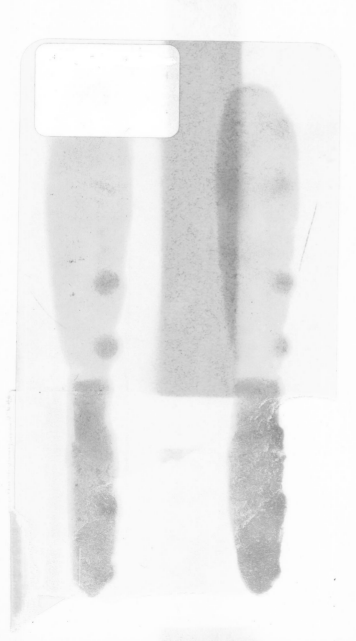

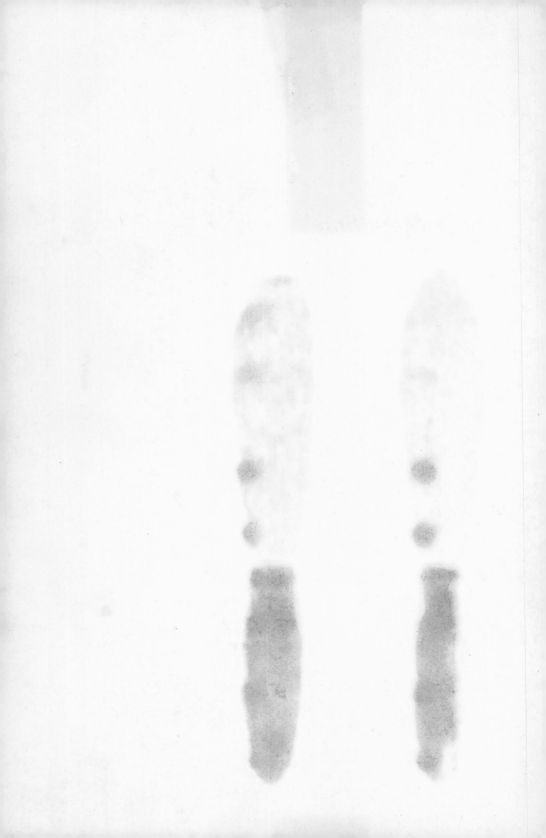

The Marathon

Also by Marc Bloom • *CROSS COUNTRY RUNNING*

THE
MARATHON
WHAT IT TAKES TO GO THE DISTANCE

Marc Bloom

HOLT, RINEHART AND WINSTON • NEW YORK

Published by Holt, Rinehart and Winston,
383 Madison Avenue, New York, New York 10017.

Published simultaneously in Canada by Holt, Rinehart and
Winston of Canada, Limited.

Library of Congress Cataloging in Publication Data
Bloom, Marc, 1947–
    The marathon: what it takes to go the distance.
    Bibliography: p.
    Includes index.
    1. Marathon running. I. Title.
GV1065.B57   796.4'26   80-18859
ISBN Hardbound: 0-03-052476-8
ISBN Paperback: 0-03-059153-8

Portions of chapters 9 and 10 first appeared in *The Runner*
magazine and are reprinted with permission of the publisher.

First Edition

Designer: Helene Berinsky

Printed in the United States of America

10 9 8 7 6 5 4 3 2 1

For Andrea, Allison, and Jamie,
future marathoners

CONTENTS

ACKNOWLEDGMENTS

I wish to thank the following persons for their assistance and cooperation: Jimmy Behr, Will Cloney, Irving Epstein, Marion Epstein, Johnny Miles, Jerry Nason, Kathrine Switzer, and Grete Waitz for allowing me time to interview them; Bernard and Helen Davis for giving me the opportunity to visit them and spend time with their son, Eric; Peter Diamond and John Lucas for lending me books from their sports libraries; Drs. David Costill, William Fink, Richard Schuster, and Seymour Goldstein for trying to find out what makes me tick; Peter Watson and Per Balke for sharing their physiological research; Deborah Mitchell and Mary Billard for tape transcriptions and clerical assistance; and Marian Pickman for her wonderful drawings.

I could not have written this book without the support of my wife, Andrea, and our daughters, Allison (age 8) and Jamie (age 2). They sacrificed a lot to allow me the time—"spare" time I carved out of half-weekends—to work on the manuscript. I only hope I can repay them now that my Sundays are free again.

I would also like to thank George A. Hirsch, publisher of *The Runner*, and Jonathan Z. Larsen, the magazine's first editor, for giving me great responsibilities in the job I'd always dreamed I might someday have.

FOREWORD

I have always enjoyed writing about people and their participation in sports. I am a fan of sports, especially running, and
have spent a good deal of time over the past decade and a half
watching people run, talking to them about it, and then writing about them. For half of this time I have been a runner,
first for my high school track and cross-country teams and
then, after an 8-year moratorium on running, just for myself.
On occasion I have written about my own running, not because I am very good at it but because it has meant a lot to
me and there were things I had to say to the large numbers
of people who had taken up the sport.

As a journalist in pursuit of runners and running, I have
found it interesting and beneficial to use my experiences and
the experiences of others to provide insight into what is by
now quite a grown-up sport. That is part of the framework
I have used in this book about the marathon. I have written,
in part, about people—people who run the marathon, a footrace of 26 miles 385 yards. Some of them are very good at it;
others, like me, are less capable—but no less enthusiastic. I

chose subjects of varying abilities, backgrounds, and ages to help give a complete picture of the sport and to show a number of different approaches to the marathon—one or more of which will hopefully relate to your own experiences.

One major section of the book deals with how the body and mind work under the influence of long-distance running, and it is here that I use myself as an example to explore a bit of the science of the marathon. There is increased professional interest in the psychological ramifications of long-distance running. I have believed for some time that emotional intervention can significantly advance or retard achievement in running, and I discuss this particularly in chapter 5 and touch on it implicitly in other parts of the book.

Additionally, I describe the marathon's leading events, examine its historical origins, and offer an analysis of its current popularity. I have sought to provide a thorough overview of the marathon by covering most of its aspects, some in greater detail than others.

When I began work on this book early in 1979, I was concerned that it would take me away from my own running. And since I believe that I actually do my most cogent thinking about running during my daily workouts, it was important that I not abandon them during this time. Fortunately, I managed to run about 40 miles a week and even to compete, although not in a marathon.

One man I know who did more than his share of running during my temporary abstention from competitive marathoning is Jay Helgerson, an ex-Marine from San Francisco. I spoke with Jay at the 1979 Boston and New York City marathons, and he told me about his progress toward a goal of running a marathon every week for a year. On the third weekend in January 1980, Jay Helgerson ran and finished the Houston Marathon, his fifty-second weekly marathon in a row. On that same weekend I completed the manuscript for this book. I think I know how he felt.

MARC BLOOM
Staten Island, N.Y.
January 1980

PART ONE

A SPORT MATURES

1

THE MARATHON TODAY

The radio alarm wakes Michael Andropolis at 6:43 A.M. Without delay he gets out of bed and begins his morning ritual. His uniform for the day is an old blue suit, a sweatband, a stubbly beard, a troubled yet cocksure look, and a pair of running shoes. In his shabby one-room apartment there is barely enough space for Andropolis to twist and stretch and get the kinks out for another long day's journey into an unwelcome environment. A man could break his neck doing sit-ups in this place. And the room is an ugly mess: a cracked lamp, a cracked mirror (in which to see his cracked life), reading matter strewn about, clothing draped over anything within reach. Ratso Rizzo could do better.

His shoelaces tied securely and his jacket knotted around his waist, Andropolis goes on his way, running through Lower Manhattan past the business district, Chinatown, Little Italy, Greenwich Village, and uptown to the Queensboro Bridge, where, on the way back, he outruns the snarled traffic and is taunted by motorists whom he acknowledges, without breaking stride, with the middle finger of his raised right arm.

Michael Andropolis runs for the better part of two hours that May morning—to the home he shared with his wife and their two daughters before the separation, to the school his children attend and in which his wife teaches, back over the bridge into Manhattan, and down to the Discount Shoe Mart where the proprietor, Mr. Maloney, fed up over Michael's cavalier attitude toward his job, fires him.

"Don't you think you'd be better off doing something you like?" Maloney asks him sincerely.

"Yes," replies Andropolis.

This was the opening segment of a film called *Running*, which played in theaters throughout the country in the fall of 1979. Had the film not received negative reviews, it might have played longer. Michael Douglas starred in the role of Michael Andropolis, the do-or-die marathon runner seeking a berth on the U.S. Olympic Team for the 1976 Games in Montreal.

That a major studio, Universal Pictures, and a box-office attraction, Michael Douglas (late of *The China Syndrome*, in which he co-starred with Jane Fonda), would join hands for a film about the marathon was an important indication that in the seventies running, and then marathon running, had become a mass movement. Films have always been the ultimate measure of cultural acceptance of new ideas and changing lifestyles, and while *Running* did not do for the marathon what *Saturday Night Fever* did for disco, it symbolized the growing appeal of marathon running and provided snippets of insight into its seductive powers.

The critics, I think, missed part of the point. While *Running*, by and large, was an artistic failure (the plot was thin, the dialogue clichéd, the climax overly melodramatic), the critics dwelled almost exclusively on the treatment of Andropolis's Olympic aspirations as a Rockyesque metaphor for his unfulfilled life and not on the marathon per se and its influence over those who aggressively pursue it. One of the paramount issues facing running in the 1980s is the extent to which we change our lives, for better or worse, because of the demands required by long-distance running and the marathon. By the end of the eighties, according to current estimates, 1 out of every 3 adults in America will be a confirmed runner.

Running already constitutes a movement; the numbers alone attest to it: numbers of runners, races, running shoes, commercial sponsors, fitness centers, sportsmedicine specialists, and so on.

Within running, the marathon has come to hold a very special place. The marathon has historical romance, as the story of Pheidippides is told again and again. It has the glamour of the Olympics, from Spiridon Loues to Emil Zatopek to Frank Shorter. It is a race with a name, not a number like the 100-yard dash or the 10,000 meters—a name that, like "the mile," reinforces its identity. It has an American tradition for which the Boston Marathon is largely responsible. It has its distance of 26 miles 385 yards, long enough to sufficiently challenge runners committed to it, yet not so long as to be beyond the capabilities of those who contemplate it. It has its physiological imperatives—the training and conditioning, the fluid replacement, the race pace—that can be both art and science in their application to human spirit and human anatomy.

Yet, until a few years ago relatively few people were motivated to run it. As recently as 1971 there were only about 100 marathons held in America, most of them drawing small fields and little public attention. But then came the Running Boom—some say it is still coming—and large numbers of people jogged and ran and raced—and started looking to the marathon. One mile, 5 miles, 10 miles—that was fine. But when you can have it all, why settle for less? So the marathon was born for mass consumption. In 1980 more than 350 marathons were run in this country, with an estimated total entry of 200,000. This is still a small percentage of the people doing any sort of running and a far cry from the number who watch "Monday Night Football," every week, but it's a movement nonetheless.

While *Running* did not sufficiently "smell" of running, as

writer-runner Hal Higdon complained, it did present a fairly authentic, if self-righteous, view of a man caught between the mainstream responsibilities of raising and supporting a family and his need to run the marathon. As runners everywhere have by now discovered, talent is not necessarily the force that drives us. Running can be a logical career for the great runners, especially as more money is being poured into the sport. But there is something in the controlled rebellion and stubborn determination of a Michael Andropolis that I suspect touches many marathoners, from Bill Rodgers on down, at least part of the time.

Andropolis's refrigerator is bare, except for some orange juice and beer. Running magazines and books pile up. He runs in his suit because on that day he must. He runs where he pleases—over bridges, to his kids' school, through threatening neighborhoods—without self-consciousness. His job is secondary to his running, and so is his marriage. Michael Andropolis loves his wife and kids, he says, but apparently he loves running and the possible prize of the Olympics even more.

And who is to say whether this is right or wrong? For Michael Andropolis running is right, the marathon is right, and in late 1970s America one could meet many others with a similar philosophy of life on line at any health food store. Their goals would be different—how many runners can realistically look to the Olympics?—but hitting the qualifying time for the Boston Marathon, a challenge that can hypnotize runners, might well be considered Everyrunner's Olympics.

Jim Fixx, of all people, points out the pitfalls of this philosophy. Fixx, who helped elevate running to a cult with *The Complete Book of Running* (1977), pointed out in *Newsweek* ("What Running Can't Do for You") that: "Running has nothing, absolutely nothing, to do with caring about other people, or with compassion or with self-sacrifice. On the contrary, devotees of the sport are likely to be incorrigible loners, sufficient unto themselves in their sweaty enjoyments. To the extent, therefore, that we let ourselves equate those enjoyments with the traditional pursuits and hard-won satisfactions of religion, we deflect our attention from concerns that are far more important than getting into a pair of Adidases and breathing hard before breakfast."

Running extracts its price, and for the marathon, the price one pays is high. Still, its rewards are coveted by increasing thousands as marathon running seeps into every realm of our culture and becomes associated with the kind of individual whom people have come to admire: fit, healthy, lean, determined, handsome, strong. Get up, get out, and get going. Do for yourself. Celebrate yourself. If you don't, who will?

In this era of aerobics, endurance is chic. Not long ago, when running was primarily a young man's sport, sprinting was de rigueur. Kids went out for track and told the coach, "Put me in the 100." Sprinting requires explosive power, not the steady state of submaximal effort physiologists associate with distance running. Explosive power—in sport, in art, in attitude—was once the ideal. To run distance was to challenge the norm. In a short period of time, however, distance running has become the norm. Frank Shorter won the 1972 Olympic Marathon. Joe Henderson espoused the ease and fun of something called Long, Slow Distance (LSD). George Sheehan said run, play, and don't listen to your doctor (unless he also knows from running and playing). Ken Cooper wrote *Aerobics*. Jim Fixx gave us *The Complete Book of Running*. Women, freed by feminism and the changing mores of the sixties, ran along. Corporate fitness was added to our lexicon, and it had nothing to do with debits and credits—and before you knew it Michael Douglas was running the Olympic Marathon in the movies, and Joanne Woodward, in "See How She Runs," was running the Boston Marathon on TV. Both protagonists made it to the finish line and both came in last, physically beaten but victorious nonetheless. Perhaps that is the lesson for the eighties: It will hurt but it will feel good, too.

In *Sports Illustrated*, Kenny Moore called the phenomenon for which Shorter's victory was the major catalyst, a "social chain reaction." Moore, fourth behind Shorter in the 1972 Olympic Marathon, wrote in *SI* in January 1979: "Growth became geometric, and fed on itself, because once past that point of no return, running was visible. All those checks on human behavior that apply when one has to go at it alone fell away. As the 'me' decade provided a fine excuse to soak in hot tubs, strut in discos and vote for Proposition 13, running became for many an exhilarating self-indulgence. Vigorous sport has always called to us from our genes, from our childhoods, but not, until recently, from our culture. When it finally did, an explosion was inevitable."

When culture calls, it is difficult to resist. Eventually we became athletes—or thought we became athletes—and after that we would not be the same. "The athlete comes to accept his body as himself," wrote Paul Weiss in *Sport: A Philosophic Inquiry* (1969). "This requires him to give up, for the time being, any attempt to allow his mind to dwell on objectives that are not germane to what his body is, what it needs and what it can or ought to do. But that to which he consciously attends is not always that which his body is prepared to realize. It becomes a prepared body only after he has learned how to make it function in accord with what he has in mind. Normally, he does this by habituating his body to go through a series of acts which, he has learned, will eventuate in the realization of the prospect to which he attends."

If anything, running is habituating. A 1978 Gallup Poll said that 47 percent of all Americans claim they participate in some form of physical exercise every day—twice the percentage recorded in 1961. Of those daily exercisers, 24 percent said they jog or run. From this we got the much-quoted estimate of 20 million Americans active in some form of running. The report, one of many that would paint runners as "upscale," also characterized them as young, single, and well-educated. One year later, the Yankelovich, Skelley and White polling organization said there were at least 30 million runners in the nation.

Also in 1979, "The Perrier Study: Fitness in America," conducted by Louis Harris and Associates, reported that 90 million adults, representing 59 percent of all Americans 18 years and over, now regularly participate in some form of physical activity. Only 15 percent, however, could be considered "high actives," those who exercise vigorously for at least 5 hours per week. Harris also reported that running and calisthenics were the fastest-growing activities, each having increased 19 percent in the previous two years. The Harris statistics reflected women's entry into sports, especially running, where the number of new female runners grew by 73 percent over the previous two years, compared to the 53 percent growth attributed to men.

Age, probably the most limiting factor in sports, has not been an acute handicap for marathoners. The very young and the very old will run slower, of course, but they will run—and with regularity. Bucky Cox, a 5-year-old first-grader from Lawrence, Kansas, created quite a stir in July 1978 when wire-service pictures of him running a marathon appeared in newspapers around the country. Though the youngster finished the run (in 5:29) and did not suffer any immediate ill effects from it, his participation fueled the debate over the exposure of children to bouts of prolonged exercise. On the other end of the scale, people have marveled at the marathoning of Paul Spangler of San Luis Obispo, California, Noel Johnson of San Diego, and Tom Pagan of Pompano Beach, Florida, all octogenarians. A few years ago, doctors gave Pagan, who had been quite ill, only six months to live. Refusing to wait idly for his presumed fate, Pagan started jogging and worked his way up to a regimen of 50 miles per week. In January 1979 he completed the Orange Bowl Marathon in Miami in 6:33. "You know you can't buy your health," says Pagan. "You can only make it. I intend to jog until I drop dead."

Just as age has not been a handicap to marathoners, handicaps have not been a handicap. Wheelchair athletes are frequent participants in marathons and other road races, and if the course is particularly suited to them—as it was in New Orleans for the Mardi Gras Marathon in February 1979—they can strong-arm their vehicles ahead of the runners. In the Mardi Gras event, Bob Hall of Massachusetts took advantage of the flat course and tail wind to win the race in 2:07:11, beating the recognized world marathon record time of 2:08:34. But Hall and his colleagues are not always welcome at races, since some consider wheelchairs to be a safety hazard. The issue went to court, and the wheelchair "runners" won the right to compete. Still the debate continues, and further legal maneuvers are forthcoming.

When Harry Cordellos competes, however, hardly anyone gives him a second look. The 40-year-old runner has been blind since birth, but he has run the marathon in under 3 hours. When Harry's not running, he's cycling, swimming, hang-gliding, or waterskiing. He likes to say he is not the greatest blind marathoner in the world, that there is a European or two that can run faster. He told writer Mark Osmun, "If I help someone, if I inspire someone by running, that is more important. I don't know, it's a reward maybe nonrunners wouldn't understand."

Dennis Rainear was born with all of his vital parts in working order, but he ran the last 16 miles of a marathon with an undeniable handicap—a bullet in his head. It happened on November 4, 1978, at the Grand Valley Marathon in Allendale, Michigan. Rainear, a 26-year-old chemist, was running comfortably when just past the 10-mile point "I felt a terrible blow to my head. I felt an immediate swelling but no blood. There was some pain but it wasn't excruciating. I just assumed I had been struck by a rock."

Rainear, who had been running for two years and had a marathon best of 3:00:31, continued his 6:30-per-mile pace with "a buzzing feeling in my head." At 22 miles, the "blow" finally took effect, and Rainear became so fatigued and dizzy he felt "pie-eyed drunk."

Still, he struggled to the finish line for a time of 3:09:37. Seeing his condition, Rainear's wife, Linda, summoned the physician in attendance. The doctor told Rainear, "I think you've been shot."

Rainear took the news in stride and was driven to Butterworth Hospital in nearby Grand Rapids, where a doctor gave him a local anesthetic and, with a pair of plastic tweezers, removed a .22-caliber bullet from his head. Apparently, the slug had penetrated Rainear's scalp but—miraculously—had not entered his skull. The wound was closed with three stitches.

Handicapped people, who feed off the challenge of everyday life, had few opportunities to test themselves in the marathon prior to the 1970s. There weren't many runners, nor marathons, around then. In 1969, the year Derek Clayton set the current world record of 2:08:34, there were some 44 marathons conducted in the United States. By 1975 that number had grown to 150, and by 1980 it was over 300.

Sometimes a sport's progress can be measured by its level of conflict. The more high-pitched the debate, the greater the issues. By this criterion, the marathon is doing very well. Generally, the issues involve the same things confronting society at large—money, politics, safety, health, the family.

There are questions about corporate sponsorship and its influence over the conduct of competition. There are questions about payoffs to top "amateur" runners. There are questions about entry restrictions and "illegal" entries.

Then there are the questions about TV's future role in covering, and thereby further mass-producing, the sport. There are questions about the international ruling bodies and their discriminatory stance against women marathoners competing in the Olympics. There are questions about what the marathon can and cannot do for you in terms of physical and emotional health—and some people wonder whether it can even cause harm. This last question is most critical, and medical authorities are not in agreement over its answer.

In an article in *The New York Times* on October 16, 1979, writer David Crossen asked: "Are long-distance runners immune to atherosclerosis, the progressive buildup of fatty cholesterol deposits in coronary arteries that leads to heart attacks, the main cause of death in the United States?"

While medical people are virtually unanimous in their view that a fair amount of running on a regular basis—say, a half hour a day—reduces the risk of heart attack, they do not share Dr. Tom Bassler's view that marathon running makes one immune to coronary heart disease. Dr. Bassler, who has steadfastly maintained his controversial view over the last few years, told Crossen: "We are monitoring marathoners and autopsy reports around the world, and to date only two marathoners have died of heart disease because of progressive atherosclerosis, and they were both smokers."

Dr. Bassler's theory is considered extreme by most of his colleagues, including Paul Milvy, Ph.D., of the Environmental Science Laboratory of New York's Mount Sinai School of Medicine. Milvy, who edited the New York Academy of Sciences exhaustive work on the marathon—*The Marathon: Physiological, Medical, Epidemiological and Psychological Studies* (1977)— said, "The real danger is that people, believing immunity awaits the marathoner, may press too hard in an attempt to run at that level while insufficiently conditioned and die in the process of seeking immunity."

Where lies the truth? Dr. Steven Subotnick, for one, has found a truth of his own. Subotnick is an enterprising podiatrist who has written a book called *The Running Foot Doctor*. He also sings and has recorded "Marathon Song," on the Subotnick label. (The flip side is "Daydreams of a Night Jogger," and the Bee Gees have not yet asked to borrow the lyric.)

Herewith, from "Marathon Song":*

> *Don't live for tomorrow*
> *For today is still young*
> *Feeling good as we're running*
> *Life again has begun*
> *When we're out on the road, friends*
> *Only one truth we know*
> *26 miles is a long, long way,*
> *26 miles is a long, long way,*
> *26 miles is a long, long way to go.*

*From "Marathon Song" © 1979 Subotnick Productions.

2

TRACING THE LEGEND

Did Pheidippides do it?

Forgive me: I know this is tantamount to questioning the probity of Little League, motherhood, the flag, Patriot's Day in Boston, drive-in movies, ice cream, the church, ole Johnny Kelley, small cars, and T-shirts that celebrate THE FIRST ANNUAL MIDDLETOWN BANKERS TRUST MEMORIAL DAY MARATHON.

Is nothing sacred? How would you break the news to a Rockwellesque little boy with a baseball cap over his cowlick, a face full of freckles, and a bat and ball in his hands that Babe Ruth was the protagonist of a fairy tale? Imagine race director Will Cloney announcing to 10,000 runners at the start of the Boston Marathon that the legend of Pheidippides was a lot of baloney. Sure, some runners would answer, "Who gives a shit—start the race," but others would be saddened. We are in an era, let's remember, with few authentic heroes.

There is a spoilsport among us, and it is none other than Jim Fixx who, in a December 1978 article in *Sports Illustrated* ("On the Run in Search of a Greek Ghost"), had the audacity to conclude, after consulting with Greek scholars and visiting Greece himself, that "there is absolutely no reason to suppose he [Pheidippides] ever lived." Talk about biting the hand, er, foot, that feeds you. Fixx, of course, is the author of the phenomenal best-seller *The Complete Book of Running*, a work that profited by a public imitating the fearless determination of Pheidippides, the Greek courier thought to have collapsed and died in 490 B.C. after carrying a message 25 miles to Athens from the Plain of Marathon.

We'll return to Fixx's argument—which is not without foundation—but first to the literati who have heralded Pheidippides' feat—and feet—as the origin of the race we call the marathon. In *Athletics of the Ancient World* (1930), Norman E. Gardiner wrote, "We have no means of estimating the performances of Greek runners or comparing them with those of our times. The Greeks kept no records. We hear of a runner who could outpace and catch hares, of another who raced a horse from Coronea to Thebes and beat it. Various feats of endurance are recorded. Herodotus tells us how Pheidippides ran from Athens to Sparta, a distance of 150 miles. It was the same Pheidippides who is said to have brought to Athens the news of the victory of Marathon. . . ."

In *Athletics of To-day* (1929), the authoritative F. A. M. Webster also spun the yarn of Pheidippides, but Webster claims the soldier ran not 25 miles but 22 miles 1,470 yards "to bring news of his countrymen's victory over the Persian hordes under Darius who had sought to invade Greece." Webster also told of Pheidippides' 2-day, 2-night run, which purportedly preceded his "marathon," and of the hero's last gasping words, the contemporary marathoner's credo: "Rejoice, we conquer!"

"The battle has always been considered one of the decisive events of history, checking as it did for many years the aggressive policy of Persia toward Greece," wrote John E. Sullivan in *Marathon Running* (1909). Sullivan, first president of the AAU, also noted, "The City of Athens awaited the outcome in feverish excitement, and the story is told that a soldier whose name is unknown ran the whole distance from the battlefield to the city to bear the news of the victory, falling dead from fatigue as the message left his lips." (The Plain of Marathon, Sullivan explained, derived its name chiefly from the battle between the Athenians and the Persians in 490 B.C. and was found on the northeast coast of Attica, containing four villages—Marathon, Probalinthos, Tricorythos, and Oinoe—which formed a Tetrapolis, or "city containing four towns.")

\ It has been convenient through the ages to embrace the Pheidippides tale as fact; this is especially so in present times when journalists of every persuasion and runners with a teary-eyed sense of nostalgia are seeking historical justification for the enthusiasm and plight of the marathoner. While *Sports Illustrated*, courtesy of Jim Fixx, is the most popular vehicle to have debunked the myth, other sources of cynicism preceded it.

H. A. Harris, in *Greek Athletics and Athletes* (1964), tells, too, of Pheidippides' 2-day run (here it is *160* miles) as documented by the historian Herodotus (who makes no mention of Pheidippides as the hero of the second, more famous run). Harris also notes: "Another and much later story told by Plutarch is that an Athenian named *Eucles* ran back to announce the victory in Athens, dying as he did so." Harris had more respect for the ancient Greeks than did their artificial mimics. He wrote, "The Greeks never raced over such a distance. They recognized the value of 'ponos' or toughness in athletics, but in all departments of life they followed their excellent principle, 'Nothing in excess.' "

These claims are echoed in *The Marathon* (1966), by John Hopkins. It seems Herodotus was born "just before the war with the Persians" and should have known from what he speaks. Hopkins also states, "Accounts other than that of Herodotus' differ considerably; for instance, Plutarch ascribes the second run [back to Athens] to a warrior called Eucles, mentions in his account that other historians credited it to Thersippus." Plutarch wrote: ". . . it was Eucles who ran in full armour, hot from battle and, bursting in at the doors of the first men of the state, could only say, 'Hail! We are victorious!' and straightaway expired."

As if that weren't enough to embarrass the Pheidippideanists, Erich Segal, marathon runner and classicist scholar extraordinaire—and, yes, one of Frank Shorter's professors at Yale—wrote in a 1977 piece in *The New Republic* how little esteem the long-distance man was accorded in Hellenic culture. Segal wrote, "Old Pheidippides . . . was no 'athlete' to the Greeks. He had the social stature of a telegram. He was no better than other members of his lowly class, *hemerochomoi* (literally 'all-day runners'), messengers who merely brought the news. Paperboys before the age of paper."

Which brings us back to Mr. Fixx, "running, sweating hard, down a two-lane road that curls through the dusty slopes of southern Greece." It is May 1978. The occasion is the Spirit of Pheidippides Marathon, to which 250 runners, most of them Americans on a vacation tour, have come like a lost generation looking for its roots. And they found it—the Plain of Marathon, about 5.5 miles long and 2 miles wide, from which the narrow road travels to the village of Marathon. The race is brutal. The second half of the course is mostly uphill and the temperature during the race is typically in the 80s, despite reports that the average temperature range for that place at that time is 51–68 degrees. It is a race that salutes the past, not one that amplifies the present. "Before many miles have passed," Fixx writes, "I begin to feel like an orange lollipop left too long in the sun."

But Jim Fixx was not in Greece for a good time; he was there to corroborate the disbelieving views of classics professors he resourcefully consulted. "Mine was a study in historical experience," wrote Fixx, "based on the hunch that the closer I came to the authentic historical experience, the more I would be able to learn about it."

The virtual unanimity among scholars past and present on the matter of the 48-hour, 150-mile jaunt to Sparta before the Battle of Marathon—by a courier named Pheidippides—was enough to convince Fixx of that; thus, he took to Athens with a three-part query: Did a messenger also run the 25 miles or so to Athens; if so, was he the same person who'd completed the 150 the previous day; and, whoever he was, did he drop dead immediately after this ultra ultramarathon?

Fixx says no, no, no. He claims Pheidippides—nicknamed "Speedy" in his piece—was a trained runner and would not have expired from such a run, that his alleged route could not have been paved and firm but tiresomely soft and thick, that such a courier might have had to run in armour and boots, that dangerous dehydration would have resulted from the absence of water stations (not to mention disorientation from the absence of mile splits), that Speedy's muscles would have been fuelless from not being carbo-loaded, that long-distance training being what it was, such a runner, however blessed with natural talent, could not have melded the proper doses of speedwork and distance running and surely would not have met the serious marathoner's daily quota of at least 10 miles per day.

Fixx exhibits more incredulity in his speculation than is called for. Surely, he is aware of the seemingly impossible feats registered over the years by extraordinary runners who conquered odds that would have put most of us six feet under. Ted Corbitt, in his salad days in the fifties and sixties, was known for his punishing training runs and "races" of up to 100 miles and 24 hours. Corbitt ran most of his 193 marathons and ultramarathons before the era of ERG (an electrolyte replacement drink), carbo-loading, lightweight racing flats, and sophisticated training manuals. Lately, hardly a day goes by that word does not come to me about another exercise in long-distance masochism performed by the likes of Park Barner, Don Ritchie, and Don Choi (who outdid even Pheidippides by running 204 miles in 48 hours for a world record). And has Fixx forgotten about 7-time Boston Marathon winner Clarence DeMar, found by physicians to have a remarkable constitution and an unusually large heart. To deny that there could have been a Ted Corbitt in Greece 2,500 years ago is historical parochialism.

And so I'm still not convinced. I'm waiting for an anthropologist like Richard Leakey to discover the remains or at least the artifacts (running sandals?) before making up my mind. For now, though, I'm going to remain true to my romantic and patriotic impulses and refuse to totally disbelieve that in 490 B.C. a noble and strong Pheidippides, as a courier in war, ran what we call a marathon, exclaimed, "Rejoice, we conquer!" and fell dead. When I run the marathon, I need to believe Pheidippides did it, too.

PART TWO

CONDITIONING BODY AND MIND

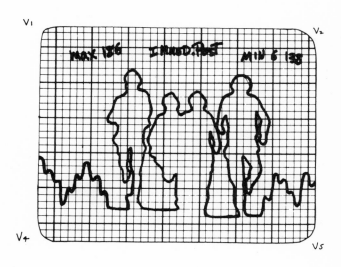

3

THE BASIC PRINCIPLES

So you want to run a marathon. While the other fourteen chapters tell you in detail how others have done it, and how you, too, can do it, here—for quick reference—are seventy-three basic pointers about preparation for and participation in the event. Some of these principles are elaborated upon in other chapters.

FITNESS

1. Marathon running, along with bike touring, cross-country skiing, and competitive rowing, is considered the most strenuous of conventional sports.

2. While marathon runners are obviously in better shape for prolonged exercise than "joggers" who might run a few miles every other day or so, the extra running they do does not necessarily make them healthier in the broadest sense of the term. Marathon training is roughly analogous to taking

large doses of medication for an infection—and continuing the medication after the infection has disappeared.

3. While there are potential dangers of both a physical and psychological nature in marathoning, they are vastly outweighed by the benefits, which include: improved fitness, enhanced self-image, a heightened sense of accomplishment, and, *some* doctors claim, an immunity to coronary heart disease.

4. People who smoke will not run as well as people who don't smoke, all other things being equal; but while it is unusual to find marathoners who smoke, it is not unheard of. Indeed, after the 1979 Boston Marathon, one competitor who had just run an excellent time of 2:26 was seen smoking a cigar.

5. Marathon runners should be trim because a great amount of energy is needed to fuel the muscles for a 26.2-mile run, and the more spare the muscle mass, the more fuel is available to each muscle. Less weight also means less heat buildup in the muscles, and heat buildup can impede performance.

6. The most important barometer of capacity for distance running is maximal oxygen uptake, or "max VO_2." This is the peak rate at which the body can take in and use oxygen, and it is measured in volume of oxygen per kilogram (2.2 pounds) of body weight per minute of exercise. Oxygen is transported to the muscles through the bloodstream and is needed to help burn energy sources of muscle glycogen and fat. This max VO_2 is measured while the subject runs on a treadmill in a laboratory.

7. While there are genetic factors that limit your ability to improve maximal oxygen uptake, persistent training will elevate max VO_2 because, among other reasons, it will cause the number of oxygen-carrying red blood cells to increase.

8. The age for optimum performance of men in marathoning is in the late 20s or early 30s since, as we get older, oxygen intake and other physiological determinants deteriorate. However, the curve is likely to shift—which way it's hard to say—as more people of all ages enter the sport. A 2:30 mar-

athoner at age 30 would be expected, theoretically, to run the distance in about 4 hours at age 80. (Since women in large numbers are so new to the sport, it is not yet possible to calculate their optimum age for high-level marathoning.)

COMMITMENT

9. Preparing for a marathon frequently requires a holistic approach to conditioning, involving not only a prescribed amount of running but also factors of nutrition, rest, injury prevention, and competitive experience.

10. The holistic approach to the marathon is sometimes referred to as the marathon life-style. It is suggested that marathoners, because of the demands of their sport, live a little differently from other people, even other athletes. This is the case with some marathoners, but a distinct correlation between this life-style and performance has not yet been proven.

11. Even if you enjoy other sports like tennis, racquetball, or bowling, you may have to give them up if you become a marathoner. It is doubtful that you'd still have the time for such pursuits or that you would continue to enjoy them while focusing so much attention on the marathon.

12. You have probably heard it said that anyone can run a marathon. This is an irresponsible statement. Perhaps the word *theoretically* should be used to qualify the statement. Given the principles of physiology, most people have the God-given equipment to develop the conditioning required for the marathon. However, since an extraordinary commitment must be harnessed and numerous intangibles play into such development, it should not be assumed that "anyone" can do it. Some people, even fine athletes, simply do not have the time.

13. The needs to achieve and to be recognized, which are strong in all of us, are readily fulfilled by marathon running, which can be done by most people willing to make the commitment.

14. Try to run every day. This, of course, does not mean that you *will* run every day; minor colds, leg soreness, adverse

weather, or family and job obligations will almost surely cause you to miss a day now and then. However, if you try to run less than every day, your continuity will be severely battered when the inevitable obstacles do get in the way.

15. If you've never run a marathon, go and watch one or two before you decide to run one. Get there early and don't leave till you've watched the slower runners finish. Keep your eyes and ears open. Pick up the "smell" of the event by observing the pre-race rituals, listening to runners discuss their training and race strategy, and capturing the trials and elation that are part of the marathon experience.

TRAINING

16. If you've done no running or jogging whatsoever but would like to start, with hopes of someday running a marathon, bear in mind that you should condition yourself for at least a year before you even think about building a training program that might eventually lead to a marathon.

17. The main theory behind any running program is that the body—indeed the mind as well—undergoes a gradual adaptation to stress, mainly of the muscles and joints and cardiovascular system. Therefore, patience and restraint are great virtues in marathon preparation. Rushing through a program is not only immature but potentially dangerous. The body is a remarkable organism and will surprise you in its ability to adapt to stress, if only you let it proceed at a natural and sensible rate.

18. Before embarking on an advanced training program specifically designed to prepare you for a marathon, you should have logged at least 1,000 miles in training or run an average of 20 miles per week for a year. To fulfill the former quota, the mileage must be consistent—it will be insufficient if it has been broken up by periods of nonrunning due to illness or injury.

19. After a basic conditioning period, you should run at least 40 miles a week for at least 10 weeks for minimum pro-

ficiency in the marathon. Within these 10 weeks, a run of 15 miles or more should be done at least 5 times. This training requirement should merely enable you to finish a marathon, not to achieve a particularly fast time.

20. Unless you are a superior runner or have been running for at least three years and have hopes of becoming a superior runner, do not run twice a day with any regularity. First of all, one strong workout does more good than two moderate ones; second, the body needs time to rest between workouts, to repair damaged tissue, and to sustain motivation. Double workouts are not altogether inappropriate for average runners but often there are diminishing returns in the good they can do.

21. If you hope to run a marathon at a certain pace, you'll have to do some of your training at that pace or faster so that your body is conditioned to use its limited energy resources at a given level of stress. For example, you could not expect to run a 3-hour marathon (6:52 per mile) if some of your training were not at that pace or faster.

22. It is important in training to occasionally simulate the conditions of racing. Otherwise, you could not expect the body to tolerate the call for an intense effort. That is why, for example, marathoners sometimes run in the heat or high altitude if they expect to run an important race under those conditions.

23. All marathoners should try to incorporate in their training at least one run per week of 15–20 miles. Among other benefits, this run conditions the body to burn alternative sources of fuel (i.e., fats) once the glycogen supply is theoretically exhausted after 20 miles.

24. While keeping a written record of your running can work against you by making you even more compulsive about your day-to-day training, such record-keeping in the form of a diary is generally advantageous in monitoring your development and in serving as a ledger of your accomplishments.

25. It is not necessary to run the marathon's distance of 26.2 miles in training, but then again it wouldn't hurt, if done infrequently and well in advance of the actual race. If you do

take the plunge and run a practice marathon, your training may suffer in the ensuing week or two as you recover from the strain.

26. Runners with 2 or more marathons under their belts who wish to improve their performances should train no more than 70 percent of the time at a leisurely (LSD) pace. The other 30 percent should be spent on various forms of tempo, pace, and speed running.

27. Two of the best forms of speedwork involve running your normal training distance at near-race pace, and going to a track to run intervals—fast, repeated laps with short rests in between each one. Just as you initially adapt to LSD running, you must gradually develop your capacity to run at a faster pace, and this speedwork should be done with great care. Running in races is also a good form of speedwork.

28. In the week before a marathon, run two-thirds as many miles as you had been running in the previous weeks. Rest is essential to prepare you for the ordeal of running 26.2 miles. Moreover, assuming you've trained properly, your condition won't be improved appreciably by another few days of heavy running.

29. Walking should not be categorically eschewed on long training runs or in marathons. Walking briefly can help relieve a sidestitch or loosen a tight muscle, and is sometimes recommended when taking periodic drinks, to ensure proper digestion.

30. Weight training is of little use to marathon runners, except for rehabilitation after injury. Running will naturally develop the muscles, and marathoners need not try to artificially develop the legs or upper body.

31. Hill running can help provide the effects of speedwork in a more appealing setting than a track. It also serves to strengthen the quadriceps and the buttocks without the heavy pounding of flat speedwork.

32. Men and women have equal abilities to train for and complete a marathon. But men, all other things being equal, have a better chance of running faster because they generally have stronger muscles than women. They also have a greater

capacity to take in oxygen, which allows them to run at a faster pace for a longer period of time.

33. While pregnant, many women continue to run and even to compete in marathons. The fitness associated with marathoning can be an aide in childbirth. Such activity during pregnancy should be done under the supervision of a physician, however.

RACING

34. Make sure the first marathon you run has: (a) mile or kilometer markers; (b) plentiful liquids at "pit stops"; (c) a looped or out-and-back course in case you are forced to drop out; (d) cool weather; (e) few hills. Why make it tougher on yourself than necessary?

35. If as a newcomer to the sport you have just run a pretty good marathon (say 3:30 or better in your first effort) and have set your sights on the elite class, this is what you're up against: The Boston Marathon, the ultimate arbiter of marathoning status, set its 1980 qualifying standards at 2:50 for men, 3:10 for men 40 and over, and 3:20 for women. The Olympic Trials qualifying standard in 1980 was 2:21:54, a mark achieved over the previous year by more than 200 men.

36. If after running for a while you then decide to compete, don't try a marathon for your first race. That would be a serious mistake. Run at least 3 or 4 shorter races to get the feel of competition and to learn what it feels like for the body to go all out. This will also give you a better estimation of your level of fitness and prevent you from running a marathon before you're ready for one.

37. The goal of an average runner entering his first marathon should be to finish, not to achieve a certain time. The confidence gained by finishing a marathon is great and can provide an incentive to enhanced training and performance. There is no sense in risking an incomplete first marathon by gambling with a fast pace or trying to outrun your neighbor. Eventually, there will be opportunity for that.

38. While energy expenditure in a marathon is most affect-

ed by pace, runners fail to realize that running form and style are also important. The more steady and streamlined one's form—that is, the more efficient it is—the less actual movement is required. This means less expended energy per stride and ultimately a better performance.

39. Racing successfully at 10,000 meters or even a half-marathon is no guarantee that you will race successfully in the marathon, especially if you are a relative newcomer to competition. Taking the body beyond 20 miles creates unique problems (see numbers 53 and 54).

40. Even most superior runners have in them only one peak marathon a year. It is hard to sustain peak condition from one marathon to the next. And although something intangible like luck may enable a runner to hit a supreme performance, one cannot expect to be lucky very often. Hence, if you're an experienced runner hoping finally to break 3:30 or even 2:20—and indeed you do—don't expect to do it again the next time out.

41. An exceptional runner who finally decides to try a marathon should, of course, set a time goal, but it should be conservative. The transition from track or road running at 10,000 meters is not to be taken for granted, even if a sufficiently heavy training foundation has been established. Experience at the marathon is not instinctive; it must be acquired.

42. Unless you are Ron Hill and do not want to break your streak of having run every single day for sixteen years, take at least one day off prior to a marathon. This will serve to renew your desire to run.

43. Author Manfred Steffney, a former Olympic marathoner for West Germany, claims that if you multiply your best time for 10,000 meters by 4.666 you will find the best possible time you can hope to achieve in the marathon. But he also cautions that this is your realistic time, not the one you can necessarily expect to achieve. This formula bears out for me, at least. My 10,000-meter PR (personal record) of 38:00, according to Steffney's calculations, would put me at about 3:00 for a "best" marathon, and 3:15 for a realistic one. My marathon PR is 3:17. Grete Waitz, to use a better runner

as an example, has run 31:00 and 2:27:33 for the 10,000 and the marathon. Steffney's figures pit a 31:15 best for 10,000 meters with a 2:26 best for the marathon.

44. All but superior runners should start a marathon at a pace slower than their anticipated average pace for the distance and keep that slower pace for about 5 miles. Since disproportionately higher amounts of fuel can be used in the early miles, this will serve to save valuable fuel for the later miles when it is needed most.

45. Arrive at the starting area of a marathon at least 90 minutes before post time. This will give you enough time to warm up by jogging and stretching, to find toilet facilities, to relax and review your race plan, to take last-minute drinks, to get your number, and to take care of other sundries.

46. Take extra clothing to a marathon since even small temperature drops prior to the start of the race might require you to put on gloves, a hat, or an extra shirt; or for a change to warmer temperatures, a porous, lightweight top.

47. Unless you are a champion looking for the slightest edge on the competition, wear your training shoes for a marathon. They are the footwear you are most comfortable with and they offer the greatest protection and stability. Lightweight, less supportive racing flats are not recommended for most marathon runners.

48. Use a lubricant such as Vaseline liberally on all areas of the body that can be irritated by friction, such as feet, thighs, and nipples. Also apply it to the face as protection against extreme cold.

49. During the marathon, there is a temptation to get lost in thought to make the miles more tolerable, but better runners tend to concentrate on their bodies in order to make adjustments, if necessary, in pace, form, or strategy. If your main objective, however, is to finish a marathon, getting lost in thought—perhaps through conversation with a partner—is psychologically advantageous because it keeps your mind off minor discomforts or periods of tedium in the middle of the race.

50. Hot weather to a marathoner is not equivalent to hot

weather for a sunbather. Temperatures as low as 60 or 70 degrees can be brutal, which is why a race like the Honolulu Marathon starts at 6:00 A.M. In hot weather, in addition to ample fluid intake (see numbers 52, 53, and 67), the body should be protected by proper clothing, such as a cap to shield the head from the sun. Forced to work harder in the heat, the body uses up energy stores at a faster rate.

51. No matter how much you sweat in a marathon, never take salt tablets. The body has enough salt to sustain loss through sweating, and excessive salt intake can harm your system, causing nausea or stomach cramps.

52. The body's thirst response becomes acute well after the need for fluid intake is established, so don't wait till you really feel thirsty to start drinking. Some medical experts even recommend drinking a pint or more of liquid (preferably water) fifteen minutes before a marathon. At the very least, drinking (8 ounces or more at a shot) should begin at the 5-mile mark. Additional drinks should be taken every few miles, the amount and frequency to be determined by the weather, level of fitness, past experience, and the body's tolerance to liquid intake.

53. If at 20 miles or beyond, you become overwhelmed by fatigue and suffer from painful cramps in your leg muscles, you have probably "hit the wall." It is sometimes wise to drop out at this point, take in fluids that will help lower your body temperature, and have someone put you in a reclining position and give you warm clothing so that your muscles will relax.

54. Even if you are still okay after the 20-mile mark, your pace (unless you are a superior runner) will still slow down considerably. Therefore, when setting your time goal you should factor into your overall pace a marked slowdown for the last 6 miles.

55. In training it is hard to enforce maximal efforts over long distances such as 10,000 meters or 10 miles. But actual racing provides a framework for this, and in the company of other runners speedwork seems to be less of an emotional strain.

56. While certain people need vitamins as nutritional supplements, there is no conclusive evidence to support the belief that they improve fitness and performance, according to Dr. Gabe Mirkin, co-author of *The Sportsmedicine Book* (1978).

57. People who engage in strenuous exercise seem to naturally seek foods rich in carbohydrates. Indeed, studies have shown that such a practice is generally advantageous to marathoners, who commonly go through a so-called carbo-loading procedure prior to competition (see number 58).

58. The principle of carbohydrate-loading, the success of which varies from runner to runner, calls for stockpiling carbohydrates in the days prior to a marathon by eating large quantities of foods like spaghetti. A week before this loading period, according to the theory, a runner should take a long run to deplete the muscles of the form of energy known as glycogen, thereby enabling them to more easily store this fuel during the period of relative inactivity before the race.

59. While beer remains popular among marathoners as a post-race refresher, medical experts disagree about its nutritional value or its use in rehydration of mineral losses following long-distance running.

60. The "simple" carbohydrates in so-called junk foods have some value to marathoners as day-to-day fuel but are less important in the pre-race carbo-loading process. Physiologists have found that complex carbohydrates, like those found in pasta, are used more beneficially by runners in a long run.

WARNINGS

61. Because of the emotional reinforcement it provides, marathoning can elicit a compulsiveness on the part of runners that can interfere with other primary sources of fulfillment, such as work and family life.

62. Even if it turns out that you are among the lucky few who can run every single day with little difficulty, I recom-

mend that you take a day off every other week or so, to rest the body and replenish the desire to do serious training.

63. Even if the marathon is your "best" event, avoid running more than 6 of them a year, unless you are a very good runner or you intend to run a few of them as "submaximal" training sessions.

64. Children under 10 years of age should not run marathons. They might damage their muscles and joints, which are at critical stages of growth, as well as their emotional stability, which is also at a critical stage of maturity. In addition, there is the danger of burning out a youngster so that he or she will turn away from running before reaching adulthood. There are ample opportunities in competitive running for youngsters without leading them into marathoning.

65. Advanced age is no hindrance to marathoning, provided one takes the well-documented precaution of a medical checkup to ensure that there are no hidden abnormalities in the vital organs and then embarks on a gradual exercise program. There are men and women today in their 60s and 70s, and even a few in their 80s, who began rudimentary running a few years ago and now compete in marathons.

66. The heavy training required for marathoning sometimes causes hormonal changes that result in irregularities in a woman's menstrual cycle. This is of concern especially when a woman is trying to become pregnant. (Similarly, low sperm count in men is sometimes associated with strenuous exercise, although there is little data to support this.)

67. Heat is the marathoner's worst enemy. That is why relatively few marathons are held in the summer. Experienced runners know that in cool-weather marathons fluid repletion is important, and in hot weather it is critical. It is absurd to think that your badge of courage will be enhanced by abstention from drinking during a marathon.

INJURY

68. Injuries generally occur for one of three reasons: (a) you have overdone it; (b) you have not taken preventive measures;

(c) you have a biomechanical weakness that is being magnified by your running. The first two factors can be avoided by using some common sense, from mileage control to shoe wear and care to adequate stretching. The third is hard to diagnose, and a sports podiatrist may be needed to check your feet and gait and correct any deficiencies that might cause you injury.

69. Injuries are inherent in marathon running. Some people are impervious to serious ailments, but sooner or later all those miles day after day catch up with you and—pop—you've got tendinitis or some such thing and cannot run for a while.

70. During periods of inactivity from running, it is sometimes useful to seek alternative forms of exercise to keep from falling entirely out of shape. This would include swimming and cycling, depending upon the nature of the injury.

71. The theory of "reversibility" claims that you lose two days of conditioning for every day you do not run beyond the normal nonrunning day(s) that are built into your schedule. Thus, after a bout with the flu or a case of shin splints, be aware of the extent to which your level of fitness may have deteriorated.

72. According to chiropractors who treat athletes, people with poor posture in general will have poor posture when they run, thus increasing the possibility of injury and limiting performance.

73. Depending on how your marathon went, it will take at least three or four days before you can run normally again. Even if it was a successful, relatively pain-free run, in all likelihood you will feel very tired for seventy-two hours or more, your arms and shoulders will be stiff, and your legs—particularly the calves and hamstrings—will ache. Such stiffness can be relieved by light jogging, which will improve circulation, and by the application of ice to tender areas.

4

PHYSIOLOGY: RACING THE TREADMILL

"Huh-huh-huh-huh-huh-huh-huh-huh-huh-huh-huh . . ."

I am breathing hard, dripping sweat, running up a grade of 8 percent at a 6:00-per-mile pace, ready to burst. My hamstrings hurt and I am starting to feel some pressure in my quadriceps. It is getting more difficult to maintain this pace, which I have held for more than a minute now. It is, I sense, my maximum effort, but my pride is at stake and I am not going to ease up until I must. I am going to run as fast as I can for as long as I can and worry about the consequences later.

"Huh-huh-huh-huh-huh-huh-huh-huh-huh-huh-huh . . ."

"C'mon, you can do it," I am told. "Lookin' good." Who is he kidding? My shirtless body reveals spare cargo where my stomach meets my shorts, shorts that are frayed at the edges and are pasted to my buttocks with sweat. I am trying to look good and even run well, but I realize I will have to settle for something less on this mid-August morning.

"Huh-huh-huh-huh-huh-huh-huh-huh-huh-huh-huh . . ."

My legs buckle from the weight of exhaustion. I have to

make a conscious effort to keep this from happening again. I lose my balance once or twice—my equilibrium is slightly amiss—and sway from the straight, narrow path that has been prescribed for me. The head clamp is starting to annoy me and my mouthpiece slips halfway out every so often. I have to strain to run a tad faster so as not to pull the apparatus out of whack—the wires and hoses can reach only so far. "Stay with it," I'm encouraged, but every part of my body feels heavier and heavier with each stride. My eyes close on and off, a habit of mine when I am running all out and know the end is imminent. Somehow, somewhere in my fading consciousness, I tell myself I have to go down swinging.

"Huh-huh-huh-huh-huh-huh-huh-huh-huh-huh-huh . . ."

Faster-faster-faster-faster . . . Finally I give up. I raise my right hand, the signal that I don't think I can run like this for more than another thirty seconds. I reach that point familiar to runners when I can barely "feel" my body, when waves of numbness wash over me and my movement becomes oddly mechanical. I get a ten-second countdown and am then ordered to stop. I grab the bars to my right and left and lift my legs and am congratulated for my "performance." I have just competed against myself on a treadmill in the Human Performance Laboratory at Ball State University in Muncie, Indiana.

The lab is supervised by David L. Costill, Ph.D., who is to exercise physiology what Benjamin Spock is to child care. Costill has written numerous articles for scientific and lay publications on how the body works when undergoing extraordinary stress, as it does in endurance sports and particularly in long-distance running. These articles have been based mainly on studies he and his colleagues have done at the Human Performance Lab, where in the last thirteen years Costill has tested thousands of runners, including America's best, with a special interest in marathoners. Bill Rodgers, Frank Shorter, Ted Corbitt, Ron Daws, and Amby Burfoot are among the top marathoners Costill has tested. In 1970, a year after Derek Clayton of Australia set the world marathon record, he visited the United States. He made certain to stop in to see Dave Costill and go through a battery of tests that it was hoped would shed physiological light on his remarkable 2:08:34 performance.

Some of Costill's most important work appeared in *The Marathon: Physiological, Medical, Epidemiological and Psychological Studies*, the 1,000-page tome published in 1977 by the New York Academy of Sciences and edited by Paul Milvy. The highlights of Costill's findings over the years are summarized in his recent book, *A Scientific Approach to Distance Running* (1979). Costill also is in great demand as a lecturer before medical, scientific, and athletic groups. When I visited him, Costill was planning a three-week lecture tour of South Africa for later that year.

Dr. David Costill is preeminent in his field of exercise physiology, a branch of sportsmedicine. Not long ago sportsmedicine consisted mainly of fixing up Sandy Koufax's left elbow so that he could pitch the Dodgers into the World Series and himself into the Hall of Fame. After that, it meant fixing up Joe Namath's knees so football would have at least one interesting player to keep audiences titillated and sponsors appeased. When running emerged as a habit-forming antidote for a people tired of just watching Sandy Koufax and Joe Namath, there also emerged a need to study what happened to these people when they put their bodies through such great stress. Enter the physiologist, the podiatrist, the cardiologist, the orthopedist, the internist, even the chiropractor—to study and probe, and to provide treatment to those whose bodies break down and get hurt.

Suddenly this esoteric craft of sportsmedicine had many practitioners, specialists (many of whom are runners themselves) who live in a professional world of treadmills, muscle biopsies, hydrostatic pools, biomechanics, anaerobic threshold, and glycogen depletion. It is the New Biology, and it has excitement and even a bit of glamour to it. But as with astronomy, which has been around a lot longer, sportsmedicine authorities frequently find that the more they investigate, the more they find they do not know. What they do know of strenuous exercise has given us a greater understanding of the marathon—the preparation required to meet the distance or do it at certain speeds, and the way to run the race itself so as to maximize the use of our faculties.

At the Human Performance Laboratory I spoke with Peter Watson, a graduate assistant, before I was to be tested. Here are excerpts from that interview:

BLOOM: What is this apparatus we're looking at now?

WATSON: You're looking at the gas analysis system, a semiautomated system that was developed by Dr. Costill and Dr. Jack Wilmore of Arizona. While the subject is running on a treadmill, we want to determine the volume of gas he is inspiring and expiring. It is processed by a micro-processing unit here and read off in liters. We need that measurement to be able to compute the amount of CO_2 and O_2 produced and used during specific exercises.

BLOOM: Is this for maximal oxygen uptake?

WATSON: Also for submaximal oxygen uptake. We can get a handle on metabolics at different levels of exertion by comparing the amount of oxygen consumed versus the amount of carbon dioxide produced. And then we can determine whether someone's burning fats or carbohydrates or what level of mixture they're using.

BLOOM: What is this gadget?

WATSON: This is the control mechanism for the motorized treadmill. We can get a visual display on it of the speed at which the treadmill is traveling and also the elevation. Most of our tests involve either gradual increases in exercise intensity or a specific intensity over a duration.

BLOOM: Since one of the things I'll be tested for by Dr. Costill is maximal oxygen uptake (max VO_2), would you define that for me, and also explain why someone who had a score of 84 like [Steve] Prefontaine [the late 5,000-meter specialist] should run a whole lot faster and for a longer period of time than somebody like myself who has maybe 50 or so.

WATSON: All the max VO_2 encompasses is the amount of oxygen (in either liters or milliliters per kilogram of body weight) your tissues can use over a specific period of time (which we use as a minute) to produce energy. An endurance bout of exercise is mostly an aerobic exercise and involves the presence of oxygen.

BLOOM: This is used only by the tissues in this context?

WATSON: We're assuming the only thing that's using up oxygen is your tissues and we're also assuming that your muscles are using such a high percentage of it since you're exercising, that, other tissue utilization is constant and can be ignored (even though we do measure it).

BLOOM: This doesn't concern the transport of oxygen?

WATSON: Well it does indirectly because if you can't get it to your tissue you just can't use it. Indirectly we're looking at your ability to transport it but directly we're looking at your ability to use it.

BLOOM: Like a fuel.

WATSON: It's only one of the fuels, along with either carbohydrates or fats. Oxygen produces ATP, which is an energy molecule that you're going to use to perform mechanical work.

BLOOM: That the muscles will perform?

WATSON: Right. And the numbers you refer to as 84 and 50 represent the volume of oxygen used over a specific period of time in milliliters per minute per kilogram of body weight. You have two people—say, Bill Rodgers and you. You are capable, say, of using 50 milliliters per minute at your maximum consumption; your tissue can only consume that much. Bill Rodgers at his maximum aerobic rate uses 78 milliliters per kilogram of body weight.

BLOOM: Is that what he tested when he was here?

WATSON: Yes.

BLOOM: Is this something that is genetically determined or does the training effect influence this figure?

WATSON: You get a large increase in your oxygen consumption with your training. But there also is a certain limit for each individual.

BLOOM: What does this limit depend on?

WATSON: Your body type, how much lean muscle mass you are going to carry with you, your bone structure, things like that. If you have a very large bone structure, you're probably not going to be able to compete with someone with a small bone structure unless your cardiovascular system is extremely efficient.

BLOOM: Large bones mean more muscle, more tissue on those bones.

WATSON: Even if there wasn't more tissue—but the same

amount of tissue—you're still going to have more inactive weight carried along with you. Certainly there are large-boned people who are good distance runners. These points are generalizations.

BLOOM: So body type and body-fat percentage and overall weight, among other things, have something to do with this max VO_2 figure.

WATSON: There are nutritional factors as well. If someone is eating a typical American diet of very high protein and fat content and low carbohydrate, he would have a tough time hanging in there in a marathon with an identical twin who eats a high carbohydrate diet. Because in an endurance bout, the twin would have the advantage of carrying more usable fuel. When you're talking on a broad scale, VO_2 max is probably our best indicator of endurance performance capability. But when you're talking about people like Rodgers and Shorter, who are within 10 milliliters per kilogram of each other [Shorter has 71 to Rodgers's aforementioned 78], there are other factors that come into play. Things like biomechanical efficiency and motivation. And in a given situation, it's a matter of how hard you want to push yourself and how efficiently you can utilize that oxygen, that energy you're producing. If one runner doesn't apply the force of the ground as well as another, he's not going to travel as fast so there's an efficiency factor involved. Max VO_2 is not the only factor that determines who is going to beat whom.

Before I underwent the test for maximal oxygen uptake on the treadmill, my body-fat measurements were taken. Body fat, a percentage of body weight, is computed most precisely by submerging the subject in a hydrostatic pool for underwater weighing. Ball State's lab had no such pool (at the time, they were trying to obtain more funds from the university for additional space and facilities), so Dave Costill used skinfold calipers to measure my body fat.

Keeping my weight down, as an adult, has never been easy for me. When I was a youngster I had a reputation in the family and among friends as a big eater, but it never showed because I spent most of my waking hours, outside of school, playing ball. When I stopped playing ball, my appetite waned but not by very much, and by 1972 my weight had climbed past 170. That's about when I started to run, and within four months I'd lost 25 pounds. Yet even with all the running I now do, keeping my weight at 150 (which is still a bit high for my 5-foot-9-inch frame) requires careful eating, restraint, and sacrifice.

I had not eaten very carefully in the weeks before visiting Ball State, however, so I approached the body-fat test with trepidation. A 1975 study of 20 elite distance runners at the Aerobics Institute in Dallas had showed a mean body fat of 5 percent for the 11 middle-long-distance runners and 4.4 percent for the 9 marathoners. Good male runners who eat sensibly rarely have more than 10 percent body fat.

First I weighed in—at an embarrassing 158.6 pounds, or 71.93 kilograms (a kilogram equals 2.2 pounds). Costill grabbed a pinch of skin from my left thigh and put the claw-like calipers around it. He did this three times, and then put the calipers around a chunk of flesh on the right side of my back. The result—a body-fat percentage of 17.4. My lean body weight, which is what I would weigh if I had virtually no body fat, was calculated to be 131. The message was clear—*Lose weight!* Bill Fink, Costill's associate, told me my body fat would plummet to 10 percent if I got my weight down to 145. "As weight goes down, oxygen consumption goes up (all other things being equal)," Fink said. With less weight, one has less tissue and therefore more oxygen per tissue mass; and one would be working at a lower percentage of one's "max," to run the same pace as before, when body weight was higher. The simple conclusion was that I could run a marathon a good deal faster if I lost at least 13 pounds and got my weight down to 145 or, preferably, to an even 140.

Another test I had hoped to undergo is a muscle biopsy. In this test, which is mildly surgical, a small piece of tissue is cut from a muscle, commonly the calf (gastrocnemius) muscle, in order to determine the percentage of "slow-twitch" and "fast-twitch" muscle fiber. The greater the percentage of slow-twitch fiber, the better one is equipped to run long distances, like the marathon. The converse is true: sprinters have an abundance of fast-twitch fiber. In the Aerobics Institute study referred to earlier, marathon runners, by and large, showed the largest percentage of slow-twitch fiber among the elite distance runners tested. For example, Gary Tuttle has 98 percent, Jeff Galloway 96 percent, Ron Wayne 82 percent, and Frank Shorter 80 percent. Oddly, Don Kardong had 50 percent. Steve Prefontaine, a 5,000-meter specialist, had 27 percent.

In his book, *A Scientific Approach to Distance Running*, David Costill explains the important role of muscle fiber capacity: "The fact that slow twitch fibers are metabolically more active during distance running suggests that they are used more extensively in this type of exercise. When these fibers have relinquished their glycogen stores the fast twitch fibers are apparently unable to generate enough tension to compensate for the exhausted slow twitch fibers. As a result the runner finds each stride more difficult and finally becomes exhausted when the slow twitch and fast twitch fibers fail to develop sufficient tension. This selective depletion of muscle glycogen is undoubtedly the cause of muscle distress often described by runners in the final stage of marathon competition."

I know this muscle distress well. In 4 of the 5 marathons I've run, my leg muscles cramped severely in the latter miles, twice forcing me to drop out of the race. It occurred to me that perhaps my body—for physiological reasons—was simply not suited to this sort of running and perhaps I should shift my priorities to shorter distances, even as short as a mile or 5,000 meters. Throughout my youth I had been the fastest kid on the block—sprinters were *fashionable* then, distance runners considered a bit wacky—and in high school I was a fair quarter-miler. Of course I had lost a good deal of speed over the years, but still I wondered if I had more potential for competitive success in my age group at the shorter distances.

Unfortunately, Dave Costill was not setting up the lab for muscle biopsies on this day—there was just no time—and I would have to earn my stripes another day. Maybe I was better off. Knowing your slow-twitch percentage is almost like knowing your destiny. I want to experiment, to be surprised by my running. To know where your theoretical strength— and weakness—lies also gives you a crutch. Sure I ran a poor race, one could rationalize, I'm not *supposed* to run well at this distance. Roger Bannister once told me, when asked what the ultimate mile performance might be, "Theoretically, it's $3\frac{1}{2}$ minutes. When you work out the oxygen requirements at a certain speed, the equation begins to cause problems. But I've always thought individuals can overcome equations."

Being prepped, finally, for the treadmill makes me feel special. It is a rare opportunity to be treated like a real athlete. Mike Sherman, the lab assistant who will record my ECG readings and track my heart rate, shaves three 1-inch squares on my chest so that the electrodes can be attached there. He rubs these shaved areas with alcohol and applies electrode jelly to the backs of the receptors and attaches them to my skin with tape. Wires extend from the receptors to the electrocardiograph, which is positioned to the right of the "mill" (as they call it); Mike takes his position. To the left is the gas analyzer, which will be operated by Pete Watson. In front of the mill, facing me, is Dave Costill, who will operate it.

It never occurred to me that there would be a *way* to run on the treadmill, but there is. First I am told to grasp the rails— which are like parallel bars in gymnastics—and lift my body, but not to step down on the treadmill, which is not yet running. Dave clicks the treadmill on, at only 3 miles per hour, and has me walk on it for a while. Then I am told how to put one foot down at a time on the moving belt, to move easily into the rhythm of the mill, and I do this with the speed set at 8 mph, or a 7:30-per-mile pace. It is an odd sensation: I wobble a bit at first and immediately it becomes apparent that I will have two things to worry about—not just whether I can run fast enough and long enough to record a respectable VO_2 max but whether I can ever get the hang of this damn machine. Of course, one cannot achieve the former without the latter. I feel the same bit of nervous tickle I feel before a race. I am being tested and I expect something of myself, but can I produce?

My attempt to run smoothly on this contraption will be made more difficult by the fact that attached to my head will be the breathing apparatus necessary to measure my maximal oxygen uptake. Costill shoves a nozzle into my mouth. Attached to the nozzle are two pale-blue hoses—much like the water hoses in your car's engine. One hose funnels to the gas analyzer, the other to a gas meter. Then he places a clothespinlike device on my nose, so that the air I breathe in and breathe out—my ventilation—will go only through the hoses. Pete and Dave explain how the initial speed of the treadmill would be set at an 8:30 pace on a flat grade and will graduate in several steps to a 6:00 pace on a grade increasing by 2 percent every 2 minutes until I can go no longer; when I feel spent I will raise my right hand as a signal for them to stop the mill within thirty seconds. I'm ready.

Running on the treadmill, I find, is hard work. You must be alert, and your concentration can never lapse. If it does, your rhythm and the rhythm of the treadmill will be out of sync and you will not run as efficiently as you must, your ultimate readings will be adversely influenced, and there is even the danger that you will completely lose your balance and dislodge the equipment mounted on and attached to you. You simply must keep up with the pace of the treadmill. At each step I feel as though I am running faster and working harder than I usually do to manage the given pace. Eight minutes a mile is slow for me in a workout; here it seems decent. I wonder if all along I have miscalculated my workout pace. (Ah, maybe that explains my slow marathon performances.) Pete assures me that the sensations I feel are common, and I am encouraged, at regular intervals, to keep it up. When I run, I tend to have a short stride and drag my feet. On the mill I must constantly remind myself to lift my legs to maintain the proper rhythm.

As I run, all I have to look at is the Perceived Exertion Chart posted on the wall in front of the treadmill, and Costill. Developed by Gunner A. V. Borg, the chart has a scale of 6–20, 6 representing extremely light work and 20 representing extremely heavy work. I play a game of choosing the point I am at, but the more fatigued I get the harder it is to focus on the chart. After 17 minutes, the test is over, blood is taken from my arm, and I cool off.

Soon enough, I am given my report card. My maximum heart rate is 186. The formula for figuring out your theoretical maximum heart rate is to subtract your age from 220. That would give me 188, but Dave Costill says the 220 formula is very general and with 186 I should feel I have hit my max.

My maximal oxygen uptake is 58.75 ml/kg/min. Top distance men commonly have a VO_2 max of 70 or higher; female runners 60 or higher. I feel okay; I passed. Costill says the best ever recorded is an 89 for Emiel Puttemans of Belgium, 1972 Olympic silver medalist in the 10,000 meters.

I test out "normal" for most of my other vital signs, such as cholesterol count and HDL's—high-density lipoproteins, the presence of which in the blood is a defense mechanism against atherosclerosis. *Most* of them . . .

I do have something wrong with me. But it's the same thing that's wrong with 5 of the 20 world-class runners tested in the 1975 Aerobics Institute study in Dallas. My ECG waves show a funny pattern at one point and Costill, whose own ECG showed the same pattern some years back, says it is probably a "false positive," which is a scientific way of saying doctors don't know what the hell it means. It could suggest that as my heart works harder, it does not get sufficient blood supply because the coronary artery, the vessel that feeds the heart, is partly blocked or impaired. "Unless there's discomfort during running," says Costill, "there is no cause for alarm."

I further checked my condition with Dr. George Sheehan, the noted cardiologist, and he shared Costill's view. "Current feeling," Sheehan explained, "is to regard most abnormalities in your age group as false positives—if you have no symptoms." Both Costill and Sheehan suggested I take another ECG in the near future as a precautionary measure.

At Ball State I was more curious about performance than "disease," and I continued talking with Dave Costill that evening.

BLOOM: Can you use that figure [58.75 max VO_2] and determine something about my condition, about my potential, or recommend training? I'm probably not all that different from a lot of runners. What does that figure mean to you exclusive of other data that you don't yet know?

COSTILL: I don't even need the other information. Based on some of the stuff we've done, that is looking at the economy with which one runs, technique, and all that, one could have a very high max VO_2 but very poor technique. Like having a big powerful engine but having it hooked up all wrong, so it wouldn't do you any good. I can look at your running and your VO_2 max and knowing a little bit about your training—if you're putting in about 50 miles a week—I have a pretty good idea that right now you should be able to run about a 3:20 marathon.

BLOOM: You get this figure based on familiarity with studies?

COSTILL: That's right. Knowing other people. And the advantage of having tested myself is that I can look at other people's values and I immediately remember what I can do and have a pretty good idea of what they ought to be able to do, given the same conditions and so forth.

BLOOM: What about my maximum heart rate of 186?

COSTILL: That doesn't mean anything. It's just an individual characteristic, like the length of your fingers. It's something that is governed internally but doesn't really have any bearing on how you're going to perform.

BLOOM: All right, here I am a 3:20 marathoner. Suppose I wanted to try and break 3 hours. What do I do?

COSTILL: You look like you could trim down. We can look at it in terms of having to "pay" to perform that well. What you pay with is the talent to consume oxygen. If you can't do that there's no way in the world you're gonna run 3 hours. Just like I knew when they moved the standard down to 3:10 at Boston [for men 40 and over] I'd seen my last Boston, because I know that the amount of training it would take for me to elevate my max VO_2—my general conditioning to be able to hold that pace—is far beyond the amount of time I have available, and the amount of physical talent.

BLOOM: So there's something inherent at work as well.

COSTILL: There is. There's a certain limitation and it's fairly well fixed.

BLOOM: Why does Frank Shorter have more of a capacity to consume oxygen than I, other than the obvious training effect?

COSTILL: The same reason he's not 7-foot-2. It's genetic.

BLOOM: Is it the size of your organs?

COSTILL: The size of your heart, the pumping capabilities of the heart, even more importantly maybe in the control of blood flow through the muscle. These are finite things that we really can't measure precisely, but we do know that they have very high values per maximal oxygen uptake, which believe me is not the ultimate answer on how you perform. The ultimate answer as to how you perform is a mosaic of different things, and max VO_2 is only one of those. It's really a holistic approach to the whole organism.

BLOOM: So there are some people who have certain inborn characteristics that enable them to consume oxygen well.

COSTILL: Having that endurance quality is somewhat like having a 200 IQ. You can have all the intellectual capabilities but unless you can develop it, you never see it. So when you look at it, you can't say, "He's a great endurance champion— all you gotta do is train him a little bit." You could be deceived.

BLOOM: What else would come under the heading of things about one's physiology that cannot be developed, that you're stuck with. I mean, that can work for you or against you in long-distance running, things that training really can't drastically alter?

COSTILL: Even how well you adapt to training. You and I could go into the same training programs starting with the same max VO_2, we do exactly the same training, you'll end up having a max VO_2 of 70 and I'll end up with 55. Or we could both start weight lifting and you'd become Mr. Universe and I'd end up looking like a scrawny runner. How well you adapt to your environment is also something that's genetically determined.

BLOOM: Would you say that body type also is an important factor?

COSTILL: There's nothing you can do about your anatomical makeup. If you've got big, heavy bones, then you've got to carry them around and that's certainly no advantage.

BLOOM: I sweat an awful lot in competition. I'm wondering how much of an effect that has in a long-distance race.

COSTILL: I ran with a guy in Indianapolis. It was 80 degrees and I was just drenched, just dying of the heat, and I ran by this guy and he was as dry as a bone. He finally pulled away from me. Well, sweat is important to keep the skin wet. But to have an excess and drip it on the ground doesn't do you any good at all. There's an efficient rate of sweating, and that's just keeping the skin wet.

BLOOM: Can't that work against you because you don't replenish the fluid properly?

COSTILL: Oh yes. It becomes more of a challenge to try and get the fluid in, so it's difficult. It's advantageous to have a very efficient sweating mechanism, but beyond that I'm not sure we could be too precise because it does vary tremendously from person to person.

BLOOM: Why would that be so?

COSTILL: I don't know. There are other major problems besides sweating in terms of temperature control.

BLOOM: I have a terrible tendency to cramp up at the end of a marathon, even when I've taken in a lot of fluids.

COSTILL: I can tell you that in Honolulu I drank so much fluid that I was overhydrated when I finished. And I still cramped. It was a point that I always cramp at, about 24 miles, sure as anything. Just when I think I've got it made, 24 miles, my hamstring goes and you think, "Oh, no, not now." You just try to keep loose.

BLOOM: The muscle cramping, is that always attributed to—

COSTILL: Nobody really knows. One of the major causes can just be fatigue, and we can guess that it may be due to changes in the membranes of the muscle fibers or it could even be somewhere up in your spinal cord. We don't really know; it suddenly throws a bunch of impulses down there to the muscle and it just begins to contract. It takes energy to relax as well as to contract so you may fire it, and it contracts but doesn't have enough energy to relax. It stays in that state until finally you stop running and force it to relax.

I left the Human Performance Laboratory at Ball State University feeling more certain I would never be a great marathoner but more confident I might one day be a better one.

5

PSYCHOLOGY:
THE IRREPRESSIBLE URGE

I admit to having only two states of mind: I am either training for a marathon, or I am not. Since I began running in the spring of 1972—I do not count my sprinting days in the Police Athletic League and grade school and the streets of Brooklyn, or my efforts on behalf of the high school track and cross-country teams—I have spent roughly half of my life getting ready for marathons and the other half lamenting the reasons (sometimes rationalizing them) why I was not getting ready for one.

Getting ready for a marathon is a marvelous lesson in psychological self-discovery. When I prepare for a marathon my running, and my life, take on a certain pattern—a pattern that is not always evident during the preparation but one that usually becomes clearer in retrospect. A decision is made, a plan is laid out, a course is followed—and then the climactic day arrives. It is all very logical, and for a goal-oriented person like myself it is another excuse to further structure my day, my week, my month as modules in a grand design to take me

26 miles 385 yards in a given time and with a minimum of duress.

For some runners, God bless them, this structure seems to come naturally. They have bodies that do not resist the added miles, or temperaments that do not allow for self-doubt, or families and careers that do not get in the way. For them, the goal and the path to it seem perfectly compatible.

The lucky stiffs—or are they? They have missed only six days of running in the last eleven years and their PR's are down to 2:28; God, what I would give for that! But do they have any fun? Nah. Fun is *not* running for good reason, like family get-togethers, or lousy weather, or aching knees, or your kid's birthday party, or because you don't feel like it today, and lowering your PR to 3:28. Sure.

The psychological considerations involved in getting ready for, and running, a marathon are based of course on the physical requirements (see chapter 6). The marathon is the only popular running event for which the usual preparatory routines are changed considerably. For a casual Turkey Trot or a 10-kilometer or even a 20-kilometer race, you follow your normal training schedule, give or take a few miles, unless you are an exceptional runner keying for a major event. And even then, Mr. or Ms. Fast Runner, you are only adding more speedwork to your regimen so you can kick down the stretch with the best of them and not get blown away by that high school upstart with two hundred college-scholarship offers and a room full of free running shoes. But 26 miles 385 yards is another matter entirely. It is enough to make exercise physiologists wax mathematic and tell us in axiomatic terms that one has to run a certain number of miles at a certain pace for a prescribed period of time in order to negotiate a marathon successfully. Unfortunately, physiologists and other soothsayers rarely agree on the exact nature of those requirements, which leaves us with a choice.

Assuming you are already a relatively serious runner logging 25 or so miles a week, Expert One says just increase your load to 40 miles and you'll do fine. Expert Two says run 50 miles a week and never miss more than one day a week. Expert Three says the prospective marathoner must run virtually every day, 60–70 miles weekly, and to hell with visiting the folks in Pittsburgh—you can't afford to miss that day's mileage.

What to do? If you want something badly enough, you don't take shortcuts. Experts One and Two offer shortcuts; Expert Three sells you insurance. If you're like me, you take it. It's all or nothing, up to a point. That's how I am. At 20 miles in a marathon, when even my hair hurts, I don't want to say to myself, "Jerk—sure it happened this way, look how many days of running you missed."

Normally, I run 40 to 50 miles a week. I run 5 to 6 days a week, rarely 7. I am somewhat lax about my diet, don't get enough rest, suffer periodic aches and pains, and am never as fit as I want to be. In short, my running is fairly hit-or-miss. Basically, I have learned to accept it this way and not let my fantasies get the best of me. But when the marathon comes along I become a different person. I forget, first, how the last one felt—the late-race leg cramps, the post-race blues, the ordeal of it all. This one, the next one, will be better. And to make sure it will be better I become a disciple of Expert Three. I become unfaithful to my wife and my kids and my job and the Sunday *Times* and acquire another partner in life: the marathon.

To get in shape to run the marathon at a respectable pace and with a minimum of pain—and of course this is different for all of us, the pace and the pain—I decide, usually four months before the day of reckoning, to run every day, to average close to 10 miles a day, to run hills, to watch my diet, to become very fit and strong and lean, to be very careful to avoid getting colds or injuries . . . and the hell with everything else. I have to believe that I am being completely disciplined and fully committed or it won't work. The marathon is an obsession. It has to be.

Running an average of 10 miles a day, every day, for three to four months is not an easy thing for most people, including me. To do it right requires not only discipline and commitment but also a strong constitution and a certain amount of selfishness. We all have our physical limitations, and for most of us those boundaries fall somewhere below 60–70 miles a week. It is a strain for me, especially in the initial weeks. Because of the strain, I cling to certain time-proven devices to minimize the discomfort and maximize the chances of completing the mileage. The focal point of the day becomes the run, and that means I must find a couple of hours (for stretching, running, showering) best suited to my running 10 miles comfortably and confidently. I have to consider the weather, my disposition, tomorrow's workout, yesterday's workout, whether a friend can join me, how tender my Achilles' tendons feel. And then peripherally, the wife, the kids, the job, and the other people and things that normally come first.

It's all in the numbers. I don't get hung up on mileage totals—except when I'm being seduced by the marathon. Maybe it's fear. Fear of failing. As I train for the marathon, perhaps there is an unconscious reminder that if I do not satisfy the requirements, at 22 miles into the race I will hit the wall. Hitting the wall, despite what you may have read elsewhere, does not have the men-at-war romance of a John Wayne movie. I know; I've been there. It is a badge of courage I can live without.

Maybe this is it. Maybe hitting the wall scars a runner emotionally for life. Maybe that torturous feeling is both awful and challenging enough to generate an obsessive need to overcome it. Please—hit me again; I know I can take it *this* time.

Thus, I stretch and I run for 70 to 80 minutes and I stretch some more and do my sit-ups. And in the shower I dwell on the 10 miles I have added to my total as though I were a collector of 10-mile workouts, and 9-mile workouts had no market value. After the shower I scrape the baby blisters from my feet, snip the funny-looking toenails, and poke and squeeze and press the muscles and tendons that are vulnerable to make sure I have not developed some soreness that will make tomorrow's 10 miles harder to come by.

This goes on for months. Inevitably, Monday through Friday does not produce 50 miles but 40 to 45, less when once every other week or so a day is missed. Therefore, the weekends must be packed to attain the desired weekly mileage. I know I am trying desperately to satisfy a psychological need. This need is wedded to physical realities, which makes it more burdensome, and it drives me unremittingly through the weeks and months to the point at which I can rise on the day of the marathon and tell myself that it will come out all right because I have averaged 64 miles a week for 14 weeks. So there. I have also read less, written less, phoned less, kept fewer appointments, missed dinners with the family, stuffed myself with vitamins at the slightest sniffle, and made a lot of people mad at me. My normally self-righteous conscience is put into storage and life becomes a bowl of ERG and beer, quadriceps and hamstrings.

No, I have to run. No, I have to eat so I can have the strength to run. No, I cannot eat because I have to run. I'll run first, then I'll do it. No, I'm too tired. *But you're not too tired to run!* I am, but I'm going to run anyway. I have to.

This fear of failing is not only associated with a fear of hitting the wall but with the pride I bring to any challenging project I undertake. I can recall years ago when I was a secondary-school teacher the extent to which I would prepare for almost every lesson, not so much because I cared more about my students' learning than the next teacher but because I recognized the art in teaching and sought to master it. Of course I did not master it; given the complexities of those circumstances true mastery was probably impossible. But not to have tried would have been anathema to me. I had to test myself, and every time I decide to run a marathon I make another commitment to test myself. Should I fail, I want to fail because my expectations perhaps were too grandiose, not because I could not measure up to my own standards.

Dr. William Glasser would surely call this a "positive addiction," a phrase he added to our language by writing the best-selling book of the same name in 1976. In his chapter on running—"the hardest but surest way to positive addiction"—Dr. Glasser opens with remarks made in the London

Sunday Times by British marathoner Ian Thompson: ". . . it's an unvicious circle; when I am happy I am running well and when I am running well I am happy. . . . It is the Platonic idea of knowing thyself. Running is getting to know yourself to an extreme degree."

Yes, the self-discovery is remarkable—we can learn most about ourselves when undergoing the most severe stress. But in Thompson there is evidence, ironically, of a pernicious symptom. Can he have happiness when he is not running well? Probably not. But Ian Thompson is perhaps entitled to running-related despair, for he is one of the best marathon runners in the world. Running, therefore, is his job. When one is not doing well on the job or when business is bad, one is commonly unhappy; when one is in a general state of "happiness," one tends to do better on the job or at least suffer less amid occupational setbacks.

I spoke with Thompson in 1979, first at the Montreal International Marathon in August, and again in October at the New York City Marathon. Thompson, who is 30 years old, married with one child, has had a somewhat troubled career as a marathon runner. In 1974, in only his second try at the distance, he came in first at the British Commonwealth Games and his performance of 2:09:12 was the second fastest marathon ever (today it stands as fourth fastest). Thompson was rightly hailed as the next great marathon runner and a potential Olympic champion. In the years that followed, however, he did not come close to matching his feat of 1974, and for that he has suffered.

In the Montreal race, on a very warm day, Thompson led a superb field for 15 miles, then fell off his 5:00-per-mile pace and came in sixth. At New York, determined not to carry the pacesetter's burden (which Kirk Pfeffer easily took on), Thompson held back in the early miles and ran strongly at the end, finishing fourth. His clockings in these two races were 2:15:24 and 2:14:43, respectively. On both occasions he said he was training very hard, trying to "unlock the door" to the 2:09 he felt he still had within him. But very soon he will have to realize that perhaps he cannot do it. To have done it once before will make this realization that much tougher to accept. But if Ian Thompson hopes to be truly happy in his running, and then in his life—as apparently he once was—he will have to recognize his limitations and pursue something other than a 2:09 marathon.

Most of us can hope for a 3:09 or 4:09 marathon. Running is not our job—it is our play. But as behavioral scientists and philosophers, and more recently the oft-quoted Dr. George Sheehan, have told us, play can—Sheehan says *should*—gain control over our lives. "Play is the motivation for running and sport is play intensified," Dr. Sheehan stressed in his address on "The Body" before the Psychology of Running Seminar at Cornell University Medical College in New York City in October 1979. "Play has to fit your temperament and body," Dr. Sheehan said. As an illustration, he told of his youth in Brooklyn, where, according to one's temperament and body, there were three kinds of kids: the stoop-sitters; those in need of body contact ("It hurts so good"); and "the rest of us." Each group had its own kind of play, according to Sheehan, and that holds true for the adult world as well.

Sam Merrill is certainly among "the rest of us." Merrill, 32, is a contributing editor of *The Runner* who has written about running's addictive hold on people. Merrill should know—he's a case study. He has written about himself, first in the classic "Diary of an Obsession," which appeared in the 1977 New York City Marathon program published by *New Times*, and in other articles. In "Diary," Merrill wrote: "And so it passed, the moment of vivid and inescapable self-realization every social deviant must eventually encounter. Until then, I'd been able to hoodwink myself and others into accepting the utterly preposterous notion that running was something I could take or leave. But after turning down the most beautiful apartment in New York because it was too far from Central Park, all pretense fell away and my politely expressed but rarely dwelt upon desire to become a marathon runner was revealed for exactly what it had become: a desperate and grotesque obsession."

Sam Merrill had been seduced by the marathon, as I had

been. And while it is obvious that the marathon is enjoying unprecedented popularity, I sought to sample a cross section of marathon runners in the spring of 1979 to find out to what extent the marathon had entered and gained control of their lives. I distributed several hundred "marathon surveys"—questionnaires that requested information about a marathoner's training, competition, performance, occupation, lifestyle, and relationships with others. These survey forms were given out at a handful of races, including the Boston Marathon. While this was clearly not a scientific study, the responses are nonetheless revealing.

I received 70 completed questionnaires, a respectable 10 percent return. Fifty-one of the 70, or 73 percent, answered "Yes" to the question: "Is there something called a 'marathon life-style' and do you exemplify it?" There was no discernible correlation between response and performance, however; indeed several marathoners who answered "No" to that question listed their best time as under 3 hours. Here are some of the affirmative responses:

John Butterfield, a 43-year-old naval officer from Annapolis, Maryland, who has run 51 marathons since 1971: "Your daily routine revolves around ensuring you get a workout(s) in, and you plan meals and sleep to keep you as healthy and refreshed as possible."

Charles Christian, a 54-year-old engineer from Schenectady, New York: "I can't accept activities that would interfere or conflict with my training schedule or interrupt routines I have established."

Nancy Pearlman, a 31-year-old teacher from Los Angeles: "Sleep and think running always; aiming for a goal. Everything gets scheduled around workouts. Diet has to be watched, plus overdoing it physically in other areas."

Nan Rollings, a 27-year-old nursing student from West Lafayette, Indiana: "My husband and I look forward to it [a marathon] for quite a while, and much of our life revolves around our next race."

M. Mittleman, a 47-year-old physician from West Hartford, Connecticut: "It requires a frame of mind and concern about health and/or body conditioning before, during, and after the marathon."

Phil Curatilo, a 22-year-old-pharmacist from Brighton, Massachusetts: "There is a marathon life-style. It is called sacrifice. I would like to exemplify it more than I do."

Lance Koll, a 34-year-old electrical engineer from Santa Clara, California: "I always enjoyed the act of running for itself before doing marathons. But racing has provided something that is difficult to find nowadays, an activity with immediate feedback. So many things we do have no visible end, or are too far off and vague to be meaningful. A race begins and *ends*; and you know immediately how well you competed against yourself (the only real competition there is)."

David Lawton, a 36-year-old foreign correspondent stationed in Hong Kong, was one of the respondents who replied at length: "It would strike me as a bit tenuous to refer to a marathon 'life-style.' Maybe a more valid point can be made by distinguishing between runners who classify themselves as athletes, and runners who describe their running in terms of a motivation such as fitness or relaxation. In other words, there are runners who run because they have become runners. Not all marathoners are that kind, but many are (including me). Their life-style is similar to that of athletes in other sports. It is pretty much a self-justifying identity.

"Deciding to run the Hong Kong Marathon last January was part of a larger decision to reorganize my life. Demanding more of my (already long-established) daily running was central to that reorganization. I am not competitive by nature, but I decided to enter races to give myself training goals. I decided I was not satisfied with my work (correspondent for the *Washington Post* in Bangkok), so I moved to Hong Kong, took a new job (editor on the *Wall Street Journal's* Asian edition), and consciously began putting less of myself into that job. I rejected some ambitions I had before. At the same time, outside journalism, I simplified my social and romantic life. I now find that much of my life revolves around running. But I wouldn't ascribe that to any gradual, mystic effect of my previous daily running for fitness and relaxation. Rather, I'd say that I made a series of very conscious decisions at the end of last year.

"I don't think it would mean much to say that my life is now better. It is certainly different and I enjoy it more. There are conflicts, which I resolve by dropping non-athletic friends. For instance, a couple of months ago a news associate and his wife—a nice couple whom I have always liked—invited me to dinner at their home. There were four other guests. Because of my running, I eat a lot—much more than average. Also, I am a vegetarian, which means that I eat different food from most. At this dinner there was sufficient vegetable curry for me to enjoy quite a good dinner. On my third helping, I suddenly became conscious of strained silence around the table. I looked up and found everyone staring at me. From their expressions I got the feeling that they possibly couldn't help finding my eating a bit disgusting—not my manners, but the sheer bulk. In any case, their dishes were cleared away, and dessert stood waiting on the sideboard; I was keeping them from it. It was an uncomfortable moment. I didn't sense any real hostility, but I had a keen *aperçu* of my difference from my friends and their other guests. I just didn't belong with them. I haven't seen them since. Since then, I have declined most invitations from non-athletic friends. I find I enjoy eating only with people who take my tastes and appetite for granted.

"My only regret in this new life-style is that I am not a better runner. My last marathon was poor (3:56). I am running in an ultramarathon of 35 miles in a few days with little realistic chance of finishing. (I will next year.) In short, in choosing running I have to accept—and face every day—my limited ability.

"However, one thing I like about racing marathons is that I get a very precise measure of my progress and limitations. In a profession, or in social and romantic life, one seldom knows where one is. Obviously, I have limitations in those talents too, but society and culture tell one to keep on trying in those areas no matter what. I decided that was unreasonable. So now I 'jog' through the rest of life and run seriously."

The dominant role that marathon running can play is not without its conflicts, as David Lawton has described. Another question on my survey was: "What conflicts have entered your life since you became a marathon runner?" A majority of those responding—including some who rejected the idea of a "marathon life-style"—indicated that they have experienced conflicts, most of them dealing simply with finding enough time to run and also do other things. A sampling of responses: "Little time to socialize except at track; nonrunners can't understand my fanaticism." "I've been injured with three stress fractures and mentally it creates problems." "Friction with my wife because of the time and emotional commitment." "Because running comes first, there is insufficient time for what used to be routine chores." "Social life has gone downhill; I work, run, eat—and that's it!" "It takes a lot of time, which conflicts with work, family, and home upkeep." "Pulled among job, family, running, and friends." "I had a thriving business which I neglected for marathoning."

That a great many runners have been captivated by the marathon, for better or worse, says a great many things about the needs and desires of people, and the ways in which marathon running can satisfy those needs and desires. Included among these: the need to play, to work, to win, to lose, to "feel good," to compete, to establish goals, to achieve, to feel superior, to seek recognition, to be challenged, to strive for perfection, to conform (or nonconform, as the case may be). In his essay, "Running, Psychology & Culture," in the Annals of the New York Academy of Science, Dr. Ernst Jokl of the University of Kentucky Medical School wrote: "Sport is indeed capable of establishing a new balance vis à vis the inequities that are caused by the steadily progressing transformation of society. Like art, sport washes away from the soul the dust of everyday life. Sport renders possible the expression and the satisfaction of many desires that the modern world awakens as well as represses; desires for recreation and social contact, for aggression and play, for self-assuredness and hero worship. True, athletics and sport are not the only means to attain such satisfaction; but they would seem to be among the most readily accessible and the most rewarding. Marathon running as it is now developing in the United States as a branch of the 'sports-for-all' movement exemplifies this issue."

"Ordinary" running—running that requires much less commitment than marathoning—can satisfy some of these desires for some people. But the marathon stands a much better chance of doing so, and ultimately for a greater constituency. If you are very hungry and eat a small meal you will become less hungry but not necessarily satisfied; a larger meal will probably come closer to satisfying your hunger.

We are all hungry people, hungry for the opportunity to prove ourselves. After a while, for a variety of reasons, the normal patterns of our family, social, occupational, and spiritual lives do not provide those opportunities, or if they do provide them they are defused by their repetitiveness. So, as Jokl claims, we turn to sport for its accessibility and reward. And in America, in the 1980s, the sport—the activity—that is most challenging, most accessible, and offers the greatest intrinsic reward to the largest audience, is the marathon.

A lot has been written about the teenager's need for peer approval, but I believe the need is at least as strong in adults. While runners frequently shrug off the need for peer acceptance and approval of their running, they tend to eventually supplant nonrunning friends with friends and acquaintances who also run. And while it may seem silly and immature, marathon runners engender respect, admiration, and envy from their peers in much the same way as teenage quarterbacks, track stars, and beauty queens do from theirs.

Indeed, I am certain that most people (especially men), given the choice, would rather perform well and have status in sport than in anything else. I believe the degree to which this would be true would rise with the hypothetical level of performance offered them. Would you rather be an Olympic marathoner or equally successful in your chosen career? I have thought about the question myself—the Olympics or the Nobel Prize for Literature. I am still undecided but leaning toward the Olympics. I love writing, but I love running a little more.

The need to express oneself through sport—which is manifest in marathon running—has been found by many behavioral scientists to be a basic human trait. In *Involvement in Sport: A Somatopsychic Rationale for Physical Activity*, Dorothy V. Harris wrote, "It appears that physical activity and sport experiences provide tremendous opportunity for the individual to experience a sense of success and satisfaction which reinforces a positive sense of self." In her section on "Emotional Factors," Dr. Harris cites *Motivation and Personality* by Abraham Maslow, among other works. "According to Maslow, when the belonging and social needs are met, one moves up the hierarchy to the esteem needs, which include the need or desire for a stable, firmly based and unusually high evaluation of himself, for self-respect, self-esteem and esteem of others. . . . Some theorists go so far as to suggest that the need for achievement and the need for recognition may be the two most important motives for involvement in competitive physical activities."

This universal need for recognition and achievement was fulfilled in the minds of the respondents to my marathon survey. One of my questions was: "How has your preparation for and participation in marathon running changed your life for the better?" Here is a sampling of responses: "I know that if I want something bad enough, I can go through any pain to get it." "Feel better, look better, perform better." "It has built up my confidence and persistence and proven to me that I can do anything I want to do." "Better appreciation of my good fortune to be healthy." "Took control of my life and am more intrinsically motivated in all endeavors." "I am convinced that marathon running has enhanced my life to the extent that I cannot conceive of life without it."

This last statement points again to the fact that many people who run the marathon become addicted to it. Marathon running provides them with so much of what they need and desire that to part with it would be so emotionally devastating as to be virtually inconceivable. This, indeed, is not unlike the feeling one gets when contemplating the loss of a loved one. This hypnotic attachment to what is basically a simple pursuit can, like another sort of love affair, produce a harmonious relationship or one that is ill-fated. If the marathoner parlays his running into a truly enhanced life-style, he has succeeded in developing a positive addiction; if, like the most pernicious kind of addict, he has become so drugged by his sport that he neglects himself and others for whom he is responsible, he has developed a negative addiction.

"We're here to play," declares Dr. George Sheehan, the author of *Running & Being,* to an audience gathered in New York for a seminar on the psychology of running. "Play—it's where we live. It is the motivation for running." Play, a persistent theme of Sheehan's, is given less compelling properties in the book *Homo Ludens: A Study of the Play Element in Culture* by Johan Huizinga. In 1938 Huizinga wrote:

> First and foremost, then, all play is a voluntary activity. Play to order is no longer play: it could at best be but a forcible imitation of it. By this quality of freedom alone, play marks itself off from the course of the natural process. It is something added thereto and spread out over it like a flowering, an ornament, a garment. . . . It may be objected that this freedom does not exist for the animal and the child; they *must* play because their instinct drives them to it and because it serves to develop their bodily faculties and their powers of selection. . . .
>
> For the adult and responsible human being play is a function which he could well leave alone. Play is superfluous. The need for it is only urgent to the extent that the enjoyment of it makes it a need. Play can be deferred or suspended at any time. It is never imposed by physical necessity or moral duty. It is never a task. It is done at leisure, during "free time." . . . A second characteristic is closely connected with this, namely, that play is not "ordinary" or "real" life. It is rather a stepping out of "real" life into a temporary sphere of activity with a disposition all of its own.

Play is superfluous. While Huizinga's work predated the 1970s running boom, I doubt he would see sport today in a light that would cause him to reevaluate his thesis. "The basic forms of sportive competition are, of course, constant through the ages," he believed. For George Sheehan and a great many marathon runners, running is not superfluous. It cannot be deferred or suspended at any time. They could not well leave it alone. Thus, to them, either play is not superfluous, or running is not play. I believe that most marathoners would say that running is not play, that running, for all of the elements of play it contains, is mainly a mission. This is not a semantic distinction but a philosophical one. By attributing greater cultural importance to play than scholarly consensus has, Sheehan provides a convenient rationale for those who immerse themselves in running.

Perhaps this is the dividing line between the positively and negatively addicted. Those on the so-called negative side have perhaps convinced themselves that to play (that is, to run) is to live; or, if they do not consciously attribute such honor to play, they have strayed in their running so far from the boundaries of play that their running becomes, as Huizinga suggests, "a forcible imitation of it."

The idea that running could become a negative addiction was first advanced by William P. Morgan, Ph.D., former vice-president of the American College of Sportsmedicine, current director of the Sports Psychology Lab at the University of Wisconsin in Madison, and author of numerous articles on sport and psychology.

Early in 1979, Dr. Morgan wrote of the plight of the exercise addict in *The Runner*. He concluded: "The gradual process leading to exercise addiction, then, is really no different from the addictive process in general. But, just as not everybody who drinks coffee, smokes cigarettes or takes drugs gets hooked on them, not everyone who runs regularly becomes a 'running-head.' The key difference between the person who becomes an addict and one who uses running sensibly is the elusive quality of moderation, or sense of perspective. Unfortunately, some runners lose perspective altogether. Their running program becomes an end in itself rather than a means to an end. At that point running is no longer an entirely healthy activity."

One of the respondents to my survey, a 47-year-old physician, wrote: "When I asked my wife about her thoughts
about this questionnaire the suggestion arose that next time
it should be addressed directly to the member of the marathoner's family. It's hard for me to be objective though I believe her response implies some unhappiness. Frankly, I'm so
involved with long-distance running that although I'm concerned a little about the above 'unhappiness,' it would not at
the moment cause me to alter my schedule."

Another respondent, a 48-year-old Cleveland attorney,
feels he overdosed on running and has decided to give up the
marathon. He wrote: "While I enjoyed marathon running, I
found no joy in marathon training. The pressure to schedule
my life so I could get in the miles in the weeks before Boston
became unbearable. And I became tedious conversationally,
with the sole focus on my running. Clothes piled up, un-
washed; mail went unopened; my apartment became a sham-
bles; stinking running gear hung from improvised clotheslines
all over my bedroom. A once flourishing social life, and the
happy physical contacts that went with it, dwindled. Time on
the job decreased, as did efficiency while there: a 10-mile run
or 8 miles plus 5 miles of intervals do not come free. So I've
tentatively concluded that marathon running was a phase,
which I've survived with reasonable honor, given my 47 years
and no previous marathoning experience. But which I shall
not repeat or extend."

To illustrate the addiction process, Dr. Morgan told of several runners who had become so hooked on running that they
continued to run vigorously even while admitting that running had impaired their relationships with others and their
job performance and that they had acquired serious injuries.
One man, a 28-year-old school counselor, reported: "I simply
cannot exist any longer without a midday run. The problem
is that I am expected to counsel students throughout the
day—that's my job. As I sit in my office, however, I start to
become very tense and uneasy between noon and two o'clock.
For this past month I have found myself going for a run in the
middle of the day in addition to my morning and evening

runs. I feel guilty, however, because I'm being paid to counsel students. . . . I know this cannot go on forever, but on the other hand I must run during midday. I know it's wrong, though—especially with the students waiting to see me. I don't know what I'm going to do."

Another runner exhibited less guilt and less perceived conflict. He said, "The hell with promotions—I achieve on the road!" Morgan commented, "Promotions are, in fact, often a bother. They can mean increased responsibility, additional stress, the possibility of relocation and less time and attention for self."

Following publication of Dr. Morgan's article in the March 1979 issue of *The Runner*, he received letters from numerous runners and their spouses crying out for help. These letters represented "true confessions" from people who were experiencing the negative side effects of a positive phenomenon. They saw Dr. Morgan as a man who had the courage to suggest that, for some people, the addiction to exercise that marathon running can generate can ultimately lead to self-destruction. Dr. Morgan sent me copies of some of these letters. One woman wrote: "I am a wife of 20 years of a man who for over a year now has jogged an easy 70+ miles a week, run 3 marathons in the last year as well as numerous minimarathons. In the last six months the fact of numerous problems has surfaced and for four months the four children (an additional oldest child is away at school) and I have lived without husband and father. The children do see him between runs! . . . I must be clear that the marriage problem is not entirely related to the running and that there are many contributing factors. However, it does seem that running does and has offered an escape from reality."

At the Psychology of Running Seminar in October 1979, Dr. Michael L. Sachs of Florida State University delivered a paper on running addiction. The paper referred to Bill Morgan's work and evoked a fair amount of feedback from the audience as well as from the other speakers on the rostrum. One person suggested that highly addicted runners were actually "running bums" and that they were in need of a sort of Runners' Anonymous. Another speaker attributed to runners this philosophy: "I run not because it makes me feel good but because I feel bad when I don't." Dr. Sachs acknowledged that because the phenomenon of negative addiction is so new there is virtually no hard data on it among runners; most of what is deduced is based on anecdotal records of "addicted" runners.

To which someone at the seminar, on that day before the New York City Marathon, noted: "They're all here today."

6

TRAINING: A REALISTIC PROGRAM

In 1909 marathon running was very popular in the United States. While people did not participate in the large numbers we find today, there were many colorful figures among the better runners, and thousands of enthusiasts came out to watch them compete in both amateur and professional races. Johnny Hayes, an American who won the 1908 Olympic Marathon (London), did much to stimulate this excitement. And other heroes of the day included Matthew Maloney, Tom Longboat, and Alf Shrubb of Great Britain.

There was such interest in distance running—some even called it a craze—that a book called *Marathon Running* (1909) was published by the American Sports Publishing Company of New York. The book was part of Spalding's Athletic Library, and it was edited by James E. Sullivan, who, in addition to being president of that publishing company, was the first president of the Amateur Athletic Union. The 128-page book, which sold for a dime, is a priceless piece of marathoning history and contains race results as well as pointers on training, pacing, diet, form, gear, and race management offered by the experts of that time. There are even some tips on "how to lay out a track on a baseball field" because races were sometimes held in ball parks. The Marathon Derby of 1909, for instance, was run within New York's Polo Grounds. While the athletes of that time were given a few strange notions, many of today's marathoning principles apparently were known more than seventy years ago. Here is an excerpt:

Training for Marathon Racing
1. Age: The pitiful sights witnessed in many Marathon races of late, where young men have been allowed to start and compete, are not examples of what we must do if we are to improve the benefits to be derived from distance running. There is no place in a Marathon race for a boy who is not mature. Promoters should absolutely insist on an age limit of at least nineteen years.
2. Work: Anyone who enters a Marathon race without having proper preparation is most assuredly injuring his constitution. Many of our present-day five- and ten-mile champions have failed at Marathon running. They seem to think that because they can run ten miles they can run twenty-five. It is an entirely different proposition.
3. Sleep: The young lad, or the old lad, who is shining in the athletic world and who thinks that because he has a nice physique and a strong constitution he can get along with five or six hours' sleep is making a serious mistake.
4. Diet: Running every day, sweating and losing weight, will soon have a man worn to bits if he does not take proper nourishment. Go on the theory that what you eat and drink is to be worked off and made into muscle and sinew.
5. Pace: There is no reason why a man should not prepare his schedule in advance; knowing his own capabilities he should go according to a schedule. In that way his advisor on a bicycle can keep him posted, and he will not run his head off in the early part of the race.
6. Shoes: The Spalding Marathon Shoe is the only shoe on the market that is suitable for both indoor and outdoor wear. It is hand-sewn with a flexible upper. The soles are of good weight

and protected on the outside with rubber, to prevent slipping of the tendon or muscles. A shoe should be light, flexible and with a good weight sole to give proper results.

7. Clothing: The most sensible and sanitary outfit for fall and winter should consist of a serviceable pair of long gray woolen or worsted tights, either coming to the ankle and to be worn with a light sock or to have feet attached as the case may be, and as the wearer may prefer. Over these tights, for the sake of looks, the regular short running pants should be worn. A very light-weight sleeveless cotton shirt and medium-weight sweater should be worn over this.

Don'ts for Marathon Runners

1. Don't allow a trainer or handler to throw buckets of water on you while in competition. It is absolutely unnecessary and a detriment.

2. Don't wear spiked shoes in a Marathon race, either indoor or outdoor.

3. Don't, in practice, run yourself to a standstill.

4. Don't smoke, and don't drink intoxicants.

5. Don't let anyone give you "dope" in a race.

6. Don't, in the winter time, take cold baths. They shock the system and are of no value.

7. Don't start in a Marathon race with a new pair of shoes.

8. Don't take any nourishment before going seventeen or eighteen miles. If you do, you will never go the distance.

9. Don't, an hour or so before the race, go out and eat a very hearty meal.

10. Don't stop at the side of the road to be rubbed down; you will never get going again.

These do's and don'ts of marathon training from the great runners of three generations ago tell us that many of the principles of long-distance running hawked today by the sport's leading spokespersons are not "secrets" at all. They suggest that common sense and trial-and-error provide the runner's most effective guidelines. But while I am familiar with the commandments of marathon training—the distance requirements, speed buildup, carbohydrate-loading, what have you—I am also a closet disbeliever. I can't help feeling that because we are all so different in our physical and emotional makeup, there is little we can take from the schedules of others. Also, marathon running is not a skill sport, unlike sprinting and hurdling. There are specific techniques that must be mastered to do well in those events. If a runner has tremendous leg speed but has not learned, for example, the technique of starting or of correct arm action, he will never be very good in the 100-meter dash, an event that requires great power and precision.

The longer the distance, the greater the differences among runners in preparing for it. Even the 1975 Aerobics Institute study of elite distance runners showed a weekly training range of 75–120 miles for the 9 marathoners in the group.

By definition, trial-and-error yields mistakes, but that is part of the thrill of conditioning, of finding through experimentation a running schedule that works for you. It would be wonderful if we could all memorize Astrand and Rodahl's *Textbook of Work Physiology* (1970) and then adapt its principles to every mile we run. But life does not work that way. And while sophisticated sportsmedicine is hard on the trail of physiological determinants in marathon running, few of us can find out our VO_2 max, percentage of slow-twitch muscle fiber, and anaerobic metabolism. Nor would we all want to. While sportsmedicine has made great advances in its studies of long-distance running, I still suspect that the human body's reaction to running long distances is so complex that the only gospel in our minds should concern our own experiences. When we run, we are both researcher and subject.

Having bared my skepticism, I will review some of the specific training doctrines espoused by runners and physiologists and also present a marathon training program of my own. I do this in part to satisfy the hunger of runners still looking for magic formulas to enhance their potential for improved performance. But remember—good magicians reveal the results of their magic, never the magic itself.

SPECIFIC TRAINING PROGRAMS

Here are four training programs that could be used for, or adapted to, marathon running. They are excerpted from the published work of Joe Henderson, Hal Higdon, Dr. David Costill, and Lasse Viren. Henderson is the author of numerous books on running. Higdon and Costill, contributing editors to *The Runner* magazine, have written extensively on training and physiology. Lasse Viren, the great Finnish Olympic champion, has written an autobiography.

Joe Henderson's Marathon Training Schedule

This program is taken from Henderson's article, "The Making of a Marathoner," which appeared in the 1977 New York City Marathon program, published by *New Times*. After detailing schedules for Basic Training, Distance Building, and Summer Break, Henderson wrote, "You have the background now to make the final push for the marathon at the end of October, and you have three months in which to make that push. Training for a marathon is a long-term commitment, even with the preparation you've already done. You must double your distance again during these months. By sneaking up on the distance, building training mileage gradually for several months, you minimize the trauma of the race—you'll gain more from it than the relief of surviving, and give more than you might realize."

AUGUST

Sunday:	25–30 minutes
Monday:	25–30 minutes
Tuesday:	45–60 minutes
Wednesday:	25–30 minutes
Thursday:	45–60 minutes
Friday:	25–30 minutes
Saturday:	60–90 minutes

SEPTEMBER

Sunday:	35–45 minutes
Monday:	35–45 minutes
Tuesday:	70–90 minutes
Wednesday:	35–45 minutes

Thursday:	70–90 minutes
Friday:	35–45 minutes
Saturday:	120 minutes

OCTOBER
Sunday:	45 minutes
Monday:	45 minutes
Tuesday:	90 minutes
Wednesday:	45 minutes
Thursday:	90 minutes
Friday:	45 minutes
Saturday:	120 minutes

Henderson added these footnotes: (1) The Sunday run each week is optional; substitute a day of rest if needed. (2) Add 1 minute at faster speed for each 20 minutes of marathon-paced running. (3) When a range of times is given, progress from the lower to higher figure during the month. (4) Do a quarter-marathon race (6.55 miles) or time trial at the end of the first month, a half-marathon (13.1 miles) at the end of the second, and finish the program with a full marathon. (5) In the last week to 10 days, cut down to 30 minutes a day.

While Henderson has set up his schedules with times rather than mileage, I might point out that at an 8:00-mile pace, the August plan computes to about 40 miles a week and September and October to about 60 miles a week. Thus, considering his point about dropping off in the week or so before the marathon, a runner following this program will run 60 miles a week for the 6 to 7 weeks prior to the race.

Hal Higdon's Marathon Training Schedule
In a December 1979 article in *The Runner* ("The Runner Marathon Training Guide"), Higdon, fourth in the 1964 Boston Marathon with a 2:21:55 and still a 2:30ish performer at age 48, took an irreverent look at training phobias through the eyes of his friend, the Gnome of Athens, the runner's equivalent of Mel Brooks's 2,000-year-old man. While Higdon stat-

ed that the ultimate training guide would be published in his 1999 book *How I Broke Two Hours at Age 65*, he did make some firm recommendations.

A SCHEDULE FOR THE NOVICE

Sunday:	15 miles comfortable pace
Monday:	1 mile
Tuesday:	10 miles
Wednesday:	4 miles
Thursday:	Rest
Friday:	6 miles
Saturday:	Rest

A SCHEDULE FOR SEASONED RUNNERS ONLY

Sunday:	20 miles steady pace
Monday:	5 miles relaxed run
Tuesday:	10 miles cross-country varied pace
Wednesday:	5 miles comfortable run
Thursday:	Intervals: 10 × 440, race pace or faster, 440 jog in between
Friday:	5 miles easy
Saturday:	10 miles fast pace, or race

A SCHEDULE FOR ELITE RUNNERS ONLY

Sunday:	20 miles (sometimes more)
Monday:	A.M.—100-yard striding or sprints on golf course P.M.—8 miles steady
Tuesday:	A.M.—5 miles easy P.M.—6 miles fartlek
Wednesday:	A.M.—5 miles relaxed P.M.—13 miles cross-country at solid pace
Thursday:	A.M.—5 miles comfortable P.M.—Intervals: 4 × 1,320, 440 jog in between

Friday: A.M.—5 miles pleasant
             P.M.—8 miles, building pace in middle
Saturday: A.M.—10 miles fast, or race
             P.M.—5 miles cooldown

Lasse Viren's Marathon Training Schedule

Unlike the programs of Henderson and Higdon, designed for general consumption, Viren's program is his own and he offers it for reference, not necessarily for imitation. It is for a 2-week period in February 1976, 6 months before he was to repeat his Olympic 5,000- and 10,000-meter victories and also score a fifth in his marathon debut.

Feb. 8:   A.M.—6 km (30 minutes)
           P.M.—21 km (65:27)
Feb. 9:   A.M.—13 km (50 minutes)
           P.M.—traveling
Feb. 10:   A.M.—10 km (42 minutes)
Feb. 11:   A.M.—10 km (42 minutes)
           P.M.—22 km (1:30)
Feb. 12:   A.M.—12 km (48 minutes)
           P.M.—15 km fartlek (1 hour)
Feb. 13:   A.M.—medical exams
           P.M.—15 km fartlek (1 hour)
Feb. 14:   P.M.—14 km (race or time trial)
Feb. 15:   A.M.—12 km (49 minutes)
           P.M.—22 km (1:26); fartlek plus 5 km nordic skiing
Feb. 16:   A.M.—12 km (no time given)
           P.M.—16 km (1:06); 400–800 bursts
Feb. 17:   A.M.—12 km (no time given)
           P.M.—20 km (1:20)
Feb. 18:   A.M.—12 km (50 minutes)
Feb. 19:   A.M.—12 km (no time given)
           P.M.—22 km (1:26); includes 5-km bursts
Feb. 20:   A.M.—12 km (47 minutes)
           P.M.—30 km (2:08)
Feb. 21:   A.M.—12 km (52 minutes)

This comes to about 206 miles for 2 weeks.

Dr. David Costill's Marathon Training Schedule

"Each cycle," Costill says, "requires the greatest distance during the second and fourth weeks, with marked reduction in total effort during the first and third weeks. Thus, the runner gains the full benefit of the difficult training sessions by permitting a more complete recovery."

CYCLE A		CYCLE B	
Week 1:	60 miles	Week 5:	70 miles
Week 2:	90 miles	Week 6:	100 miles
Week 3:	70 miles	Week 7:	80 miles
Week 4:	100 miles	Week 8:	110 miles

"Based on previous research," writes Costill, "it seems that the total work performed serves as the strongest stimulus for an endurance training response. . . . Since most physiological systems require three to four weeks to show a response to a given training stress, it seems the runner's training load should be judged on the basis of total distance covered in a four-week period."

Now it is my turn. Here goes . . .

Marc Bloom's Realistic Marathon Training Program for People Like Himself

PHILOSOPHY

Earlier today I was out running with my friend Jimmy Behr (see chapter 11). Jimmy said he felt he was getting a little run-down and decided it was time to cut his mileage from 122 to 113. A week. Instead of doing 18 miles Monday through Thursday (in double workouts), 9 Friday, 18 Saturday, and 23 Sunday—which can get a man down—he'll drop back to 16 miles Monday through Friday and clip a mile from Saturday's workout. I hope Jimmy doesn't suffer withdrawal and do a 9-miler on Sunday night just to keep himself honest.

Jimmy never misses a day of running, never incurs an injury, and runs the marathon in 2:38. (If he cut his mileage and did more speedwork, he'd probably run a lot faster, but that's another matter.) There are other people like him. They should turn to Lasse Viren's training program, not mine. All of you who suffer no great interference in your running—all you 2:15 and 2:30 and 2:40 marathoners—study Lasse Viren's training or, better yet, ignore anything you hear about training because you're probably so routinized that any shift in your running would ruin its consistency. Why tamper with success?

MINIMUM REQUIREMENTS

If you do not run at least 20 miles a week and have not been running for at least a year, stop: Go out and run and reach that point and then try to prepare for the marathon. You simply don't have the foundation and experience to take the plunge. (Moreover, people who run marathons a couple of months after they start running make people like me look foolish.)

DESIGN

This is a 6-month program, since it takes at least that long to build to the marathon. Actually, it could take less time—even 3 months—but this schedule, unlike most others, allows for hypothetical setbacks and recoveries in keeping with the theme that there are the Lasse Viren's of the world and there are the mortals. I have also built into this program "acceleration points" so that runners who discover they have more talent than I will not have their progress moderated by the "average" developmental steps.

APPLICATION

Portions of this schedule can be used independently for runners at various stages of development and proficiency.

CONSIDERATIONS

People like me have several things in common when it comes to running. Here are nine of them.

1. It is almost impossible to run for more than 10 days in a row without missing a day.

2. Attempting to run at 6 A.M., before work, is self-defeating.

3. Attempting to run at 10 P.M., after dinner has been digested, is self-defeating but not as self-defeating as attempting to run at 6 A.M.

4. It is almost impossible to run "hard" for 2 or more consecutive days.

5. It takes 3 days or more to fully recuperate from a session of speedwork, such as 5 × 440 in 75 seconds with a 440 jog in between.

6. After running 5 × 440 in 75 seconds with a 440 jog in between, parts of the body that do not normally hurt start hurting.

7. Given the choice of eating a meal or running, we will choose eating a meal almost 50 percent of the time.

8. It is almost impossible not to get the flu or a bad cold at least once in the fall or winter.

9. It is very difficult to run consistently for more than 3 months without having to take a week off because of injury, family emergency, job responsibilities, or concern over the threat of a coup in a foreign land.

WEEK 1 (25 MILES)

Monday:	4 miles normal pace
Tuesday:	no running
Wednesday:	4 miles normal pace
Thursday:	4 miles faster pace
Friday:	no running
Saturday:	5 miles normal pace
Sunday:	8 miles slower pace

Comments: Not everyone's running "week" starts on Monday. Begin on any day and continue in 7-day installments. "Normal" pace is the pace at which you feel most comfortable in your training. Comfort should not be confused with "ease." Some runners feel comfortable training at a rather quick pace. Fine; soon enough, you will find out if the pace is *too* quick.

Faster pace is about a minute per mile faster than your norm, slower pace about a minute per mile slower than your norm.

WEEK 2 (27 MILES)
Monday: 4 miles normal pace
Tuesday: no running
Wednesday: 4 miles faster pace
Thursday: 4 miles normal pace
Friday: no running
Saturday: 5 miles normal pace
Sunday: 10 miles slower pace

Comments: Two important changes here. You switch your faster midweek run from Thursday to Wednesday to see which day you feel most like running fast. You start building on your weekly long run and aim to complete the distance even if you have to slow your normal pace considerably.

WEEK 3 (30 MILES)
Monday: 2-mile jog (the 10-miler knocked you out)
Tuesday: 5 miles normal pace
Wednesday: no running
Thursday: 6 miles faster pace
Friday: no running
Saturday: 7 miles normal pace
Sunday: 10 miles slower pace

Comments: Weary from the 10-miler, you alter your running somewhat in the early part of the week. Also, the previous week you felt uncomfortable running the faster midweek workout on Wednesday so you switch back to Thursday for what will become a fixed faster session.

WEEK 4 (25 MILES)
Monday: no running
Tuesday: no running
Wednesday: 5 miles slower pace

Thursday: 5 miles normal pace
Friday: no running
Saturday: 5 miles normal pace
Sunday: 10 miles slower pace

Comments: Coming back in Week 3 with 7 miles on Saturday and another 10 on Sunday has irritated your right Achilles' tendon. It even hurts a little when you walk. Play it safe and rest it, and when you resume running hit a slower-than-normal pace for the remainder of the week so you will be ready for another 10 on Sunday. (If you're not hurt or otherwise cranky, repeat the schedule for Week 3.)

WEEK 5 (32 MILES)
Monday: no running
Tuesday: 6 miles normal pace
Wednesday: 4 miles normal pace
Thursday: 6 miles faster pace
Friday: no running (A: 5 miles)
Saturday: 6 miles normal pace
Sunday: 10 miles faster pace

Comments: On Friday of this week we begin the Acceleration Points for runners with talent and a higher threshold for day-to-day running. On Friday, when the rest of us are eating more because we feel guilty that we're not running, go out and run 5 miles. Also, in Week 5, you are ready to test your conditioning by trying the 10 miles at a faster pace. If you can complete the distance at 30 seconds to a minute per mile faster than your normal pace, you're doing fine.

WEEK 6 (35 MILES)
Monday: no running
Tuesday: 6 miles normal pace
Wednesday: 5 miles normal pace
Thursday: 6 miles faster pace

Friday: no running (A: 5 miles)
Saturday: 6 miles normal pace
Sunday: 12 miles slower pace

Comments: I'm betting you'll feel terrific on the 12-miler, but don't overdo it; restrain yourself from going too fast or farther than 12 miles.

WEEK 7 (37 MILES)
Monday: no running
Tuesday: 8 miles normal pace (A: 10 miles)
Wednesday: 5 miles normal pace
Thursday: 6 miles faster pace
Friday: no running (A: 5 miles)
Saturday: 6 miles normal pace
Sunday: 12 miles normal pace

Comments: The better runner covers 44 miles this week, but bear in mind that no one is yet advised to try to run every day.

WEEK 8 (40 MILES)
Monday: 3 miles slower pace
Tuesday: 8 miles normal pace (A: 10 miles)
Wednesday: 5 miles normal pace
Thursday: 6 miles race pace
Friday: no running (A: 5 miles)
Saturday: 6 miles normal pace
Sunday: 12 miles normal pace

Comments: You're feeling great on Thursday, so why not go for it? That feeling is rare—capitalize on it. Now that 8 weeks of base conditioning have passed, some faster work can be injected into the program. Still, this will be a very minor part of the grand plan and an optional one at that. It is the first thing to put aside should problems develop.

WEEK 9 (40 MILES)

Monday:	5 miles normal pace
Tuesday:	8 miles faster pace (A: 10 miles)
Wednesday:	5 miles normal pace
Thursday:	8 miles faster pace
Friday:	no running (A: 5 miles)
Saturday:	3 miles slower pace (A: 5 miles)
Sunday:	A.M.—10-km race
	P.M.—4-mile jog

Comments: You have added a second faster workout, and this is also a good time to run a race.

WEEK 10 (45 MILES)

Monday:	no running
Tuesday:	10 miles normal pace
Wednesday:	5 miles normal pace
Thursday:	10 miles faster pace
Friday:	no running (A: 5 miles)
Saturday:	5 miles normal pace
Sunday:	15 miles slower pace

Comments: Your first 15-miler is very important. After you've run 15 miles, the marathon, psychologically, starts to seem less imposing. Run the first 5 miles of the 15 slowly to store your energy for the last few miles when you want to feel good about the long workout.

WEEK 11 (35 MILES)

Monday:	5 miles normal pace
Tuesday:	10 miles faster pace
Wednesday:	5 miles normal pace
Thursday:	10 miles faster pace
Friday:	no running (A: 5 miles)
Saturday:	no running (A: 5 miles)
Sunday:	5 miles normal pace (A: 15 miles)

Comments: Although you did the 15, you were fatigued toward the end and developed some groin soreness. Early in the week it got worse and you had to lay off. Accelerated runners do not have much trouble with minor soreness.

WEEK 12 (33 MILES)
Monday: 5 miles normal pace
Tuesday: no running
Wednesday: 8 miles normal pace
Thursday: 5 miles faster pace (A: 10 miles)
Friday: no running (A: 10 miles)
Saturday: 5 miles normal pace
Sunday: 10 miles normal pace (A: 15 miles)

Comments: You're still being prudent to make sure the soreness is gone so you can do more running.

WEEK 13 (50 MILES)
Monday: 5 miles normal pace
Tuesday: 10 miles normal pace
Wednesday: 5 miles normal pace
Thursday: 10 miles faster pace
Friday: 5 miles normal pace
Saturday: no running (A: 5 miles)
Sunday: Race—half-marathon

Comments: Essentially, this is not an advance from the 33 miles of Week 12 but from the 45 of Week 10. During Weeks 11 and 12, as you nursed a hypothetical groin injury, you didn't lose any conditioning, you simply stood pat. As you enter the second half of this 24-week program, competing in a half-marathon is not only appropriate conditioning in and of itself, but also a litmus test for your development. Noting how fast you run and how well you feel will help you determine the effectiveness of your workouts.

WEEK 14 (48 MILES)

Monday: no running (A: 5 miles)
Tuesday: 8 miles normal pace (A: 10 miles)
Wednesday: 5 miles normal pace
Thursday: 10 miles faster pace
Friday: 5 miles normal pace (A: 10 miles)
Saturday: 5 miles normal pace
Sunday: 15 miles normal pace

Comments: From this point you are very careful to build the week's long run so that there will be sufficient opportunity to run 20 miles once a week for at least a few weeks prior to your marathon.

WEEK 15 (50 MILES)

Monday: 5 miles normal pace
Tuesday: 10 miles normal pace
Wednesday: no running (you planned to run in the
               evening but work got in the way)
Thursday: 2 miles jogging, 2 miles speed, 2 miles jogging
Friday: 8 miles normal pace (A: 10 miles)
Saturday: 5 miles normal pace (A: 7 miles)
Sunday: 16 miles normal pace (A: 17 miles)

Comments: On Thursday of this week we introduce speed-work, which can lessen the inevitable monotony of homogeneously paced running and also increase your anaerobic threshold to pave the way for a faster marathon. The 2 miles of speed can be composed of 440 intervals on a track, or 1- to 1½-minute runs on the road, with 3- to 4-minute recoveries between each run.

WEEK 16 (54 MILES)

Monday: 5 miles normal pace
Tuesday: 10 miles normal pace
Wednesday: 5 miles normal pace (A: 7 miles)
Thursday: 2 miles jogging, 3 miles speed, 2 miles jogging

Friday: 3 miles normal pace (A: 5 miles)
Saturday: 7 miles normal pace (A: 5 miles)
Sunday: 17 miles slower pace (A: 20 miles)

Comments: Here, in the last third of the schedule, try to make sure you run every day.

WEEK 17 (60 MILES)
Monday: 6 miles slower pace
Tuesday: 10 miles normal pace
Wednesday: 7 miles race pace (you feel great)
Thursday: 2 miles jogging, 3 miles speed, 2 miles jogging
Friday: 5 miles normal pace (A: 10 miles)
Saturday: 7 miles normal pace
Sunday: 18 miles normal pace (A: 20 miles)

WEEK 18 (60 MILES)
Monday: no running (dog-tired from the weekend)
Tuesday: 8 miles normal pace
Wednesday: 10 miles normal pace
Thursday: 2 miles jogging, 3 miles speed, 2 miles jogging
Friday: 8 miles normal pace (A: 10 miles)
Saturday: 7 miles normal pace
Sunday: 20 miles slower pace (A: normal pace)

Comments: Your first 20-miler is another important test. If you can't run 20 miles comfortably in training, you won't be able to run 26.2 without severe discomfort in the marathon.

WEEK 19 (60 MILES)
Monday: 2 miles slower pace (A: 5 miles)
Tuesday: 10 miles normal pace
Wednesday: 10 miles normal pace
Thursday: 2 miles jogging, 2 miles speed, 2 miles jogging
Friday: 8 miles normal pace (A: 10 miles)
Saturday: 5 miles slower pace
Sunday: 30-km race (18.6 miles)

Comments: A 30-km race, or any event that approximates that distance, should be used as a workout and not run at optimum pace at this point.

WEEK 20 (NO RUNNING)
Comments: You've got a bad cold with a light fever and your muscles ache terribly from yesterday's race, which was on a hilly course. You chalk it up to experience and although you feel better by the weekend do not resume running till Monday, so you can be as fresh as possible.

WEEK 21 (50 MILES)
Monday: 4 miles normal pace
Tuesday: 7 miles slower pace
Wednesday: 10 miles normal pace
Thursday: 5 miles faster pace
Friday: 7 miles normal pace (A: 10 miles)
Saturday: 5 miles normal pace
Sunday: 12 miles normal pace (A: 15 miles)

Comments: You've fully recovered; and although you feel a bit weak, you're confident that the layoff has only delayed your progress.

WEEK 22 (61 MILES)
Monday: no running (A: 5 miles)
Tuesday: 7 miles normal pace (A: 10 miles)
Wednesday: 10 miles normal pace
Thursday: 2 miles jogging, 2 miles speed, 2 miles jogging
Friday: 10 miles slower pace
Saturday: 8 miles normal pace
Sunday: 20 miles slower pace (A: 22 miles)

Comments: You had to try for the 20 again, and I'm betting it felt good and gave you even more confidence for the upcoming race. Even though every day counts now, you had to take Monday off to rest for substantial running the rest of the week.

WEEK 23 (70 MILES)

Monday: 6 miles normal pace
Tuesday: 10 miles normal pace (A: 12 miles)
Wednesday: 10 miles normal pace
Thursday: 2 miles jogging, 2 miles speed, 2 miles jogging
Friday: 10 miles faster pace
Saturday: 8 miles slower pace (A: 10 miles)
Sunday: 20 miles normal pace

Comments: If next week is the marathon, this is your last heavy week of training before the period of cutting back for ample rest. If the marathon is some weeks away, maintain the 70-mile schedule but be prepared to cut Tuesday's or Wednesday's 10-miler to just a few miles of jogging if you feel worn out.

WEEK 24 (29 MILES*)

Monday: 7 miles normal pace (A: 10 miles)
Tuesday: 10 miles normal pace
Wednesday: 7 miles normal pace
Thursday: 5 miles slower pace (A: 7 miles)
Friday: no running (A: 5 miles)
Saturday: no running
Sunday: THE MARATHON

Appraisal: You have averaged 43 miles for 23 weeks (not counting the hypothetical 1-week layoff). In 9 of those weeks you totaled 50 miles or more. Four times you ran 20-milers. Accelerated runners averaged 50 miles a week, reached 60 or more in 6 weeks, and ran 20-mile workouts 6 times. Chances are you suffered a few minor setbacks and one major one—which were built into this schedule—but you are now in excellent shape and fully prepared to run a marathon. If you have been faithful to the schedule, you have not overtrained since the program allowed for "easy" days and recuperative periods following hard workouts.

*Plus the 26.2 miles for the marathon.

"Too often," writes Dr. David Costill, "both coach and runner ignore the important contribution of rest to running performance. From a physiological point of view, the purpose of physical training is to stimulate the biological systems essential for prolonged, high rates of energy production. As a result, the systems are often overused and require rest to compensate for the stresses of training. It is in this way that the systems get stronger and the runner's endurance improves."

OTHER SYSTEMS

There is no lack of training approaches to the marathon. Of the 47 usable responses to a training question that appeared in the marathon survey I distributed in the spring of 1979, 21 runners said they trained 40–50 miles a week prior to their first marathon, 11 runners said they trained 50–60 miles a week, 10 ran 60–70, and 5 did 70 or more miles per week. Emil Zatopek of Czechoslovakia, who won the first marathon he ran—the 1952 Olympic Marathon in Helsinki—trained mostly on a track where he did repeated sets of fast intervals. "When his training was designed for long distance," his biographer Frantosek Kozik wrote, "he kept up the 60 × 400-meter stretches for ten days without a break." During a 1979 visit to New York, Zatopek said, "I knew how to run slow. I wanted to learn how to run fast."

One of the respondents to my questionnaire prepared for the 1979 Boston Marathon by cross-country skiing an average of 15 kilometers (9.3 miles) a day for a month and then running an average of an hour a day for a month. His time was 2:58:14. Dr. Alex Ratelle of Minneapolis, one of the most determined runners I've come across, supplements his 80-mile-a-week training regimen with regular stints on a stationary bicycle. "Though there are specialized skill areas of running, such as tempo and stride length," he says, "running performance is ultimately a reflection of work capacity—and stamina, strength, and work capacity may be enhanced in a variety of ways, which all involve work and effort. If this can be accomplished without risk of injury, then consideration should be given to logical ancillary training." Ratelle, 55, has run more than 80 marathons since 1967, and his best time of 2:31:56 set a U.S. age-54 record in 1978. Claire Gesalman's system is a bit different. In an article in the magazine *Running*, she told of competing in the 1976 Skylon Marathon in Buffalo, New York, after running only 173 miles in the 14 weeks preceding the race. "At the time," she said, "I was in the throes of finishing the research for my M.S. degree. I ran when I could find time and entered the marathon for fun, but aiming to finish. I knew it would be slow and possibly painful, but I figured I could make it anyway. I had been running since 1970, so I had a fairly good fitness base." She finished in "nearly 5 hours."

Success comes in different forms. For the past few years Bill Rodgers has run about 130 miles a week, give or take a mile. In 1978, when Rodgers won 27 of 30 road races including the Boston and New York City marathons, his exact mileage for the year was 6,296, an average of 125 per week. While Frank Shorter's regimen is similar to Rodgers's, Craig Virgin says, "I've never run 100 miles a week," apparently embarrassed that somebody would think he had. But Virgin, unlike Rodgers and Shorter, is first of all a 10,000-meter runner and only secondly a marathoner; at least that was the case through the end of 1979.

In a survey of participants in the 1978 Atlanta Marathon, Jeff Tucker of Georgia State University found the 32 respondents had run a total of 416 miles a week in the 8 weeks leading up to the race and had run 20 miles an average of $2\frac{1}{2}$ times during that period. Their average time in the race was 3:23. Broken up by performance, the 9 runners who averaged 2:50 ran 510 miles during those 8 weeks, while those averaging 3:18 and 3:48 ran 451 and 334 miles, respectively, during that period.

While the training of marathon runners depends on many things, two factors are essential: One is how much the body can take, and the other is what is believed to be the "right" amount for the goals in mind. If we could take it, most of us probably would run a lot more than we do; but even if we had the time, high mileage would wreck us. So we run in a progressive manner as far as we can and tailor our efforts according to principles of endurance that have come to be accepted after years of experimentation and study.

A training program should be composed of two types of running—long, slow distance (LSD) and fast, higher-intensity work. LSD enables the runner to build up the body's capacity to work for an extended period of time while avoiding major stress to the body. The cumulative effect of daily or near-daily bouts of LSD running is a high degree of aerobic metabolism. The heart and lungs will become stronger and more efficient, and the body will develop the capacity to take in greater volumes of oxygen and transport it faster and more efficiently to the cells, where oxidative enzymes serve to fuel the muscles with energy. Thus, one would acquire the physiological properties needed to sustain relatively slow-paced running for a distance of 20 miles and more.

Speedwork
When goals extend beyond the mere completion of a distance such as the marathon to the pursuit of a given (i.e., faster) time, LSD training alone is insufficient because, according to David Costill, "it fails to develop the neurological patterns of muscle fiber recruitment that will be employed during races which require relatively higher speeds." Costill also notes, "We have observed that men who use only the LSD method of training seem to show marked improvements in performance when they race frequently. This suggests that the faster speeds of competition serve to supplement the runner's aerobic endurance with patterns of movement that make his efforts more efficient." Thus, the need for occasional speedwork, such as intervals of 440 yards or repeats of fast runs of, say, a mile, or even near-maximal efforts of 5, 8, or 10 miles. What high school track coaches call "time trials."

That there is a relationship between training speed and racing speed became apparent to me in the 1977 New York Marathon. I had built up for the race by running 65–70 miles a week for 10 weeks. During these 10 weeks, I missed 2 days of running. I handled 10-mile workouts with ease and felt I was in excellent shape, perhaps the best of my life. I thought I'd go out at a 7-minute pace and see how it felt; even if I slowed up after a while I'd still be assured of breaking my PR of 3:17.

What I did not take into account was the fact that in those 10 high-mileage weeks my training pace was 7:15 to 7:30 per mile and that, intent on adding up the miles, I rarely ran 7:00 or better. Nor did I race much during that period. The result? I was able to run 7-minute miles for 17 miles, after which I slowed to an 8-minute pace from miles 18 through 20 and then, in a textbook case of marathoning deterioration, I hit the wall. It took me an hour to shuffle the final 6 miles, and my time was 3:25. I had worked above my "anaerobic threshold" at an early point in the run, which ultimately caused premature glycogen depletion and a lactic-acid buildup in the muscles, severely limiting my performance.

Some researchers believe anaerobic threshold is just as important as maximal oxygen uptake (VO_2 max) in serving as a barometer of training state. Operating under that premise, Per Balke of Penn State University—son of Bruno Balke, a pioneer in exercise physiology—has been studying anaerobic threshold, which he defines as "the point at which you could work for extended periods of time with oxygen being the sole source of energy." He has been monitoring ventilatory responses of runners under ambient conditions and at high altitude, through the use of an altitude chamber. Balke collected data by having runners run on a treadmill, taking special note of the inflection point in ventilation—the change in breathing that signals the anaerobic threshold. "By finding anaerobic threshold," Balke claims, "we can find what percentage of their 'max' would be ideal for training. You should be able to train continuously at levels just under your anaerobic threshold. It's an optimum training intensity."

While most top-flight marathon runners have VO_2 max values of 70 or higher, certain marathoners have lower values (for many reasons) but can run as fast or faster than the others not only because factors other than VO_2 max influence performance but because they train at a higher percentage of their VO_2 max than do the more well-endowed runners. Training at this higher submaximal level will cause anaerobic threshold to increase and the runner in competition will be able to sustain a faster pace for a given period of time.

Nutrition

While most researchers agree that some combination of long, slow running and short, fast running over a period of time will enable one to run a marathon at a respectable speed, there is no consensus among experts as to nutritional factors governing long-distance running performance. Books and magazine articles abound with theories, diets, recipes, and miracle formulas, with claims and counterclaims about protein, carbohydrates, vegetarianism, vitamins, bee pollen, and beer. My view of food and drink parallels the conclusions of Dr. Ralph E. Nelson, assistant professor of physiology and associate professor of nutrition at the Mayo Medical School, Rochester, Minnesota. Writing in *The Physician and Sportsmedicine* in November 1975 ("What Should Athletes Eat? Unmixing Folly and Fact"), Dr. Nelson asserted, "There is no simple food or nutrient that, when added to the diet, will produce special beneficial effects. . . . Better athletic performance should be accomplished through physical and psychological training not through excessive eating, special supplementation or other food fads."

Dr. Nelson did endorse, with reservations, one nutritional technique that has gained a wide constituency in running. This is carbohydrate-loading. Carbohydrate-loading seems to have gained such popularity that its actual effectiveness is secondary to the psychological lift it provides to large numbers of believers. I am reminded of dinner the night before the 1979 Boston Marathon. Italian restaurants, for their carbo-rich fare, were filled to capacity all over Boston. I was having a late dinner that evening with another journalist covering the race, and by 10:00 P.M. the restaurant we'd gone to had run out of Italian bread, spaghetti, and most other pasta dishes. We'd recognized many other runners there, most notably a group of

Englishmen including the world-class Trevor Wright. We chatted with the hostess about the run on pasta, and she said it was their biggest night ever, that they'd dished out eight times as much pasta as they normally would on a Sunday. Among the dietary nonconformists in Boston that weekend was that well-known nonconformist, Frank Shorter. Shorter dined on Chinese food. The next day he did not run well but cited biomechanical imperfections, not gastronomical ones, as the culprit.

By now, if you've ever leafed through a running book or magazine, you're familiar with the method of and rationale for stocking up on carbohydrates in the week before a marathon. The theory, advanced by Dave Costill and others, is that since our main energy source is the carbohydrates stored in the muscles and liver as glycogen, the more glycogen we have on reserve the day of a marathon the better our chances of running well. The method used to increase these glycogen reserves is first to deplete the glycogen by running a long workout the week before the marathon, then to take in a minimum of carbohydrates for a few days, and finally to consume great amounts of carbohydrates for the next few days when you would not use them up because you'd be running very little before the race.

Spaghetti, for example, is broken down in the stomach and intestines and absorbed through the intestinal wall so that it appears in the bloodstream as simple glucose. It is then transported by the blood to the liver, where—still as glucose—part of it is stored and part goes on to the muscle. When that glucose reaches tissue in the muscle that has been exhausted by exercise, it takes on other glucose molecules, which link together and form glycogen, a storage form of glucose.

Sometimes carbohydrate-loading works, in terms of enhancing performance, and sometimes it doesn't. The opportunity to refine carbohydrate theories so that they can be of more value to more runners has kept physiologists active in the areas of nutrition and strenuous exercise. The degree to which carbohydrate-loading works is, like other training devices, subject to psychological dependency. If you believe it works and can feel more ready and confident on race day, fine; whether it provides you more energy may not matter. On the other hand, the depletion phase can be tough on a runner because you are not getting your normal intake of carbohydrates while you are putting in your normal schedule of training. Some runners, because of this, report feeling irritable and fatigued at this time, hardly the way you'd like to feel in your final week's preparation for a marathon.

When I visited the Human Performance Lab at Ball State, Dave Costill and his associates were busy testing specific diets to determine their relative effectiveness in increasing runners' glycogen levels. Their findings suggest that the concept of carbohydrate-loading should be replaced by carbohydrate-*filling*—as much as the body can tolerate—since it appears that the greater the amount of carbohydrate intake, the better the chances of storing more of it for a long-distance run.

7

RACING:
CLIMBING THE WALL

The finest runners, like the rich, are different from you and me. They run faster—so much faster that it seems incongruous for them to take part in marathons together with the rest of us. They have a head start, of course—in body fat, muscle fiber, oxygen transport, energy utilization, biomechanical efficiency, and in thousands of miles and scores of races, all of which, more or less, enable them to run 26 miles 385 yards at a pace of close to 5 minutes per mile.

It is a fact that gets repeated over and over again wherever marathon runners meet. When talk turns to running, to the marathon, people shake their heads in awe and remark reverently that Bill Rodgers and Tony Sandoval or someone of their ilk just ran another marathon in 2:11. That is the pace of 5-minute miles. Yes, it *is* unbelievable. It is such an extraordinary feat that by the end of the 1970s only 19 runners in all the world had done it. (Another 30 or so had come close.) Bill Rodgers had done it 4 times, more often than anyone else. Toshihiko Seko, his Japanese rival, had done it 3 times.

The 5-minute-per-mile marathon is the stuff of Olympians. Go to any running track and find out—not by watching the champions but by trying it yourself. Try to run a mile in 5 minutes. Just one. Unless you are a trackman or woman or a very good road racer, you won't be able to do it. It hurts. And after you have run your 5:08 or 6:08 or even 4:52, sit down and let your heartbeat slow to rest and contemplate the athletes who run 26.2 of them in a row. Without stopping. Or, if you prefer, one hundred and four 440s in 75 seconds . . . in a row . . . without stopping.

That these runners are of special stock was impressed upon me in 1979, from the press bus as I watched them race one another in the Boston, New York City, and Montreal International marathons. Watching world-class runners in the front lines of a major marathon makes 2 hours pass very quickly. Five, 10, 15 miles go by, and then the runners who can sustain a 5-minute pace or close to it shed the hangers-on. Life at the front of the pack is a playbook, not a poem

There is speed, but patient speed. The runners do not look that fast. How could a 5-minute pace look slow? The same way your 8-minute pace might look slow to a nonrunning friend. Until he tries it. It is an economical speed and some of us, because of posture and energy expenditure and other things, are more economical than others.

While the finest runners are different, they and all the rest of us approach the marathon with two main factors in mind. These are level of conditioning and goals. They are interdependent, of course. One's goal cannot be to run 2:30 after training 40 miles a week at an 8-minute pace. Goal must match conditioning. In other, shorter events you can sometimes reach goals that would seem beyond your capabilities. Even if you fall short, you can still salvage a fine performance. But the marathon allows for little experimentation, little miscalculation, little disrespect.

Imagine a marathon god with a file for each of us. In his file he has stored the essential physiological information—our natural physical attributes and our training. And based on this information, we are programmed to run, say, 3:15–3:30; 3:15

is our limit, even if the weather is ideal and we feel terrific. Try for 3:05 and you risk everything.

As punishment the god curses you from the heavens, or at least from the Skywalk of the Prudential Building in Boston, eating away at your energy sources so that by about 20 miles—you fool!—you have almost nothing left. (If you were stranded on an island with only a loaf of bread, would you eat the whole loaf on the first day?) As your energy supply is being used up, a wall is being constructed much like a scale in which one arm is raised while the other is lowered. Both arms cannot be high. When the god's servants have cemented the last brick to the wall, you will begin to suffer, and as your suffering intensifies, you will be on Marathon's Death Row. "Next time," the gods intone, "you will have more respect."

It is not impossible to rise above the dictates of physiology in the marathon. Through some rare combination of psychological resourcefulness and luck, a runner occasionally delivers an extraordinary performance, one he is not likely to deliver again. This is much more apt to occur in skill sports or in running's shorter distances. In *The Psychic Side of Sports* (1978), authors Michael Murphy and Rhea A. White include a chapter on extraordinary feats, where John Walker is quoted after his 1976 victory in the Olympic 1,500: ". . . when I hit the front, I got a flash of compelling certainty. I didn't look over my shoulder, but I sensed someone coming up on me fast. . . . I was already at full stretch. But I went into a sort of mental overdrive, and my subconscious mind took over completely—I've experienced it in races before, and I can't explain it. I burned Wohlhuter off and went to the tape with my hands over my head." Walker, it should be noted, won with a rather slow 3:39.4, but what is significant is the credit he gives to psychological powers, powers no doubt in full bloom in his world-record mile (since broken) of 3:49.4 in August 1975.

I saw this intangible "power" exhibited in the 1979 Boston Marathon by George Hirsch, publisher of *The Runner*. George went into the race having trained consistently, but moderately, in the months before it. He was in fair shape—I know;

we'd run together at lunchtime—and said he was shooting merely for a time under 3 hours. His best was the 2:40 he'd run the previous fall in the New York City Marathon, a race for which he'd trained hard. I figured him to do 2:52–2:54 at Boston and no better. Like the rest of us from *The Runner*, George would be working during the weekend, concerned more with participating in the celebrity of the Boston Marathon than with running it.

But early in the race, George hooked up with Sue Krenn, who would place third among the women, and later with Joan Benoit, who would be first. This so inspired George that he held his sub-2:40 pace, unconsciously blotting out the doom one would have thought was impending, with about 10 miles to go. As he explained in his publisher's letter, "I lost track of my pace. They say the right side—the logical, reasoning side—of the brain begins to wander after prolonged exertion. I can certainly attest to that. I hit a marker saying 8⅞ miles to go, looked at my watch and realized there was no way I could work with those numbers. I kept trying to calculate my pace, but I couldn't get it to come out below three hours. This seemed strange since I kept saying to myself: 'I'm the third woman in the Boston marathon.' "

George ended up as the "fourth woman," with a time of 2:38:54—"Well over my head," he admitted. How he savored that run, a run he probably will never replicate.

When these once-in-a-lifetime performances occur in the marathon, they should not be confused with authentic marathoning breakthroughs. Because there is so much room for improvement in the marathon, runners can drop their times appreciably after a period of continuous training finally yields its much trumpeted effects. After Ron Breichaft, 36, of Michigan City, Indiana, increased his training from 70 to 85 miles a week, his marathon PR went from 3:07 to 2:49.

That George Hirsch could not determine his precise pace and even worried that it was not on 3 hours raises the question of how perceived exertion can influence performance. That he fed off the companionship of others makes one wonder to what extent such companionship can influence performance. Most runners come up against these questions in training, and there the answers are fairly evident. If we run a measured 10 miles, for example, we will know the fatigue we are supposed to feel after 7 or 8 miles. If we just go out to run "for a while" on unfamiliar grounds, we may pass 7 or 8 or 10 miles and not realize it, fixed not on the fatigue associated with time or distance but on the simple pleasures of the run.

Similarly, engrossed in conversation or merely supported by the presence of others, we tend to sublimate fatigue and can run longer and/or faster. But under competitive circumstances, when trying to run at our best, we may be affected less by these factors. "Perception of effort is directly related to actual exertional cost in 90 percent of all subjects tested," according to Professor William P. Morgan, a sports psychologist at the University of Wisconsin. "It is a perfect linear function." Under laboratory conditions in which one runs at maximal or submaximal speed, the subject's perceived exertion is determined generally with the use of the Borg Scale, which grades exertion from 6 (very light) to 20 (very, very heavy). "In many situations," according to *The Textbook of Work Physiology*, "the heart rate mirrors the physical strain experienced subjectively."

This is how it should be, theoretically, for optimum performance to be achieved. Should we not realize we are as tired as the workings of the body have actually made us, there is the danger of overextending in the early stages of the marathon and hitting the wall later on.

On the other hand, the mind plays great tricks on the body. The runner thinks he can run 3:30, finds his halfway time is 1:30 even though he feels as though he has done a 1:45. One of two things can happen. Spurred by performing better than his perceived exertion, he continues or even quickens the faster pace, armed with greater motivation and self-confidence. Or suddenly he feels very tired and slows down because he thinks he *should* feel that way after running at such a pace. In the latter case, performance influences exertion; usually, however, the converse is true.

I am reminded of high school track coaches I have known who relied on facile psychological ploys rather than expert training methods to get the most out of young runners. One of these ploys was to shout to runners in the midst of a 1-mile or 2-mile race split times that were either slower or faster than these runners thought they should hit. Whether the slower or faster times would be called depended on the coaches' knowledge of the competitive sensitivities of the runner. Some runners would respond to faster times, encouraged by improved performances they might achieve. Others responded to slower splits, fearful that if they did not pick up the pace they would fail to achieve even their minimum goals.

Apparently, marathoners also benefit from psychological devices, which are needed to help them cope with the painful ordeal of the race. In an article, "The Mind of the Marathoner," in *Psychology Today* (April 1978), Professor Morgan compared mind–body tricks applied by world-class runners and by runners with no special gifts. Morgan had found that elite runners "associate" with the pain and discomfort of competition, constantly monitoring "bodily signals of respiration, temperature, heaviness in the calves and thighs, abdominal sensations and the like." The other runners "dissociate," says Morgan, who characterizes the technique as "a kind of self hypnosis." He stated, "The runner who dissociates purposely cuts himself off from the sensory feedback he normally receives from his body."

An example of the dissociative thinking of the non-elite runner goes like this: "I know that I will eventually come up against the wall. The pain will become unbearable and I need to prepare myself. Mainly, I try to think about other things. I try to get my mind away from the pain. I try to fight through the wall. I know if I can't break through the wall, however, I will usually drop out somewhere around the twenty-first and twenty-third mile."

From the elite associative runner: "I not only pay attention to my body as I run, but I also constantly remind myself to relax, hang loose, not tie up—that can be disastrous. A lot of good runners will tie up; you can't be tight, however, you have to be loose. There is no wall for me . . . I stay away from the wall. I think a lot of guys are so concerned about the wall that they psych themselves out."

As Morgan says, such runners can afford to associate because "they suffer less during a race." They can flirt with the wall and know it will not seduce them. Not so for other runners. The wall. It is what makes the marathon the marathon. If history had settled the marathon at 20 miles, what would we want with it? Give us 26 miles 385 yards, 6 miles more than the body by all logical accounts is supposed to be able to take, and we will propel ourselves in the interests of sport. That is where the marathon begins, after 20 miles. The first 20 are just another long workout.

"It is at this point," says Morgan, "that a runner's homeostasis, or internal function, breaks down. The breakdown is associated with depletion of glycogen supplies in the working muscles; there is a loss of blood volume; core or rectal temperatures sometimes rise to 106 or 107 degrees, and the body starts to become dehydrated. The runner often develops what is known as paresthesia: his fingers and toes begin to tingle, a sort of queasy feeling overcomes him, and this is followed by muscle tetany or paralysis. He may also become dizzy or lightheaded, and may even faint."

So that's what I have had: paresthesia. It has happened in 4 of the 5 marathons I have run. The one in which I avoided it was beautiful, not because I'd run my best time of 3:17 but because of the feeling of beating the distance without having to take a beating. I could walk away from it. The others—hell.

My first marathon, back in 1973, was the least troublesome. Back then, the New York City Marathon was 4 laps around Central Park (plus one smaller loop), and any race that has laps invites quitting. And I did, at 20 miles, about 3 miles after the leg cramps started. The next year was a virtual carbon copy, only this time I was more determined to finish and trotted on past 20 miles with leg cramps, trying to climb the wall but being forced to lie down in the dirt on the upper east side of the park. It would have been utterly impossible to make it up the 110th Street Hill one more time, so I cut through the park to the West Side, circumventing the big hill and shaving about a mile from the total distance. I shuffled to the finish line in just under 4 hours, a wreck. People congratulated me for finishing a marathon for the first time, but I felt so defeated I kept my transgression a secret, even from my wife, Andrea. I would not leak the truth for a year and a half, at which time I provided full disclosure in a piece about turning 30 for *The New York Times* "View of Sports" page.

Thus, I was 0 for 2 in 1976, the next time I put my self-respect on the line, the year the New York City Marathon spilled out of Central Park and onto the pockmarked streets of the city's five boroughs. I was in good shape, after a summer of running almost every day, hardened by my past experiences. But this time I had another monkey on my back. Two and a half weeks before the race I came down with a serious case of bronchitis, which forced me to stay in bed for a week. When I resumed running my spirit had waned but apparently not my conditioning. Two doctors told me that running a marathon after what I'd gone through would be suicidal. I ran anyway, thinking I would drop out (what an excuse I had this time) if things got rough.

At the start I hooked up with Ed Bowes, a buddy of mine who coaches track and cross-country very successfully at Bishop Loughlin High School in Brooklyn. Ed had been a runner for the better part of twenty years and a very good one at that. But for this one he'd done little running and hoped to merely cruise it. We talked track for mile after mile, were cheered by people who knew Ed, and reached 16 miles at a 7:12 pace. Bowes excused himself, picked up his pace considerably, and finished in 3:01. I slacked off conservatively and ran my 3:17. The best part was seeing, within 100 yards of the finish line, one of the doctors who had told me not to run. I would have broken 3:17 had I not momentarily stopped to call his attention to me.

The next year my experience was more educational than exultant. I got sucked into a group of runners aiming for a 7-minute pace and as we clicked off those 7s, on the button, I decided to stay with it for as long as I could. When the time came to slow down, I thought I would, and then I'd coast home. I knew I was in excellent shape. I passed the half-marathon in 1:31, feeling great, and hung on to that pace for another 4 miles. And then I did slow down—to an 8-minute pace for miles 18 through 20, and then finally to a walk-jog-survival shuffle for the last 6, which took an hour.

My homeostasis had broken down. My glycogen was used up like pocket money in Vegas. I had paresthesia. I was dehydrated. I was a racing car without gas or oil or water sputtering to a pathetic end. The first muscle contraction ominously signaled the beginning of the end. I felt it in my right calf, the gastrocnemius muscle, what physiologists call the gastroc for short. I stopped to massage it and then the left one started to act up. There I was, in Harlem, keeled over like a wounded soldier, unable to run, barely able to walk while those crippling cramps set in like vibrating metal clamps. Any movement triggered new and more painful contractions; any halt did the same.

I would have quit right there, the hell with finishing. But I couldn't just lie down in the Harlem gutter miles from the finish line, with no prospects for immediate medical aid. That much I could still figure out. So I kept going, an engine without fuel, walking stiff-legged, jogging, trying different strides and rhythms, trying to concentrate on the pain and then trying to forget it, desperate to rid my body of the demons inhabiting the muscles and joints and tearing them apart. My mind was still alert: I kept figuring what my final time might be. Each time I figured it the estimate got slower, but that didn't matter anymore. It is amazing how easily one's values change in the midst of such trouble. My body felt compressed with hurt and fatigue—the pain was no longer confined to the gastroc or the hamstrings or the quads, but like a cancer had spread to the buttocks, the shoulders, the back—and all I wanted to do was lie down, make it go away, and fall asleep.

As an experienced runner, and one who had lost the war of the wall before, I should have known better. This was my punishment for being the kid who pleaded for one more toy, for wanting more than I was entitled to. I foolishly broke the rules of common sense, and I was apprehended. My sentence was the final miles, when pragmatism carried me to the finish line long after my body had started to plead for mercy.

As if that weren't enough, the MASH unit at the finish had no Hawkeye Pierce to come to my immediate aid. The medics stretched me out on a cot and left me in my damp clothing. I got the chills and felt as though I had a high fever of the kind I experience when I get the flu. My calves and hamstrings continued to buckle with pain, and that frightening feeling of paralysis kept coming and going. My wife had my sweatshirt and she couldn't find me. My mother, I found out later, was peeking under blankets in the medical area looking for me. Thank God she never found me. Finally my chiropractor, Doc Goldstein, located me. He removed my wet clothing, massaged and bent my legs to reduce the pain, and applied ice to the ravaged muscles. "The whole thing is relaxation," he said. And eventually I was able to relax, make it home, eat, soak in a warm bath, and go to sleep. I promised myself I would never run a marathon again.

I carried scars of my ordeal for days, unable to go up or down—especially down—stairs without pinches of pain in my legs. My time was 3:25 and change.

The next year, in '78, I was not very fit, but, caught up in the growing excitement that had enveloped the event, I ran the New York City Marathon again. This time 3:25 was my goal. And again, even with my prudent 8-minute pace, I came up short after 20 miles. I harnessed enough mental gymnastics to get me through the final miles, hurt but not crushed. My time was 3:54. Never again, I said again.

That was a lie, of course. As 1980 began I was getting ready for another marathon. But this time I had isolated a goal and would be directing my efforts toward achieving it. I wanted to finish a marathon without hitting the wall. To facilitate this, I planned to: (1) run a marathon in cool weather when I would be more able to negotiate long distances comfortably; (2) lose weight to remove some of the strain on my energy sources; (3) eat no red meat, cakes, or candies both as a dietary experiment and to harden my self-discipline; (4) run 20 miles or more at least 4 times in training prior to the race; (5) carbohydrate-load the week before the race (this might not help but I figured it couldn't hurt either); (6) start out slowly in the marathon to conserve glycogen stores; (7) drop out of the race if, at 20 miles, I again hit the wall, and then reevaluate my running.

Long-distance running is one of the few mass-participation sports where success is easily measured. Your competitive performance is both feedback and reward, and in this context goals—identifying them and going after them—are crucial.

There are probably as many different goals for the marathon as there are runners. Begin with the select few trying to run 2:10 or thereabouts and work all the way up to those trying simply to finish. But this vast group can be broken down into four general categories: the champions who are contenders for victory; the second echelon of fast runners somewhere under 3 hours and hoping to dip further below it; the runners seeking to break 3:00; and the runners for whom "just" finishing is the main goal.

Ironically, the first group cares less about time than the rest. The contenders are out mainly to beat other runners, not the clock. To do this, they have several strategies at their disposal, dependent upon their condition, the opposition, the course, the weather, the importance of the race, even the next race coming up. Flat course? Hilly course? High altitude? Sea level? Very hot? Very cold? In between? A field of international stars? The best runners from the local Y? A small-time race or the Olympic Trials? Are there hills at key junctures, like Heartbreak in Boston, or the bridges in New York, where specific tactics will be called into play? Will the weather be more like the summery Honolulu Marathon or like the Washington's Birthday Marathon in Beltsville, Maryland, where in 1978 a storm brought the windchill factor to 20 below? Are there strong-willed pacesetters like Tom Fleming or Ian Thompson?

"Road racing technique," Bill Rodgers wrote in *The Runner* ("Road Racing Strategy," May 1979), "requires that you have a thorough knowledge of the strategies and instincts of your opponents. This includes knowing their best times at various distances (good 440 speed, for example, often translates into a strong finishing kick), their experience at the distance at which you'll compete, and their style of racing."

Style of racing seems to be changing a bit in the marathon, as top runners become able to maintain control over the tenor of the race to the very end. When Craig Virgin returned from the 1979 Fukuoka Marathon in Japan, he was a little shell-shocked by the sprint to the finish waged there by Toshihiko Seko, Shigeru Sou, and Takeshi Sou, with Bernie Ford not far behind as all 4 men broke 2:11. Virgin speculated that raw speed and late-race sprinting would become a more important part of the marathon.

For runners like Craig Virgin, the marathons like Fukuoka hold a lot of meaning. For the rest of us they are nice to talk about and watch on TV, but what we really want to know, beyond the pacing considerations alluded to earlier, is how to replace the fluids lost during the exertion of the race, especially when it is warm and fluids will be lost in abundance, thereby restricting performances.

Fluid replacement has been the battle cry in attempts by physicians and physiologists to educate the marathoner. This is so because severe fluid loss can injure—and even kill—runners. Human beings are very sensitive to changes in body temperature, and an elevation of just a few degrees can mean a medical emergency. One of the most important responsibilities of race organizers is to have sufficient amounts of water and other drinks available to runners before, during, and after a race. This is one of the reasons race directors feel compelled to limit the size of their fields. There is always the danger that fluids—especially out on the course in a marathon—will be used up by the first few thousand runners, leaving the slower ones, who need them the most, without an ample supply.

Even in a short race like the Falmouth Run, a 7.1-miler, amid 73-degree temperatures and 70 percent humidity as there were at Falmouth in 1978, heat can be a villain. After the race, 11 runners were hospitalized (and later released) for heat-related injuries. One of them, Alberto Salazar, who finished tenth, collapsed at the finish. His rectal temperature had risen to 108. He was given fluids intravenously at the site, then rushed to the hospital, where, before his condition stabilized, a clergyman was summoned to administer the last rites.

At the 1976 Boston Marathon, temperatures were in the 90s for most of the race, but remarkably, relatively few participants were stricken with serious injury. Boston area hospitals treated only 16 runners, according to *Physician & Sportsmedicine* magazine, which attributed the low casualty list to, in one doctor's words, "the voluntary withdrawal of several runners who knew their physical limitations." The magazine also noted: "Local radio stations and police cars with loudspeakers asked householders along the route to spray the marathoners with hoses and sprinklers and offer drinks of water. This was credited by medical people and marathon officials with helping the runners reduce the danger of extreme dehydration."

One runner apparently not helped quite enough was Kim Merritt, the women's champion. At the finish, after her 2:47:10, according to medics, "she could hardly focus her eyes and her pulse fell to 36 beats a minute." But, like Salazar at Falmouth, Merritt recovered quickly after hospital treatment. An attending physician, Dr. Warren R. Gould, said Merritt's temperature was 103 but she wasn't sweating. "The heat couldn't get out. It was like a blown fuse," he said.

Dr. David Costill has shown that the more one is prone to heavy sweating during a marathon, the more one is likely to encounter great difficulty. Naturally, I was thrilled to learn this, since I must hold the world record for sweat loss per mile, and this physiological factor could help explain my disappointing marathon performances. It may be my only chance to make the *Guinness Book of World Records*. Physiologists are not quite sure why one person sweats more than another, but the fact of high sweat loss is significant because it is virtually impossible to replace fluids during a race in equal measure with large amounts lost.

In *Conditioning for Distance Running* (1978), by Jack Daniels,

Robert Fitts, and George Sheehan, the authors state: "Fluid loss can be as great as eight to ten percent of body weight. Beyond about two or three percent loss of body weight, the effects of further fluid loss become more critical. . . . Among the disadvantages and dangers of excessive fluid loss are reduced circulation to exercising muscles (which reduces work capacity) and ultimate loss of ability to continue putting out sweat. Severe adverse effects of further temperature rise can result, including the possibility of death."

In *A Scientific Approach to Distance Running*, David Costill suggests that "fluid therapy" in distance running should conform to these guidelines: (1) The drinks should contain less than 2.5 grams (.0875 ounces) of glucose per 100 milliliters (3 ounces) of water; (2) the drinks should contain few, if any, electrolytes—at most .2 grams of sodium chloride (salt); (3) the drinks should be ingested at frequent intervals and in volumes of 100–200 milliliters; and (4) the drinks should be cold (40°F. or 4°C.).

A 1975 American College of Sports Medicine position paper on the "Prevention of Heat Injuries During Distance Running" states that "runners should be encouraged to frequently ingest fluids during competition and to consume 400–500 ml (13–17 ounces) of fluid 10–15 minutes before competition." Costill agrees that in warm weather "the runner should drink 400–500 ml of water or a dilute sugar solution 30 minutes before the start of the race."

In a June 1979 article for *The Runner* ("Heat: The Runner's Worst Enemy"), medical writer James C. G. Conniff provided a chart of do's and don'ts for coping with the heat. One of his points is to drink before you feel thirsty because "the body loses 2–4 pounds of fluid before thirst signals the need for rehydration." Those runners whose psychological ploy is to "dissociate" will suffer because even runners who monitor such things as thirst have trouble reading their body signs. Ignoring such signs will compound the problem.

While Costill and others say there should be small amounts of glucose in replacement drinks (because blood glucose levels, a source of energy, fall drastically during prolonged activity), Dr. William J. Scheyer offered another opinion in a review of replacement fluids for *Running* magazine in the winter of 1979. "My advice to the marathoner," he wrote, "is to go to the starting line with a can of Tab in his hand, take plenty of water during the run, and have a couple of beers afterward." Water is the important ingredient because the primary aim of any replacement fluid is to maintain blood volume, and only water can do that.

Scheyer claims Tab or its counterpart Diet Pepsi are "very dilute for good absorption and contain just enough glucose and caffeine to stimulate the mobilization of fatty acids. This spares glycogen and delays the inevitable collision of the marathoner and the wall." Still, water is preferred because "the more dilute the solution placed within the intestine, the more rapid will be the absorption—anything put in that solution, be it electrolytes or sugar or whatever, will decrease or delay the absorption."

MARATHON PACING CHART: I
For an Even-Paced Marathon

Pace per mile	5 miles	10 miles	15 miles	20 miles	25 miles	Finish
5:00	25:00	50:00	1:15:00	1:40:00	2:05:00	2:11:00
5:30	27:30	55:00	1:22:30	1:50:00	2:17:30	2:24:06
6:00	30:00	60:00	1:30:00	2:00:00	2:30:00	2:37:12
6:30	32:30	1:05:00	1:37:30	2:10:00	2:42:30	2:50:18
7:00	35:00	1:10:00	1:45:00	2:20:00	2:55:00	3:03:24
7:30	37:30	1:15:00	1:52:30	2:30:00	3:07:30	3:16:30
8:00	40:00	1:20:00	2:00:00	2:40:00	3:20:00	3:29:36
8:30	42:30	1:25:00	2:07:30	2:50:00	3:32:30	3:42:42
9:00	45:00	1:30:00	2:15:00	3:00:00	3:45:00	3:55:48
9:30	47:30	1:35:00	2:22:30	3:10:00	3:57:30	4:08:54
10:00	50:00	1:40:00	2:30:00	3:20:00	4:10:00	4:22:00
10:30	52:30	1:45:00	2:37:30	3:30:00	4:22:30	4:35:06
11:00	55:00	1:50:00	2:45:00	3:40:00	4:35:00	4:48:12
11:30	57:30	1:55:00	2:52:30	3:50:00	4:47:30	5:01:18
12:00	60:00	2:00:00	3:00:00	4:00:00	5:00:00	5:14:24

Our success in the marathon will always depend on a mosaic of elements. Running it well is truly a work of art. Some runners are both athlete and artist, but those who cannot be both should be glad for the times in which we live and the chance to try.

MARATHON PACING CHART: II
For an *Uneven*-Paced Marathon

Studies have shown that a prudent pace in the first several miles will enable the marathoner to conserve fuel (i.e., glycogen) for the latter part of the race when it is most needed. Here, then, is a recommended pace for a slowish start, faster middle, and a stable ending.

Avg. pace/mile	Slow 5 miles	10 miles	Faster 15 miles	20 miles	25 miles	Slow Finish
5:00	26:00	51:00 (25:00)	1:15:00 (24:00)	1:39:00 (24:30)	2:05:30 (26:30)	2:11:00
5:30	28:30	56:00 (27:30)	1:21:30 (26:00)	1:49:00 (27:00)	2:18:30 (28:30)	2:24:06
6:00	31:00	1:01:00 (30:00)	1:29:30 (28:30)	1:59:00 (29:30)	2:31:00 (32:00)	2:37:12
6:30	33:00	1:06:00 (32:00)	1:36:30 (31:00)	2:09:00 (32:30)	2:43:30 (34:30)	2:50:18
7:00	36:00	1:11:00 (34:00)	1:44:00 (33:00)	2:19:00 (34:00)	2:56:00 (37:00)	3:03:24
7:30	39:30	1:16:00 (37:30)	1:51:30 (35:30)	2:29:00 (37:30)	3:09:00 (40:00)	3:16:30
8:00	42:00	1:21:00 (39:00)	1:58:30 (37:30)	2:38:30 (40:30)	3:21:30 (43:00)	3:29:36
8:30	45:00	1:26:00 (41:30)	2:06:00 (40:00)	2:48:30 (43:00)	3:34:00 (45:30)	3:42:42
9:00	47:30	1:31:00 (44:00)	2:13:30 (42:30)	2:58:30 (45:00)	3:46:30 (48:00)	3:55:48
9:30	50:00	1:36:00 (46:00)	2:21:00 (45:00)	3:08:30 (47:30)	3:59:00 (50:30)	4:08:54
10:00	53:00	1:41:30 (48:30)	2:28:30 (47:00)	3:18:30 (50:00)	4:12:00 (53:30)	4:22:00
10:30	56:00	1:47:00 (51:00)	2:36:00 (49:00)	3:28:30 (52:30)	4:24:30 (56:00)	4:35:06
11:00	59:00	1:53:00 (54:00)	2:43:00 (50:00)	3:38:00 (55:00)	4:37:30 (59:30)	4:48:12

MARATHON PACING CHART: III
Various Goal Paces

Time goals	Pace per mile
2:00	4:34.6
2:10	4:57.5
2:20	5:20.4
2:30	5:43.3
2:40	6:06.2
2:50	6:29.0
3:00	6:51.9
3:10	7:14.8
3:20	7:37.7
3:30	8:00.6
3:40	8:23.5
3:50	8:46.4
4:00	9:09.2
4:10	9:32.1
4:20	9:55.0
4:30	10:17.9
4:40	10:40.8
4:50	11:03.7
5:00	11:26.6

8

INJURIES:
THE LATEST TREATMENTS

I am lying facedown on a chiropractic table, staring at the floor, listening to Muzak, and holding in my right hand the switch that controls the electric currents being used to stimulate the muscle in and around my left hip. These currents give my hip a tingly feeling, a feeling that becomes less acute, even soothing, after a few minutes pass. The electricity is applied to my ailing hip through contact pads that are wired to a device called a Medocollater, which is attached to the wall on my right. The Medocollater's chief function is to stimulate muscle. It is no bigger than a bread box and can be regulated as to the type, intensity, and duration of electricity it transmits. I am in one of the three treatment rooms at the Brooklyn, New York, office of Seymour Mac Goldstein, a chiropractor. I have been here before—many times. I come here when I am hurt. Doc Goldstein makes me better.

This injury is my own fault. I cannot blame it on defective shoes, the strain of competition, the weather, genetic abnormalities, other runners, or a freak accident. In the past, those things have caused me injury, although most of my problems have been the result, simply, of overdoing it. Like the time I developed Achilles' tendinitis after repeatedly running up and down the stairs of the seven-story apartment building in which I lived. Or the time, on the first nice day of spring, I ran 18 miles to avoid "wasting" the day, only to develop a knee injury because I hadn't run much that winter. Or the time, a week after a marathon that left me with groin pain, I ran a hilly 15 miles—14 miles, that is; I had to walk the last mile and then take a full month off because I had made a bad situation worse. We learn, especially if we are marathon runners, how far we can go, but frequently the desire to advance our conditioning poisons the normal logic we bring to other tasks. We become irrational in pursuit of the marathon.

I am being "put back together," Doc Goldstein's favorite phrase, on a Wednesday morning in early December. This past Saturday I ran for 1 hour and 50 minutes, about 15 miles. It was a hilly run—there are no unhilly runs on the South Shore of Staten Island. A few weeks earlier I had decided that, based on my current condition (which was reasonably good) and the time I'd be able to devote to running in the coming months (a bit more than usual), I would consider running a marathon early in March. That would give me about three months to improve my conditioning. Training time frequently is blocked out in three-month installments. Because of the way the body works under stress, it commonly takes ten to twelve weeks for substantial progress to become evident. I'd also decided that in the ensuing weeks of training my main focus would be on the long run.

The long run is to the marathon what the jump shot is to basketball: You can't be good without it. By doing a run of 20 miles or more once a week (more frequently if you can take it)—either as a regular part of your training or as a special feature in the weeks prior to a marathon—you condition the body to use sources other than glycogen for energy; you gain valuable familiarity with your body's overall responses to running 20 miles and beyond; and you acquire confidence in your ability to sustain the distance, which can be applied in the race.

"Burning fat with muscle glycogen is up to thirteen times more efficient than burning glycogen alone," Dr. Gabe Mirkin wrote in *The Sportsmedicine Book.* "It's like a sailboat with two power sources: gas for an outboard motor, and wind for the sail. When the wind blows, gas is saved."

TRAINING BUILDUP

In the last eight years I have run close to 20,000 miles. Aside from my 5 marathons, I have run 20 miles or more a total of only 4 times. This, I realized, had been my downfall. I was determined this time to eliminate that deficit from my program and run 20 miles once each week in the 6 weeks before the marathon. I had a plan. First I would calculate my weekly long run in time, not miles; somehow that would take the edge off my weekly quota, and it seemed as though it would become easier (mentally) to increase a workout by 10 or 15 minutes than by a mile or two. The first week I would run for 90 minutes and then increase the time by 10 minutes each week until I was doing 150 minutes, or $2\frac{1}{2}$ hours. Then I'd run at least $2\frac{1}{2}$ hours once a week for 5 more weeks in a row. Since my pace would be roughly 7:30 per mile, those last 6 sessions would give me the 20s. The other components of my training would be somewhat secondary—they would revolve around this long run. In the past I'd done it the other way, so that when it came time to run 20 miles I was not rested enough—mentally or physically—to handle it. The other three facets of my training—speedwork, overall mileage, and day-to-day consistency—would have to evolve naturally, with a minimum of conscientious guidance.

I believe it is almost impossible for all but the small percentage of runners who have extraordinary talent and/or spare time to carry every aspect of marathon training to its ideal climax. I know I can't, so for this go-around the thrust of my effort would be toward my long run; in a sense, I would be isolating a variable in order to evaluate its role in my training after running the next marathon.

TRAINING GREED

I was right on schedule until I strayed from my plan, and it cost me. I ran 90 minutes the first week, 100 the second, and 110 the third. Following the first two long ones, I took a day off, in a version of the "hard/easy" concept of training. At the end of the 110 I felt a minor irritation in my left hip, which I attributed later to not wearing heavy-duty shoes, the hills, and the possibility that in running slowly (an 8:00-mile pace) for several miles to ensure completion of the distance my stride changed and extra pressure was levied to the joints. Instead of jogging or not running at all the next day, I ran 8 miles, half of this consisting of intervals and windsprints on the nearby track.

That is why, three days later, I am stretched out in Doc Goldstein's office, calling myself a jerk. Perhaps I am another case study for Hal Higdon, who has advanced the theory of the "Unfairness Doctrine." The Unfairness Doctrine, Higdon wrote in the December 1979 issue of *The Runner*, "states that just when you get your mileage up to the point where you feel you are really getting in shape, something happens. This is the Catch-22 of marathon running. You catch cold. You twist an ankle. Your knees start aching. You suffer a stress fracture."

While I do not have a stress fracture, my left hip hurts and two days ago I could not walk without a limp. One reason for this, Goldstein told me, is that I foolishly applied heat instead of cold to the inflamed area. When muscle is inflamed, there is already too much heat in the area. An ice pack should be used to reduce the heat, stimulate circulation, and expedite the breakdown of waste products that accumulate in the injured area.

MUSCLE STIMULATION

The Medocollater transmits three types of sensations, and in the past they have been applied (in slightly different ways) to my quadriceps, hamstrings, shins, calves, knees, buttocks, and lower back. One sensation is a steady one, used to increase muscle tone. "I use it to bring the muscle to the point of fatigue," says Goldstein, "because we want to start from scratch. The muscle hasn't got what is called normal myotonic variance. Once we fatigue the muscle, we go into the next type of sensation." This one grabs the muscle, then lets go, grabs and lets go—"to bring the muscle to a point of 'normalcy,' so it would not be strained or sore, so it would respond to stress." The third type of current, which grabs the muscle and holds it for several seconds before releasing it, is administered to see if the muscle is functioning properly; this imitates the running process to gauge the muscle's response to stress. Electrical stimulation per se also reduces muscle tension and serves as a relaxant. If muscles are not able to relax, they will not perform and will be more inclined to become injured under stress.

SAINT AND SAVIOR

Doc Goldstein is an institution in New York, and his reputation extends far beyond its borders. His office opens five mornings a week at 8:00 A.M., "and it goes until I finish," which is usually about 9:00 or 10:00 P.M. depending on the season—which dictates the prevalence of running injuries. There are no appointments, no receptionist, no one to answer the phone other than Goldstein himself. You just show up and wait your turn. His waiting room is so tiny and so crowded that if those seated extended their legs, they would intersect in the middle of the room.

About 70 percent of Goldstein's clientele are athletes—swimmers, wrestlers, figure skaters, gymnasts, basketball players, tennis players, football players, and runners. He estimates that half of the athletes who see him are long-distance runners who take part in marathons. Goldstein is the attending medical specialist for the Colgate Women's Games, the world's largest track meet, and for other major track meets like the Millrose Games and U.S. Olympic Invitational. He has served in the medical depot for the New York City Marathon since 1976. He treats whole teams, like the hugely successful Atoms Track Club, serving as their unofficial team doctor. Sometimes, even when he is not asked, Goldstein appears at races and track meets because he knows runners will need him and the physicians on duty either will be ill-equipped to treat runners' ailments or will be unfamiliar with the personal nuances of the many runners whom Goldstein has adopted as his own. Goldstein's position is similar to that of the more publicized Dr. Leroy Perry of California, another favorite of runners, who has been subject to scorn from a medical establishment that looks at chiropractors with disdain.

To his patients, the runners, Doc Goldstein falls somewhere between saint and savior. There are countless examples of runners who hobbled into his office following a weekend of hard competition and competed the next weekend with remarkable success. "Putting them back together as quickly as possible" is Goldstein's foremost goal. He also talks to his patients with the sincerity and reassurance of a clergyman. He gives them faith and hope and sets the errant ones straight. No lectures. No dogma. Just talk about ideas that are reinforced with each visit. Runners confide in him. Like the man says, he puts them back together.

His patient list includes Lorna Forde, Mary Decker, Francie Larrieu, Ellison Goodall, Nina Kuscsik, Dana Slater, Steve Williams, Mike Sands, Alfred Daley, Vinnie Matthews, and Marty Liquori. Also Bozo the Clown: "Thanks for fixing my aching back," says the crudely framed autographed photo hanging in Goldstein's waiting room. Scores of other tributes are found on his walls and shelves—plaques inscribed "Thanks for all your help" from high school teams and running clubs and international medals, ribbons, and trophies won by patients who returned from London and Oslo and Leningrad to give their awards to Goldstein. "I don't like anybody to lose time," says Goldstein. "If you're an athlete, you don't stop. There is no stopping."

I have stopped for three days and tomorrow, Goldstein insists, I should resume running. I walk out of his office free of pain and hoping to do an easy 4 miles the next morning. If there are no complications I will try 90 minutes for my long run on the weekend, but at best I'll still be three weeks behind schedule. This was my week to run for 120 minutes. If I don't knock off the 120 soon, I won't be able to run enough 150s before the marathon. I may be forced to come up with an alternate plan.

THE INEVITABLE

Injury to a marathon runner is like chicken pox to a child—sooner or later you're going to get it. You can hide from it for a while, but eventually it catches up with you. Learning this is important because it lessens the psychological pain of being forced to curtail training or competition as a result of injury.

As a marathon runner you are taking a chance, whether you run 2:10 or 4:10. Man was meant to move—but not on concrete for an hour or two a day—and not, every once in a while, for 26 miles 385 yards. There is a risk factor. For the person who has been at it for many years, there is the danger of cumulative abuse finally humbling a muscle or joint. For the person just getting started, there is the danger of new and shocking stress to the muscles and joints.

"Runners are the fittest group of sick and injured people in the world," states *The Runner's Complete Medical Guide* (1979), an excellent reference written by athletic trainer O. William Dayton and Drs. Peter Jokl and Richard Mangi. The injuries common to average runners and joggers are not much different from those common to marathon runners. Like the potential for extraordinary performance, injury depends on our individual approach to the sport modified by the way we are built and the way we run. Mile-a-day joggers can suffer more grief than the most ardent marathoners. Jay Helgerson entered the *Guinness Book of World Records* early in 1980 after having run a marathon every week for 52 weeks, and he had not incurred one serious injury. Most of us are not so fortunate. Even Frank Shorter, who seems to float as he runs, has suffered a serious injury and needed surgery to correct the problem that caused it.

RISKY TREATMENT

The Runner's Complete Medical Guide has some basic pointers worth repeating.

Beware of:
- Anyone who claims to have the only answer.
- Quick "magic" cures.
- Anyone who ridicules honest professionals and praises himself.
- Aids, pills, and supplements promoted by slick advertisements.
- Anything that offends your common sense.

WHY INJURIES OCCUR

Injuries often occur, says the guide, when a runner neglects any one of the following:
- Adequate conditioning.
- Sufficient warm-up and cool-down periods.
- Proper running style.
- Adequate equipment.
- Attention to mechanical and environmental problems.
- Treatment of minor injuries.

BASIC TREATMENT

Five basic steps to the treatment of injuries:
- Immediate therapy to minimize damage.
- Assessment of damage.
- Assessment of cause.
- Healing of injury.
- Rehabilitation.

AFTEREFFECTS

"Loss of ability," say the authors, "starts after 2–3 days of immobilization. It takes about three days of rehabilitation to recover for every day lost to injury." After an injury you can expect the following to happen:

- Atrophy or loss of muscle size.
- Loss of strength.
- Loss of endurance.
- Loss of flexibility.
- Loss of coordination.
- Loss of mental confidence.

REHABILITATION

Rehabilitation, say the authors, can include isometric exercises, muscle stimulator therapy, weight training, and such substitute sports as swimming, cycling, and rowing. Another sportsmedicine authority who recommends swimming as an appropriate rehabilitative measure is Dr. Leroy Perry, the noted chiropractic orthopedist. "Swimming," says Perry, "is recommended for all common running ailments because it increases neuro-muscular coordination without placing stress on injured parts of the body."

Perry also is a great believer in proper posture as a tool for effective running and for injury prevention. "Let your weight work for you," he says. Writer Eric Olsen, interviewing Perry for *The Runner* in April 1980, related Perry's view of proper running posture: "The pubic bone should be tilted forward, as always, to prevent the buttocks from protruding, and the foot should land about one-half to three-quarters of an inch in front of the heel bone. The foot should then roll forward onto the ball and then the runner should push off from between the first and second toes." Notes Perry: "Only about 25 percent of the runners I see know how to use their toes properly when they run. Most don't use their toes at all. You can look at the bottom of your shoe and tell if you use your toes properly. Is the toe area worn? If it isn't, you're not using your toes."

STARTING WITH THE FEET

Podiatrists also are concerned with posture, which they evaluate through biomechanical analysis. In running, biomechanics focuses on the feet and legs, at rest and at work. Its scope
is so encompassing that it would be hard to diagnose a running injury and not relate the symptoms to a biomechanical
abnormality. Rather, to a "normality," for as Dr. Richard
Schuster is wont to point out, most of us have something
"wrong" with our feet or legs but only when we run 5 or 10
miles a day do these aberrations manifest themselves in discomfort or pain. Then it is time to pinpoint the weakness—
limited range of motion of the ankle, forefoot imbalance,
what have you—and in many cases treat the injured runners
by providing them, perhaps, with custom-made orthotic foot
devices to compensate for the biomechanical deficiency.

Most of the specialists who work in biomechanics are podiatrists like Dr. Schuster, and their clientele consists mostly
of runners. It is ironic that podiatrists have replaced orthope-
dists, at least in running, as the darlings of sportsmedicine.
Podiatry, in sports, is no longer a blister and bunion business.

"The foot is the foundation of the body," Schuster says.
"Foot problems can cause other problems all the way up to
the arms and shoulders. Most people, you see, have some imbalance in their feet. I manage to help almost everyone who
comes in here, but it should be made clear that I don't really
cure. What I'm doing is shoring up people's feet, balancing
them, tilting them, untilting them. It's like taking a chair and
leveling off the legs so that the chair doesn't rock. It's simple
mechanics."

DR. SCHUSTER'S GENIUS

In 1974, while in training for the New York City Marathon,
I came down with an injured right knee. Nothing I did, including rest, helped, and several doctors later I found myself
in Richard Schuster's College Point, Queens, laboratory having my feet and legs scrutinized with the single-minded care

**Biomechanical Evaluation of the Lower Extremities
by Richard Schuster, DPM.**
Patient: Marc Bloom
Height: 5'9"
Weight: 150
Born: 1947

BACKGROUND:
Patient runs about 50 miles per week. There is a history of intermittent knee pain and Achilles' tendinitis which appears to be controlled reasonably well with orthotic foot devices. Present concern is tenderness in the area of Achilles' tendon (right side) and occasional groin pain (left side). The patient has been wearing extra-soft-soled running shoes.

EXAMINATION:
Rotary range of the hip: Left, 75°; Right 65° approx.
Both hips show more outward rotation than inward rotation. However, this should have no bearing on the running.
Leg Lengths: Left hip approx. ¼-inch lower than right.
The slight difference in leg length does not appear to be significant in this case.
Forefoot balance: Left, 15° varus; Right, 13° varus.
Beyond average readings. High "varus" imbalance can be a contributing cause of occasional symptoms of "runner's knee."
Ankle motion: Left, 12°; Right 15°.
The ankle has more than the average amount of up and down motion associated with flexible calf muscles. It may be significant.
In-out motion of the heel: Left, 0° out/20° in; Right, 5° out/20° in.
The left heel has limited outward motion which could contribute to groin pain on the left side.

an auditor gives to a set of books. Schuster examined me with the tools of a carpenter and architect, scratched out a dozen numerical computations, and told me the cause of my "runner's knee" (or chondromalacia) was a "high varus imbalance of the forefoot that causes the foot to flatten." During running, he explained, the flattening of the foot caused irritation in my knee.

Schuster put my feet in a tub of gook made up of auto-

Arch depression: Left, $4/16$"; Right, $5/16$".
Within average limits and not significant.

DIAGNOSIS:

The occasional pains in the groin and knee are quite likely overuse symptoms. The groin pain is probably related to the lack of outward motion of the left heel. (The groin muscles tend to pull the leg in as the unstable ankle tends to move the leg out.) The knee pain is probably due to the varus imbalance of the forefoot which causes the foot to flatten. Achilles' tendinitis in the presence of an excessive range of ankle motion suggests overstretch symptoms—probably aggravated by wearing running shoes with extra soft soles.

RECOMMENDED TREATMENT:*

1. Orthotic foot devices modified for almost the full amount of total imbalance.

2. Quarter-inch heel elevations added to the orthotic devices.

3. Soft-soled running shoes to be replaced with shoes that have firm soles and thick heels.

4. Calf stretching exercises to be reduced by about 50 percent in effort and time.

5. There is to be no increase in running until further notice.

6. Hill running should be avoided until symptoms have subsided.

---

*I changed my running shoes (wearing my old orthotics while new ones were being made), reduced my stretching, cut down my running, and did no hill work, and gradually over a three-week period the tenderness in the groin and Achilles' tendon disappeared. During this period I also applied ice to the sore areas.

mobile grease and sawdust and took an impression of them. One month later I had a pair of leather orthotics to insert in my shoes (now they're made of other materials such as plastic) and, miraculously, I resumed running with no pain whatsoever.

I have been back to Schuster's lab several times over the years, for one pain or another or to have my orthotics adjusted (I must have one of the oldest pairs in continuing use found anywhere) and hope to have him film my running on a treadmill with new equipment he'll soon install as part of a lab expansion. On a recent visit my ailment was Achilles' tendinitis, and I have provided my chart for reference. (The chart, as originally printed in *The Runner* in September 1979, stated I run 50 miles per hour, not 50 miles per week, a slip that caused colleagues to observe aloud that anyone who runs so fast would certainly court injury.)

I strongly urge every runner who runs 5 miles a day or more to visit a reputable sports-oriented podiatrist, even if you are not injured. Take my word for it—you probably have something wrong with you. Every runner has a breaking point, and those in pursuit of the marathon are likely to reach it as their training intensifies. Take cover before lightning strikes.

PART THREE

THE
MAIN EVENTS

9

THE
BOSTON
MARATHON

"They came from 50 states and 28 foreign countries to the celebration, which one Boston paper trumpeted as 'The World Series of Distance Running.' Eight thousand qualifiers and 3,000 interlopers—from Rodgers and Benoit to Superman and Cowman—made the pilgrimage to Mecca, where they listened to prophets, fondled gadgets, devoured pasta, and tested their gut on Heartbreak Hill. Bill Rodgers wore a woolen hat with a Snoopy patch and was hailed by the finish-line announcer as 'the greatest distance runner in the history of the world!' Joan Benoit wore a baseball cap backwards as she and Patti Lyons bettered the winning time run by Clarence DeMar in 1928. Johnny Miles, who won it 50 years ago, watched for the first time; Jerry Nason, The Source, watched for the forty-sixth time; while Johnny Kelley, 71, ran it for the forty-eighth time. The men's and women's American records fell, and 76 runners exceeded the Olympic Trials qualifying standard. One who did not was '72 Olympic champion Frank Shorter, who rushed into town after assisting his wife in the delivery of their first child. Thirty-five hundred runners broke 3 hours, but many, according to race director Will Cloney, will not be invited back next year. PBS put it on the tube. A Vegas bookie had Rodgers at 7–5, Benoit at 8–1, and, because his mother asked, Dan Nichols at 15–1. Jimmy Carter phoned his congratulations to the winners in a symbolic gesture once reserved for Super Bowl champions. The Boston Marathon, by almost every measuring stick, is the world's greatest footrace. In its eighty-third edition it became, possibly, this year's greatest sports event."

That was my introduction in *The Runner* to our coverage of the 1979 Boston Marathon. It was a race that had every ingredient of a classic, and a race weekend that had every ingredient of a snowballing phenomenon. It was arguably the most important Boston Marathon ever, in that it boldly symbolized—for better or worse—everything the running movement had come to mean in a nation increasingly addicted to vigorous exercise.

It was all there, in Boston: great runners and great followers; official entrants and unofficial "bandits"; men and women from 18 to 80; new records and new heroes; one international cause célèbre, one alleged domestic fraud; one sweet old man who showed off his 1926 and 1929 gold medals; numerous parties, receptions, press conferences, exhibits, product displays, speeches, clinics, pedantic ruminations about the whys and ways of running, restaurants cleaned out of pasta, hotels decked with a conventionesque ambience, audiences in large numbers, enormous media exposure, on race day a cast of millions, and administrative threats to knock this effusive outpouring of marathoning down to more manageable size the next time around.

The most significant symbols of the American Age of Running surrounding the 1979 Boston Marathon occurred not only in Boston but in Las Vegas and Washington, D.C. In Vegas, a well-heeled bookie established a betting line on the race and took in "about $100,000" worth of action. In Washington, President Carter, who's been seen jogging his way through summit meetings in far-off capitals, invited the winners, Bill Rodgers and Joan Benoit, to attend a State Dinner at the White House in honor of a visiting head of state two weeks later.

It is fitting that when institutionalized sports betting came to running, it came first to the Boston Marathon. The Boston Marathon, more than any other race, can be considered the cradle of American distance running. Through the history of its heroes, its oddballs, its supporters, its zealots, its competitions, its conflicts, its legends of character, commitment, and circumstance, its influence at home and abroad, its latter-day entry standards—from its humble beginnings on a 24.5-mile course in 1897 to the commercialized convention of 1980—the Boston Marathon has represented and frequently magnified every element in the growth of American distance running. The Boston *Herald-American* was right—the Boston Marathon is the World Series of distance running. Just as great ballplayers are commonly remembered for their heroics in the Series, great runners are recalled for their achievements in the Boston Marathon.

There was, first and foremost, Clarence DeMar, who won 7 Bostons, the first in 1911 at age 21 and the last in 1930 at age 40. There was Ellison ("Tarzan") Brown, the Narraganset Indian who won in '36 and '39, the latter being the first sub-2:30 in Boston annals. There was Jimmy Hennigan, who, after dropping out in his 8 previous Bostons, won his ninth attempt, at 38, in 1931. There was Johnny Miles, the 20-year-old Canadian who registered the greatest of all Boston upsets in 1926 and won another title in '29. There was Leslie Pawson, a converted 2-miler, who won in 1933, 1938, and 1941, the last one at age 37 over three past champions. There was Johnny Kelley, the 1945 victor who placed among the leaders year after year and ran his forty-ninth Boston, at 72, in 1980. There was Gerard Coté, the Frenchman from Quebec, who triumphed in 1940, '43, '44, and '48 and was the all-time victory leader behind DeMar until Rodgers tied his record. There was Aurele Vandendriessche of Belgium, back-to-back champion in '63 and '64; the first ever 2-time Olympic marathon champion Abebe Bikila, widely recognized as the all-time greatest marathon runner. And then there is Bill Rodgers, the first Boston hero to be a product of the current running boom, who won it in 1975, '78, '79, and '80, setting American records with his first and third victories.

The person who knows more than anyone about the DeMar years, Tarzan Brown, the Kelleys, the Finns et al., is Jerry Nason, retired sports editor of the Boston *Globe.* He's seen them all since he first covered the Boston Marathon as a reporter for the *Globe* in 1934. Nason, a warm, active gentleman of 70 who lives in Winchester, a Boston suburb, has covered 46 consecutive Bostons, and his account of the '80 race was the *Globe*'s lead story on page 1. Nason is the acknowledged historian of the Boston Marathon, and he's got about a half-century's worth of checkpoint splits, weather variances, funny stories, rundowns on the greats, near-greats, and eccentrics chronicled in diary form. I caught up with Nason on the morning of April 16, 1979, before the press bus was to take us along the route to view the progress of the race from the start in suburban Hopkinton to the finish in front of the Prudential Center in downtown Boston. It was 10:00 A.M., and as we sat on the moist field adjacent to Hopkinton High School watching runners warm up, Jerry Nason reminisced about the Boston Marathon, and I listened.

Nason was born on the day of the 1909 Boston Marathon, and right near the racing course, in Newton Hospital (since renamed Newton-Wellesley Hospital). "My mother would tell me that when the runners came by, the nurse stood by the window watching while holding me in her arms. I'd always lived on the course. When I was a kid, in the early twenties, runners had attendants so we'd get on our bikes at Newtonville, pedal up to Ashland, where the race then started—"

"That must have been a long ride," I said.

"We didn't mind," said Nason. "We were tough kids. We'd pick up a lower-case runner who had no attendant and take his jug of water for him, his oranges, his lemons, whatever. We were permitted to stay with a runner on the course."

A little more than a decade later, as a reporter in 1936, Nason watched the race that motivated him to name the series of elevations in the latter part of the route Heartbreak Hill, an enduring appellation that to this day signals victory or defeat for many a top runner. "It was an Olympic tryout year and Boston was the U.S. qualifying race. There was a 22-year-old Indian boy down on a reservation in Rhode Island, a Narraganset Indian named Ellison Myers Brown. 'Tarzan,' they called him. Totally untrained as we understand it. Possibly the greatest physical talent that ever sat in this footrace. He was loaded with natural speed, he was strong. Well, he took off like a deer and broke all the course records (for each checkpoint) down to Coolidge, which is 23 miles. He was $4\frac{1}{2}$ or 5 minutes ahead of the overall course record. Going into the hills, at 17 miles, Johnny Kelley—this is Old Johnny Kelley who was then Young Johnny Kelley—elected to chase the Indian, and he ran superbly over the hills, erasing Brown's half-mile lead and finally catching Tarzan at Boston College with 5 miles to go.

"I'll never forget this," Nason said emphatically. "Just as he was going by him, Kelley slapped Tarzan on the butt, as if to say, 'Nice run, boy.' Well, Tarzan took off as though Kelley had touched him with a blowtorch. It ended up Tarzan staggering home first, after walking and jogging the last mile and a half and Kelley finishing fifth, not making the Olympic Team."

Nason laughed as he continued to talk about Tarzan Brown. "In the early forties—it might have been '41—it was a hot day and Tarzan Brown looked beautiful coming into Natick, which is about 10 miles out, with a bunch of other fellas— Kelley, Scottie Rankin of Canada, a good field. They all looked good, running well, but Brown looked better than anyone. Suddenly, they're going by Lake Cochituate in Natick and Tarzan busted clear off the road, jumped the little fence, and plunged into the lake. He waved to everybody. He didn't like the heat."

Turning to Brown's strength again, Nason asserted, "If he were running today and being coached and getting a proper diet—he didn't know anything about diet; he trained on beer—he'd be right up there. Most of his training was done chopping wood."

The same could be said of many of the old-timers, whose performances, in retrospect, seem almost miraculous in light of their inadequate or unscientific preparation. I had the pleasure of meeting and chatting with one of these superstars of yesteryear on the weekend of the 1979 Boston Marathon. Let's go back a few years . . .

UNKNOWN KID SMASHES RECORD IN GREATEST OF ALL MARATHONS. That was the banner headline on the Boston *Post,* April 20, 1926, the day after John C. Miles of Sydney Mines, Nova Scotia, recorded what remains today the greatest upset in the history of the Boston Marathon. Even though he had never competed in a race longer than 10 miles, the 20-year-old Canadian defeated Clarence DeMar, winner of 4 previous Bostons, and Albin Stenroos of Finland, the 1924 Olympic Marathon champion. The distance that year was 26 miles 209 yards, and Miles, who beat Stenroos to the finish by 4 minutes, was timed at 2:25:40—"and two fifths," he says. Three years later Miles won his second Boston Marathon.

Johnny Miles returned to Boston for the 1979 race, his first visit to the city since '29, to commemorate the fiftieth anniversary of his second victory. At 73, he is the oldest living winner of the Boston Marathon. A retired executive of the International Harvester Company, Miles now lives in Hamilton, Ontario. He has not run since the early 1930s.

Miles, although a good deal heavier than the 130 pounds he carried in the twenties, looks fit and strong for a man his age. He is quick-witted, articulate, and modest, and he reminisced about his achievements with tempered pride. Miles showed me his gold medals from Boston (which he keeps locked in a vault) and said his 1926 victory holds greater significance to him than the one in '29. He recalled it this way:

"About 2½ hours before the race I ate breakfast on the side of the road in Hopkinton. I had a big steak that had been cooked the night before, dry toast, a Thermos of tea with lots of sugar. At about 6 or 7 miles, Stenroos started to pull away from DeMar and me. I didn't worry about it. I figured DeMar knew what he was doing, so I stayed with DeMar. When Stenroos got too far away, I got nervous and went after him. DeMar stayed back. I caught Stenroos at about 12 miles but was afraid to pass him. I said to myself, 'He knows what he's doing. I don't.' He never looked behind. When we got to the Newton Hills, he started to come back to me and I said to my-self, 'What am I supposed to do now?'

"I got up alongside of him and looked at his face and his eyes were sunken-in and glassy, and he looked as if he'd just about had it. So I passed him at 22 miles. I kept going, and I gained a minute a mile on him for the last 4 miles. After-wards, I talked to DeMar—Stenroos' English was not very good—and he told me they'd thought this race was for mid-dle-aged men and were surprised to see a kid come along and change their thinking."

Miles's victory drew an outpouring of tribute, not only be-cause here was an unheralded young runner decisively defeat-ing the two overwhelming favorites but because Miles was depicted as a grateful son, a model of self-discipline, self-control, and self-respect.

The Boston *Herald-Traveler* raved. "This Johnny Miles is a subject for fiction. As a youth he was developed physically, and in great part mentally, by his father, also John Miles, who in his own day was a runner and prizefighter. Miles senior is a man with a staunch belief in the value of physical culture work. The boy, John, early learned to swing dumbbells, skip rope, punch the bag and above all live an outdoor life. The fa-ther had no special athletic future planned for him but when the boy in 1923, only 17 years of age, manifested an interest in running and then held that interest, the father mapped his athletic life and the boy followed the advice of the man who had been over the unknown road before him."

If Johnny Miles was the Wunderkind of the Boston Mar-athon, Clarence DeMar was its monarch. DeMar made a ca-reer out of running and winning the Boston, a career that never really received the attention it deserves. But Clarence

DeMar's record at Boston, which spanned forty-three years and included 33 races and 7 victories, compares favorably with that of the most acclaimed athletes in other sports.

DeMar, at 22, won the Boston Marathon the first time he entered it, in 1911, with a time of 2:21:39—breaking the course record by almost 3 minutes. (The course was then 24.5 miles.) Before the race a doctor had warned him that he was flirting with death because of a heart murmur, and, the next year, when Alberto Lazaro of Portugal collapsed in the Olympic Marathon and died a day later, DeMar panicked and called it quits—at age 23. For ten years DeMar didn't run—ten years when he would have been in the prime of his life for marathoning, when he might have won another 5, 6, or conceivably 10 more times at Boston. There can be no underestimating this hiatus. After a decade of inactivity, when the spirit and the flesh no doubt succumbed to his sedentary ways, DeMar came out of self-imposed retirement and, at 33, won the 1922 Boston Marathon in 2:18:10—another course record.

Two achievements comparable to DeMar's two-part Boston career come to mind. One is the career of boxer Muhammad Ali, who regained the heavyweight title after a demoralizing layoff following a clash with authorities over his draft evasion. The other is the career of Al Oerter, who won the Olympic gold medal in the discus in 1956, 1960, 1964, and 1968 and who, at age 43 in 1980, was in the midst of a rather successful comeback before the United States boycott ended his hopes of competing in his fifth Olympics.

DeMar's feat alone of two record-breaking victories a decade apart is the stuff of which legends are made. But for Clarence DeMar there would be 31 more Boston Marathons, 5 of them triumphs—in 1923 (2:23:37); 1924 (2:29:40, course lengthened to 26 miles 209 yards); 1927 (2:40:22, course lengthened to 26 miles 385 yards); 1928 (2:37:07), and 1930 (2:34:48). DeMar was 41 in 1930—to this day he remains the oldest runner ever to win at Boston.

DeMar's durability was truly impressive, but his uneven disposition is recalled with equal awe. DeMar—who died of intestinal cancer in 1958, at 70—was a hard, fiercely determined man, an honor student, a Harvard graduate, a printer and teacher of the printing craft. In a May 1979 article for *The Runner* ("King of Heartbreak Hill"), Jerry Nason wrote of DeMar: "In assorted incidents over the years, Clarence punched out a spectator who threw cold water on his legs, shoved a thoughtless autograph seeker backward over the curbing, and mowed down several juvenile bike riders who persisted in penetrating his running space. . . . He tolerated post-race interviews, but woe to the scribe who approached him with an inane query. 'That's a stupid question,' Clarence would say, bringing the unfortunate reporter's interview to a quick end."

DeMar is gone, of course, and so is Tarzan Brown; and while Johnny Miles is alive and well, he has not run for forty years. Of the Boston legends, only Johnny A. Kelley—not to be confused with John *J.* Kelley, Boston winner in '57 and no relation—is still running. In 1980, Kelley, 72, wearing number 72, ran his forty-ninth Boston Marathon (and 106th marathon overall), and his time was 3:50. "Thousands of people wait for me," he said. "It brings tears to my eyes. I hope I can go till I'm 100."

Looking at Kelley, one believes he will make it. He has a full crop of white hair, the narrow firmness of a runner's body, the charm of the gracious past champion he is. His speed has waned but not his vitality.

Kelley is the most popular runner in Boston annals, but make no mistake about it—he is not the token grandfather there to be patronized. He is a serious runner. Always has been. And just as the Boston Marathon has symbolized the development of distance running in America, Johnny Kelley has symbolized the development of the Boston Marathon.

In 1928, when Calvin Coolidge was President, Kelley entered his first Boston. He dropped out, with severe blood blisters, after 21 miles. (Clarence DeMar won that year.) Through 1980, Kelley had run Boston 48 more times and finished all but twice. He'd won 2 times, placed second 7 times, and 19 times he placed in the top 10.

Kelley's victories came in 1935 and 1945. The first time, he outran Finnish-born Dave Komonen of Canada. Komonen, who had beaten him in 2:30:07 the previous year, dropped out of the '35 race. The second time, Kelley ran a smooth 2:30:40 and said at the finish: "Life begins at 40—and I have three more years to go!"

Of course Kelley had decades to go and is still going strong, running almost every morning at 5:30 near his Cape Cod home, putting in an hour a shot for about 60 miles a week.

Johnny Kelley has been doing things his way for half a century. It has required great self-assurance, as illustrated in a story he related to writer Joe Falls for his book, *The Boston Marathon* (1977). According to Falls: "When he was representing the United States in the 1936 Olympics (he was the only American to finish), the German soldiers taunted him. How could this fragile man be an athlete? They removed his straw hat and replaced it with a helmet. When the helmet slid down over his eyes, the soldiers laughed hysterically.

" 'Are you on the United States checker team?' one of them asked.

" 'I'm a runner,' said Kelley defiantly. 'I'm a marathoner.'

"The soldier took a step back.

" 'They were a lot more polite after that,' said Kelley."

The first Boston Athletic Association Marathon was held in 1897, on a 24.5-mile course that started on Pleasant Street in Ashland and finished at the Irvington Oval on Exeter Street in downtown Boston. It drew 15 starters, and John J. McDermott, 25, of New York City, won in 2:55:10, after running through a funeral procession on Massachusetts Avenue. McDermott, who'd won a marathon from Stamford, Connecticut to New York City the previous fall, stopped and walked three times in the last 10 miles and still outran his closest pursuer by more than 7 minutes.

Each race has its special story. Runners who fell and still won, who were allegedly drugged, who insulted one another, who collided with cyclists, whose path was blocked by a freight train, and so on through the DeMar years (when the course was lengthened, first to 26 miles 209 yards and then to the standard 26 miles 385 yards); the Finns, Tarzan Brown, Gerard Coté, Johnny Kelley; the foreign dominance of the fifties and sixties (during which Americans won only twice in twenty years); and then the seventies, the era of women's participation, large fields (as recently as 1971, only 887 runners started), qualifying standards, illegal entrants *en masse*, the tail wind of '75 (when record numbers posted fast times), the Broiler of '76 (when 90-degree temperatures caused a 40 percent dropout rate), and Bill Rodgers.

In 1965, for better management, the finish was moved from the old Lenox Hotel to the Prudential Center, and to retain the prescribed distance, the start was moved back in Hopkinton to the Hopkinton Common. Hopkinton is a charming New England suburb of 5,981 people, a town that holds no distinction 364 days a year, but on day 365, the third Monday in April, Patriot's Day in the Commonwealth of Massachusetts, it surrenders its bucolic cast and opens its arms to, now, thousands of people who come from every state and 25 to 30 countries to be part of the world-famous Boston Marathon.

After mingling at the traditional mega-race bazaar, the field leaves Hopkinton along Route 135 and travels east through Ashland (5 miles), Framingham (6.75), Natick (10.5), and Wellesley (halfway), checkpoints where large, boisterous crowds greet the procession. The first 17 miles or so constitute a slight downhill grade, making it an "easy" run for the well-trained, but wise runners apply restraint because from Lower Newton Falls to Boston College are 4 miles of uphill grade known as Heartbreak Hill, which pop up at just the point in a marathon where a breakdown of will is common. This section takes in Woodland Park, Auburndale, and Newtonville, past Boston College. The runners continue onto Lake Street at 21.5 miles, then to Beacon Street, past Coolidge Corner at 24.12, for the last 2 miles to Ring Road and the final stretch to the Pru.

In 1980 the patrons of this route included 450 women, about 9 percent of the official starters in the eighty-fourth Boston Marathon. Women had been accorded the proper respect in that they, too, had to qualify with a minimum performance—3:20. Only a decade earlier, women's participation in marathons (see chapter 13) was frowned upon, and women were not permitted to compete officially at Boston until 1972. Before that they competed, in small numbers, unofficially. Credit for being the first is given to Roberta Louise Gibb, who as a 23-year-old in 1966 wore black leotards and a beret and ran undetected from start to finish. Her time was 3:21:40, and she finished ahead of more than 100 men. Of course, afterward various crybabies either denied that Gibb had run at all or that she had run the whole thing. She must have jumped in at Wellesley or Boston College—she must have, she's a woman, isn't she?

The next year another woman challenged the Boston constitution, and the to-do over that eclipsed the Gibb milestone. That woman of course was Kathrine V. Switzer—*K. Switzer* to the Boston authorities who processed her application and had no inkling that this was the entry blank of a woman, a modern-day athletic pioneer, one whose picture would appear in newspapers throughout the world on April 20, 1967. You know the picture—in hundreds of papers and in countless publications thereafter it ran as a sequence of three shots, taken by UPI. It showed Kathy Switzer being shoved by Boston's Jock Semple, who had leaped from an officials' vehicle, and Semple, in turn, being shoved by Kathy's running partner and boyfriend, Tom Miller, a nationally ranked hammer thrower. When it was all over, Semple was swearing to anyone who would listen, his co-director Will Cloney was stewing in embarrassment, but Switzer had run her 4:20. Reporters besieged her with questions, the AAU suspended her, she was invited to appear on the Johnny Carson show. The Boston Marathon, and all of women's running, would never be the same.

"It was unbelievable," recalled Switzer, then a 20-year-old Syracuse University student. "I got about two hundred letters a week." All favorable? "No," she said, "about fifty-fifty."

Some of Switzer's admirers would soon run Boston themselves, as sprinklings of "illegal" entrants until 1972, when women finally were given the right to run. That year, 8 women ran and their leader was Nina Kuscsik, a 33-year-old mother of three from Long Island. Her time was 3:10:26. Kuscsik, like Switzer, has been one of the most instrumental figures in women's distance running.

From 1973 through 1980, women's titles went to Jacquelyn Hansen (3:05:59), Miki Gorman (2:47:11), Liane Winter of West Germany (2:42:24), Kim Merritt (2:47:10), Gorman again (2:48:33), Gayle Barron (2:44:52), Joan Benoit (2:35:15), and Jacqueline Gareau (2:34:28). This is hardly a homogenous group. Jackie Hansen went on to set a world record (2:38:19) and dabble in ultramarathoning. Miki Gorman, the 4-foot-10-inch Japanese-born Californian, became the darling of the press and at 42 in '77 a kind of runners' elder stateswoman. Kim Merritt, half Gorman's age, was a shy Wisconsin college student. Gayle Barron is a glamorous Atlanta woman who became a TV sportscaster and needed a PR agency to manage her numerous promotional engagements. Joan Benoit is the first track specialist to win Boston, a runner as at home in the 5,000 and 10,000 meters as she now is in the marathon. Before her record-smashing run in '79, Benoit had run only 1 marathon, the Bermuda Marathon three months earlier in 2:50:54.

Benoit was recuperating from surgery and did not defend her title in 1980 when Gareau, a French-speaking medical technician from Montreal, broke her course record with a brilliant run on a warm day. But it took a week for Gareau to be declared the official winner.

Gareau was the second woman to cross the finish line that day. While men's champion Bill Rodgers (2:12:11) was being awarded his fourth Boston gold medal, a tall unknown woman with no grace in her stride crossed the line in 2:31:56, stumbled into the arms of police—and soon became one of the most controversial figures in the history of the sport.

She said her name was Rosie Ruiz. She was 26 years old, was born in Cuba, and came to Miami with her mother and other relatives at age 7. She lived in New York City and worked as an administrative assistant for an international metal trading firm. Questioned about her running, Ruiz could not help but show her ignorance of the sport, and within a day's time the whole country was talking about the woman who cheated in the Boston Marathon.

Ruiz, despite enormous pressure and mounting evidence against her, maintained that she had run the entire course. But this could not prevent her disqualification—first from the previous fall's New York City Marathon, after race officials discovered the twenty-fourth-place 2:56:29 credited to Ruiz was a phoney, and then from the Boston Marathon after an exhaustive investigation that took a week to complete. Ruiz, it was concluded, jumped into the Boston race somewhere in the last few miles, intent either on finishing among the leaders (but miscalculating her position), or, indeed, on winning.

A week after the Boston disqualification, I arranged a dinner meeting with Ruiz, Steve Marek (her advisor), Sam Merrill (the writer I'd assigned to the story for *The Runner*), and myself. Sam and I had hoped that in the relaxed atmosphere of a good meal we'd get the prized confession from her. We didn't. We caught her in obvious lies and contradictory statements, but she would not budge. "I ran it," Ruiz insisted.

Rosie Ruiz was a mystery, and in his article ("Ruiz: Anatomy of a Fraud," July 1980), Merrill provided an analysis, based not only on her Boston ruse—the greatest in running since Fred Lorz rode in a car for part of the way during the 1904 Olympic Marathon—but also on other aspects of her life that he had uncovered. Merrill said she was a sociopath—one who, among other traits, shows "a cavalier attitude about telling the truth and [is] unflappable about lies being detected."

The Switzer incident did more to enhance Jock Semple's reputation as a crusty, stubborn, temperamental overseer of Boston's traditions than all the people he's thrown off the course for running without numbers and all the spectators and cyclists and motorists he's sparred with for interfering with the race. From Semple's standpoint it was simple: The AAU barred women from marathons and here was a woman who had (surreptitiously) gotten a number and was actually running, so git 'er t' hell outta the race.

Semple, who is 75 years old and still works as a masseur at the Boston Garden, came to the United States in 1923 from Clydebank, Scotland. Six years later, he ran Boston, and in 1930, the year Clarence DeMar won for the seventh and final time, Semple placed seventh. He had hitchhiked from Philadelphia to take part. Since then, as runner, coach, and co-director, Semple has been married to the Boston Marathon, and during this half-century he has not lost his stinging Scottish brogue nor his tendency to strike those who do not show proper deference to the Boston Marathon.

While Semple has been an exhibitionist, Will Cloney, his administrative sidekick, is subdued and dispassionate, though strong-minded. When I visited Cloney two weeks before the 1979 race, expecting to find him and his staff working at the pitch of a newspaper's city room on election eve, his headquarters on the seventeenth floor of the fifty-two-story Prudential Center was as calm as the rest of the office complexes in the huge insurance company building. A few people examined entry applications, most of them received after the March 16 deadline and most of them accompanied by notes with very good reasons for their delay. Also evident was the predictable Boston memorabilia, but mostly there were stacks of paper—leaflets with instructions for the runners. There were also piles of processed entries grouped by "acceptance" and "rejection" and by reason for rejection, such as listing a qualifying time that Cloney's people determined to be untrue. As I glanced over the applications, Cloney picked one up and told me, with a snicker, how a Pennsylvania man claimed he'd run 2:20 in a marathon no one had ever heard of. Cloney shook his head. If you're going to try to cheat, Cloney said, at least have the brains to make it less obvious.

It is a game. There are two sides: On one side are the people who have not qualified for the Boston Marathon but try to get accepted by lying on their entry blanks or by sending pleading letters that claim extenuating circumstances; on the other side are the Boston officials, led by Will Cloney and Jock Semple, who, through hardened cynicism and years of experience, spot the liars and get rid of them.

Will Cloney is director and president of the Boston Athletic Association (BAA) Marathon. He is 68 years old. He went to the Boston Latin School and Harvard (class of '33), wrote about sports for the Boston *Herald* and Boston *Post*, and worked for Keystone Custodian Funds, Inc., for thirty years, retiring as a vice-president in 1977. In the forties Cloney kept advising the Boston officials on the conduct of their race until in 1946 they finally suggested he take charge of it himself. Will Cloney has been Boston's backbone ever since. That's why the country of the winning runner now receives the Will Cloney International Marathon Trophy.

Cloney, who lives in Scituate, about 40 miles from Boston, worked simultaneously for Keystone and the Boston Marathon over the years. He received no money from the marathon, just a small expense allowance. It had to be this way: Will Cloney would not permit the Boston Marathon to become a commercial venture, even though commercial ventures have sprouted around it like crab grass in the spring. Boston has no commercial sponsors. It has two "supporters," the Prudential Company and Honeywell, which donate services and equipment. If the BAA relented and let it be known that it was looking for major sponsors, the bidding would go well into the six figures. It would be tantamount to corporations fighting for commercial air time during the network telecast of the Olympics.

Cloney's work on the race is tireless. "Would you believe the first meeting we had about this year's marathon was in this room the day after last year's?" he asked rhetorically. "We had a meeting with the secretary of public safety of the state of Massachusetts. That was Tuesday. Wednesday we met with the commissioner of police in Boston. Friday we met with . . ." After that, Cloney gathers his lieutenants for monthly meetings the rest of the calendar year and then, after January 1, for weekly meetings and daily work, frequently day and night, up to race day.

Over lunch in the Skywalk restaurant, near the balcony where priceless old photographs of the Boston Marathon are on display, Cloney seemed tired, torn by the self-imposed pressures of a man determined to preserve the quality and purity of the Boston Marathon, determined to prevent the race from being victimized by the indulgences of the day. In a sense, Will Cloney's main job now is to keep certain people out of the Boston Marathon. Telling people they cannot be part of something very important to them is not one of life's pleasures. "I bleed," says Cloney, in reference to the more stringent qualifying standards (now, as of 1980, set at 2:50 for men under 40, 3:10 for men 40 and over, and 3:20 for women).

All the anxiety over who should run the Boston Marathon and who should not seemed remote at 2:15 on the afternoon of April 16, 1979, as Will Cloney stood behind wreath-capped Bill Rodgers on the victory stand, amid the kind of excitement that accompanies the climax of the greatest sporting events the world over. It was a compelling reminder of the importance of the Boston Marathon in the history of modern-day sport and of the role it must not forfeit as a model for long-distance running in the years ahead.

10

THE NEW YORK CITY MARATHON

Drum roll, please. Fred Lebow, in running attire, and Ed Koch, in mayoral attire, step to the fore in the Blue Room at City Hall. Lebow rolls the drum and opens the latch. Martin Van Buren stares out regally from a Henry Inman painting. Mayoral aides, public-relations types, and the press lean forward in their seats. Cassette recorders click, cameras are primed, and heartbeats quicken, even those of low-pulsed runners.

Koch sinks his right hand into the bin where it wades through 5,138 New York City Marathon entries (all that fit), grabbing the first of 6 symbolic "winners" of the 1979 New York City Marathon Lottery.

Koch pulls out the name and announces to perfunctory applause: "Jay Sidman, Newton, Massachusetts." Sidman is absent from the proceedings, but I reach him later in Fort Meade, Maryland, where he is on army reserve duty. "I'm tongue-tied," says Sidman, a 26-year-old Boston State University student. "I've never won anything before." Sidman is an excellent runner. He runs 75 to 100 miles a week, has a marathon best of 2:37:07, and hopes to break 2:25 in New

York City, to atone for his DNF in 1970—the only time he's run New York.

No. 2: "Howard Kirschenbaum, Camp Uncas, Rackett Lake, New York." More applause. Kirschenbaum is a 35-year-old teacher, who is spending his summer chasing kids at camp.

By this time, rumor has it that in this soon-to-be-completed sextet there will not be one honest-to-goodness New Yorker—no one from Bay Ridge, Forest Hills, the Upper East Side, or Harlem. And when a woman from Richardson, Texas, is selected next, someone calls out that the fourth inductee could very well be from anywhere in the world. The envelope please: Cicero, Illinois. Followed by White Plains, New York, and Lynnfield, Massachusetts, to complete the tally. The Road Runners Club packs up its entries and returns to midtown headquarters to pick the remaining 1,994 lucky souls the same way that afternoon.

The lottery is the latest in a series of plans designed to cope with swelling race entries—a way to avoid divisive qualifying times à la Boston. It was the opinion of New York Road Runners Club officials that if there was not an early entry deadline, a screening system, and periodic warnings that applications would be carefully scrutinized, as many as 40,000 marathoners would position themselves at the Verrazano Bridge Toll Plaza at 10:30 A.M. on October 21, spelling doom for a race that thus far had been a model of efficient management.

The scare tactics seem to have worked. The New York Road Runners Club (NYRRC) received 30,000 requests for entry applications, all of which were honored. About 22,500 people were serious enough to return completed applications, and of those, all but 250 were correctly filled out—despite severe timing restrictions such as a requirement that requests for applications (mail only) be postmarked no earlier than midnight, June 1.

(And at midnight there were several hundred people waiting at the main branch of the post office to file entry requests—for themselves and as favors for friends in other states who did not trust the long-distance mail service.)

At 4:00 P.M. on June 26, the NYRRC received the last of the 12,000 entries that marked its first official cutoff. On July 15, they sent out 12,000 acceptances. The August 1 lottery selected the final 2,000 from the additional entries and, according to race coordinator Allan Steinfeld: "One hundred to 200 are still coming in every day." Lebow and Steinfeld cited numerous examples of panic and pressure, like the man from down South who wanted to make a "generous" donation to the NYRRC to ensure a place for himself in the race, and the secretary of a Hollywood producer who called to explain she'd forgotten to enclose the mandatory self-addressed, stamped envelope with her boss's entry, and would they let her send it separately so she could keep her job.

It was quite warm in New York the week before the 1979 race, in contrast to an early October that was unseasonably cold with a bit of frost. This turn in the weather dominated pre-race speculations, amid radio reports that the weekend would be a killer (sunny and warm, in the 80s). Was this race headed for the same fate as the Boston Broiler of '76?

Thankfully not. Race day dawned cool and foggy, so foggy that the Verrazano Bridge was barely visible to the first runners bused to the starting area at Staten Island's Fort Wadsworth at 7:00 A.M. The fog remained dense through the early morning hours, keeping media-ordered helicopters from their appointed rounds and photographers from getting those elevated shots that have become the trademark of the New York City Marathon.

Runners sprawled over the 226-acre fort, making it look more like a summer camp for kids than a military installation. It was a placid setting, with runners lying under the circusy orange-and-green tent set up by the race organizers (in case of sudden cold or rain), as well as on the baseball diamonds, the tennis courts, and the grassy fields. They read the Sunday papers or simply sat down on them to avoid getting wet from the moist ground. They stood in line at the Red Cross trucks for coffee and doughnuts and at "the world's longest urinal." Mostly they displayed their personal idiosyncrasies—odd costumes, unorthodox calisthenics, meditation, sharp-smelling liniment, the bandaging and re-bandaging of their toes and feet. If there is anything elite runners and novices have in common, it is the compulsive ritual of trying to make everything just right before the start of the marathon. At 10:00 A.M. they gathered in front of the Verrazano Bridge Toll Plaza, the 9,000 who had run marathons before and the 3,000 or so who would soon be, as one T-shirt declared, a MARATHON VIRGIN NO MORE. Physicians, attorneys, teachers, forest rangers, security guards, and "housepersons," they had come from all 50 states and from 39 countries.

At just about 10:30 the 10-second countdown began, but halfway through it runners in the front row broke from the start, creating the kind of confusion and near-disaster that keeps Fred Lebow and directors of races this size up late at night. Some top runners, caught by surprise, got stuck in the pack and were unable to break free for almost a mile. Bill Rodgers was among them. "I did a lot of zigzagging," he said.

The convoy of pace vehicles got caught in the jump-start and was too close to the runners. The photo truck assigned to follow the leading men was caught so far behind that it had to trail the field over the Verrazano, take a different route through Brooklyn, and rejoin the convoy at the 10-mile point. The reporters' minibus was outrun by several hundred runners and had to honk its way through the middle of them, nearly brushing several marathoners and drawing outraged verbal hostility from them. One steadfast runner, hearing the honking behind him, shook his head and refused to move. He was Frank Shorter. (Shorter's love affair with motorists goes back to his law school days in Gainesville, Florida, when he and Jack Bachelor made their famous run up and over a car whose driver had intimidated them earlier in their workout.) Shorter finally moved to the right, and the bus got through.

After the race, Rodgers, Kirk Pfeffer, and other runners who were asked about the confused start, said: (1) It was not perfectly clear where the actual starting line was; (2) a rope used to prevent a false start didn't work because runners feared they might get caught behind it; (3) slow runners lined up in front where they did not belong; and (4) foreign runners (of whom there were some 1,200) were particularly impatient and may have intentionally jumped the gun, or rather the cannon, because of such customary practices in their home countries.

The next day the New York *Post* claimed that a *Post* reporter, Elli Wohlgelertner, a 4:51 marathoner, positioned himself at the front and jumped out before the cannon fired, bringing the rest of the field with him. The *Post* had the photos to prove it—there was the charlatan, No. 8905, wearing a NEW YORK POST T-shirt, smiling and waving while runners with low numbers jostled for better position behind him. "For one glorious moment," he wrote, "the marathon was mine. I led for the first hundred yards."

The field unraveled on the Verrazano, and coming off the bridge, at 2 miles, the leader was Kevin Shaw. The split was 9:17. Shaw is a South African and as such is barred from international competition by the International Amateur Athletic Federation. A late entry, he was admitted to the race because he listed the United States as his place of residence. Had Shaw kept up the pace and won, he might have been technically disqualified by the IAAF, and Fred Lebow would have had a lot of explaining to do.

Shaw stayed ahead through Brooklyn's Bay Ridge section, and along Fourth Avenue. He passed 5 miles in 23:57, 6 in 28:52. Zakarea Barie of Tanzania and Steve Floto of Boulder, Colorado, ran behind Shaw. It was Barie's second marathon (he ran 2:23:24 in Montreal) and Floto's first. The pack 100 yards behind Barie and Floto included Kirk Pfeffer, Benji Durden, Fernand Kolbeck of France, and Frank Shorter. At 7.3 miles, Barie moved into the lead. At 8, Pfeffer took it from him, while Shaw drifted back. The time was 38:44.

Pfeffer is a 23-year-old University of Colorado graduate from Boulder who, twenty-four hours before the race, decided that he would run the tenth New York City Marathon. He notified race officials, hopped a plane, got into town at 9:00 P.M., bringing with him several months of hard training and a victory, two months earlier, in the Enschede Marathon in

Amsterdam. His time there was 2:11:50, a course record. Prior to Enschede, Pfeffer had not run a marathon for 2½ years, although some time ago he set U.S. age records (2:17:44 at 18, 2:17:08 at 19, 2:16:03 at 20) for the marathon that still stand. "It was a little ridiculous the way I did it," Pfeffer would say of his last-minute entry.

Ridiculous or not, Kirk Pfeffer, who had never been to New York before, "came to race and run as hard as I can." He looked as though he was working at it, running with a somewhat stiff gait uncharacteristic of good marathoners. Pfeffer headed out toward the end of Brooklyn, past mile 8, then 9 and 10 and the ethnic communities of people whose roots could be traced to at least as many countries as were represented in the marathon. At 10 miles his time was 48:21 and his lead over Barie and Floto was 30 yards. Shaw had fallen to seventh. Frank Shorter was fifteenth. Bill Rodgers, who said he was somewhere between sixtieth and seventieth at 2 miles, still was far off the leading pace.

Pfeffer did not give any indication that he might intentionally slow up. "Once you're going fast, there's not too much you can do about it," he reasoned. He kept going at 4:50–4:55 per mile and reached the halfway point, in the middle of the Pulaski Bridge, in 1:03:51. When Derek Clayton ran his world record of 2:08:34 in 1969, he reached the halfway point in 1:03:07. When Bill Rodgers ran New York in 2:10:10 in 1976, his intermediate time was 1:03:57. The challenge had been bared—Kirk Pfeffer would not relent easily. The other runners would have to catch him.

The fling into Queens is a short one, and at 15 miles up the Queensboro Bridge, Pfeffer's lead had increased to about 500 yards. He made the sweeping left turn off the bridge, the steepest "hill" on the route after the Verrazano. At 16 miles he was urged along by thick crowds on both sides of Manhattan's First Avenue at what is traditionally the most popular spectator haunt outside Central Park. As Pfeffer worked his way up First through the Upper East Side, the sun broke out for the first time. It was just about noon, and there were fewer than 10 miles left; if Pfeffer was to be taken, barring a complete collapse on his part, it would have to be set up pretty soon.

The stage was being set by the leading player in this cast of leading players. Bill Rodgers, running with Steve Kenyon (who had not run a marathon in six years), had gained ground on the leaders through north Brooklyn and had finally caught up to Frank Shorter on the Pulaski Bridge.

"Who are those guys?" Bill kidded.

"I don't know," Frank said.

Two miles later, on the Queensboro, Rodgers and Kenyon pulled up to the lead pack. There were now 8 men in it, running double-file as partners on the carpeted surface: Benji Durden and Ian Thompson (Great Britain) out front; then Barie and Jukka Toivola (Finland); Rodgers and Shaw; Kenyon and Dave Black (Great Britain).

Durden was the only one running on the grating and not the padding, which seemed to be most responsible for the tidy grouping at mile 16. The symmetry of the group was shattered when the runners left the bridge and went on to First Avenue, where there was some room to spread out and force the issue. Durden moved ahead, followed closely by Toivola, Thompson, Rodgers, Barie, Kenyon, Black, and Shaw.

As Durden put a bit more distance between himself and the others, Rodgers sped to his shoulder and asked Durden how far ahead Pfeffer was.

"Almost 2 minutes," Benji told him.

"You're kidding," Bill said.

Durden stepped up the pace and had 30 yards on Rodgers when Pfeffer, leading by roughly 90 seconds, reached 17 miles in 1:22:40. Rodgers would have to outrun him by almost 10 seconds per mile to win.

Pfeffer's eighteenth mile was 5:01, then his slowest mile of the race. His nineteenth was 5:17, and his twentieth 5:22. Rodgers had passed Durden and closed to within 1:23 of Pfeffer. Pfeffer looked worn out going over the Willis Avenue Bridge and into the Bronx. A sign in the distance flashed the temperature: 71°. A barefoot woman in full sweats joined Pfeffer for about 50 yards. Spectators told Rodgers how far ahead Pfeffer was. As Pfeffer, and then Rodgers, returned to Manhattan via the Madison Avenue Bridge, Bill closed the gap to about a minute with his patient, well-calculated pace. "I knew it would be hot and I wanted to run a moderate pace," he said.

New York is a marathon of bridges. The stretch along First Avenue from the Queensboro Bridge to the Willis Avenue Bridge—miles 16 to 20—is crucial. In a marathon, that is where the body begins to fail, where the stride changes, where the self-doubts surface. "I knew I had a lead and knew I was gonna die," Kirk Pfeffer said afterward.

At 22 miles, the course turns onto First Avenue for a mile through Harlem, on a gradual incline, to Central Park. Here Pfeffer and Rodgers could be seen together for the first time. Pfeffer ran this mile in 5:52. "The way I was running, I knew he would catch me," Pfeffer said.

With 3 miles to go, just inside Central Park, and within yards of Dick Traum, the runner with an artificial leg who had started out at 7:00 A.M., Rodgers caught Pfeffer and passed him. "Hi, Kirk," Bill said, and then took off, glancing back once to make sure he had it. Rodgers looked oddly aggressive, just as he'd looked six months before when he caught Toshihiko Seko of Japan at 20 miles in the eighty-third Boston Marathon. Rodgers ran the last 3 miles in about 14:50 for a time of 2:11:42, 1:27 ahead of Pfeffer, who held on to second and ran 2:13:09.

"I didn't expect the hills at the end," said Pfeffer, barely able to stand up as reporters gathered around him. "I didn't know the course; I'd just seen a map of it."

Rodgers was relieved. "You don't want someone with you the last few miles of a marathon. I had never had anyone with me in Central Park before. All I was seeing was the headline, PFEFFER UPSETS RODGERS. He put me through a wringer."

Bill Rodgers ran the 1979 New York Marathon in 2:11:42. He also won New York in 1976 (2:10:10), the year it first became a five-borough race, and in 1977 (2:11:29) and 1978 (2:12:12). He made his New York debut in 1974, when he placed fifth in 2:35:59. Norbert Sander, Art McAndrew, Larry

Frederick, and Art Hall will never forget that race—the day they beat Bill Rodgers.

Steve Kenyon, who ran with Rodgers from mile 2 to mile 16, finished third in 2:13:30. He had no knowledge of Pfeffer's run and thought he had come in second. It was Kenyon's best time by 5 minutes. For the second year in a row, Lasse Viren dropped out. Viren, a 4-time Olympic champion, was running a 2:18 pace at 20 miles when his calves tightened and he withdrew from the competition.

Tom Fleming, who has won New York twice, also dropped out but insisted he hadn't intended to finish. "I said so all weekend, but people don't believe you. I had a good workout —18 miles at 5:30 pace, went back to my hotel, showered, and watched 'Tarzan.' I see no point in running 2:20 in the heat."

The only outstanding male runner expected to run who did not show up was Mark Smet of Belgium, who had run 2:10 in his second marathon in September. Smet, according to the Belgian contingent in the race, was "afraid to run again" for fear of hitting a poor performance and gaining disfavor with the Belgian authorities who would be selecting its Olympic runners.

Can that possibly make sense to Ron Hill? Hill, the durable British runner who is now 41, placed forty-seventh in 2:23:20 and had the best performance of runners 40 and over, the masters. He has not missed a single day of running in more than sixteen years—"since the Tokyo Olympics"—in what is believed to be the longest running streak in the world. Lately, Hill has been running with pain because of a knee injury.

Fritz Mueller of New York, who has run 2:20:47, was the second masters finisher in 2:27:55. He felt he'd run a good race and he remembered a woman passing him in the last mile.

Last year, Grete Waitz ran the second half of her first marathon 4 minutes faster than the first half. This time, wiser and even faster, Waitz distributed her speed more evenly. She ran the first half in 1:14:51, the second in 1:12:42. "I was more tired this year," she said. "The heart and the lungs—that was okay. But after 22 miles I got tired and stiff in the legs. My legs are not trained for a marathon."

Indomitable Grete. The 26-year-old Norwegian who runs in Central Park as she does in Oslo. Grete Waitz, you see, is "still a track runner." That was her first comment to the press at Tavern on the Green after the race, as though to anticipate the first question. "I am still a track runner. That's what I train for."

Grete Waitz serves two masters—the people of Norway and Europe, who count track and the Olympics as the only pinnacles in running, and the people of New York and America, who put her on center stage in road races and marathons.

Central Park, for now, is Waitz's Olympic Stadium. A Norwegian flag would look just fine in the Sheep Meadow. Stitched on it should be the numbers *2:27:33*. That is how long it took Grete to run the 26 miles 385 yards of the tenth New York City Marathon. It is 4 minutes 57 seconds faster than she ran it the year before, when she broke the world record by 2 minutes 18 seconds. It is exactly 11 minutes faster than the second-place woman, Gillian Adams of Great Britain, ran. It placed Waitz sixty-ninth in the field of 10,602 finishers in the New York Marathon, and it is a time that would have gotten her second place overall in America's Marathon, held that same October 21 in Chicago, with a field of 7,500 starters. It is a time that would win many of the 350 or so marathons run in America; a time that would have won every Olympic Marathon through 1948 (as recently as 1956 the Olympic bronze medalist ran 2:27:47); a time that would have won the New York Marathon in 1970 and 1972 and come close in '74. It represents a pace of 5:37 per mile.

Instead of counting her miles and regulating her schedule in the weeks before the marathon, Waitz competed in 6 races. She ran the Virginia Ten-Miler on September 22 in the world-record time of 53:05, then returned to Europe to compete in Bern, Lillestrøm, Stockholm, and her hometown of Oslo. She raced 2 miles, 13 kilometers, 16 kilometers, and even a 3,000-meter race between periods of a soccer match against a two-man relay of Norwegian Olympic rowers. She outran the rowers, and she outran all the women she faced, and when the numbers were added up Grete Waitz realized she had run 41 races and won 36 of them in the 9½ months of 1979 prior to the New York City Marathon.

One she lost was the World Cup 3,000 in Montreal, and for a track runner this was not an easy defeat to swallow. So Grete Waitz started out in New York with a bit of status to regain—in her own mind if not in others'. She got off to a fast start, and Gillian Adams "saw her on the first bridge" but not after that.

Waitz quickly established her record pace and saw her first important landmark at 8 miles—her husband, Jack. "I complained as I normally do when I see him," she said, laughing. Grete told Jack her legs felt sore and her stomach hurt, but he had little compassion for her. "He knows I am always complaining," she said.

This time, however, something really was wrong, and at about 10 miles Waitz stopped running and darted between two parked cars to relieve the knot in her stomach. She lost only a few seconds' time, resumed running, and 6 miles later saw her next important landmark—Jack. He gave her an orange slice and she continued her run, passing several men along First Avenue, into the Bronx, back to Manhattan, and finally to Central Park, where she had run 31:16 for 10,000 meters last June, a performance almost as sensational as the marathon she would soon complete. "When I reached the park, I knew I could break the record," said Waitz. "I tried not to slow down."

Inside the park, as she tired, Waitz was coaxed along to the finish by 32-year-old Jose Revyn of Belgium, a 2:13:41 marathoner apparently not having a good day. He finished a step ahead of her. Soon afterward Grete Waitz patiently sat for interview after interview, tolerant even of the reporters who usually cover football and politics and who asked her and the other top runners if they had "hit the wall."

Gillian Adams of Great Britain, runner-up in the field of 1,800 women, was more interested in talking about Grete

Waitz than herself, after the race. "It's amazing . . . fantastic. It'll make a lot of men sit up and think." Adams, 24, finished second in 2:38:33 after running seventh for most of the way. She did not pass Jacqueline Gareau of Montreal to move into second until the final mile. Gareau, who had her hoped-for split times written on her left hand, finished third in 2:39:06 and became the sixteenth woman to break 2:40.

It is appropriate that Bill Rodgers and Grete Waitz ran so well again in New York, for the New York City Marathon, if not New York City itself, has been the springboard, the pace-setter, for the unbridled zeal with which people in this country have embraced running. Running happened in the 1970s, and New York '79, with Rodgers and Waitz and a field that had to be shrewdly limited to an official 14,000 entries, symbolized a decade whose yen for fitness and good times through aerobic exercise changed the life-styles and waist-lines of millions of Americans.

The first New York Marathon, organized mainly by Fred Lebow and Vince Chiapetta, was run on September 13, 1970. There were 126 starters and 72 finishers, and the winner was Gary Muhrcke in 2:31:39. The course was routed entirely within Central Park. The lone woman participant was Nina Kuscsik, running unofficially because the AAU had yet to sanction marathoning for women. Kuscsik had run 3:11 in Boston that year (also unofficially) but dropped out of the inaugural New York Marathon at 14 miles because of a virus.

In the next five years men and women would join the field in larger numbers, buoyed by all the talk about how running was good for you, and by 1975, 491 runners would start and 339 would finish. Tom Fleming won for the second time in three years and brought the course record down to 2:19:27. There was a separate women's "division," and that year the race served as the National AAU Women's Marathon Championship. The title was won by Kim Merritt in 2:46:15.

Soon after the 1975 race, the New York Road Runners Club proposed that the race be run through the city's five boroughs. Reluctantly at first, Fred Lebow agreed to press Manhattan Borough President Percy Sutton for approval, and Sutton, in turn, took it up with Mayor Abraham Beame. Beame said yes, and the Road Runners Club promptly set out to line up sponsors, design a spirited, well-organized race in keeping with the 1976 Bicentennial, and attract many of the world's best marathoners. They did all of this with miraculous success, and even though Bill Rodgers, Frank Shorter, Ron Hill, Miki Gorman, and 2,000 others showed up to run, and another half-million people showed up to watch them, no one could have predicted that in the next three years the New York City Marathon would become a 26-mile celebration of running the likes of which is not to be seen anywhere else in the world.

Runners now train for New York as they do for Boston and, for better or worse, plan months and months of running around the New York City Marathon. The eyes of their friends and neighbors and co-workers and the major media are on them, and, even if they run exceedingly well in a score of other races throughout the year, their athletic reputations and self-respect will hinge on how they do in New York.

In 1979 more than a million people turned out to watch the race and cheer the runners with Rockyesque encouragement. As in the past, the 1,000 police on duty at the 400 intersections through which the course passes reported not a single incident of violence or crime, save a few articles of clothing stolen in Central Park. Is it that the police do such a magnificent job of crowd control or that the marathon is something so special—even sacred—that would-be snipers, muggers, pickpockets, and the assorted crazies who prey on New York call a moratorium on mischief to honor the occasion?

As at Boston, the race has spawned a host of ancillary activities. Macy's had Bill Rodgers, Dr. George Sheehan, Jim Fixx, George Hirsch, and other dignitaries stop by the sporting goods department and chat with runners eager to sop up every morsel of time-honored advice. A medical association held a press conference that again brought to the fore the debate over whether marathon running and its attendant life-style prevent heart attacks. The American Medical Joggers Association held a seminar on long-distance running, physiology, and society. New York Hospital–Cornell Medical Center conducted a symposium, "The Psychology of Marathon Running." A four-day trade show, consisting mainly of displays from shoe and apparel companies, was held at the Sheraton Centre Hotel, race headquarters. The Brooks Shoe Co., Avon, Inc., and *The Runner* magazine threw pre-race parties. At *The Runner's* bash, the guest of honor was Emil Zatopek of Czechoslovakia, winner of the Olympic distance triple at the Helsinki Games of 1952 and widely acclaimed as the greatest distance runner ever. *The Runner* brought Zatopek to New York for a week to be Grand Marshal of the marathon, and the day before the race he also attended a "fun run" for foreign racers that started at United Nations Plaza and finished at Tavern on the Green, where a free breakfast was served to the participants. The night of the marathon, about nine hours after most of the runners had finished the race, 500 runners who could still move their legs attended a post-race party at the Electric Disco, and for the first time that anyone could recall, no smoke of any kind was seen inside the discothèque. Marathon Entertainment, Inc., a firm that produces and distributes such TV sports films as "Greatest Sports Legends," put together a two-hour national telecast that because of the fog obscuring the course and other difficulties was something of a disaster.

For Fred Lebow, a flawed production is anathema. Lebow is the race director of the New York City Marathon, and he worries not only about keeping sponsors pacified, signing world-class runners, limiting the field, hosting press conferences with the mayor, and whether the Verrazano Bridge will fall into the Narrows, but also about water cups, safety pins, mile markers, and bridge padding. Fred Lebow is consumed by the production of the New York City Marathon in much the same way the entrants are consumed by their running of it.

While Lebow has gradually delegated more responsibility

to his support staff—mainly to race coordinator Allan Stein-field—the New York City Marathon has been primarily Le-bow's act; everyone else is an understudy.

Lebow was born 47 years ago in Arad, Transylvania, and at 14, with his five brothers and two sisters, he was smuggled out of Romania by his father. Lebow retains traces of an East European accent, which adds flavor to the unremitting pessi-mism he expresses wherever he goes to talk about the mar-athon. At a press conference three days before the 1979 race, Lebow said, "I heard this morning it will be 80 degrees on Sunday. It really scares me." You can see it in his eyes—the fear, the concern, the worry. Fred Lebow is a worrywart, and a worrywart rarely smiles. When he does permit himself a re-prieve, it is more a sly grin than a verifiable smile.

Lebow orchestrates the greatest show on earth in road rac-ing, but he is after more, the perfect marathon, if one is even possible. As Connie Bruck observed in her profile of Lebow ("The Man Behind the Marathon") for *The Runner* following the 1978 marathon: "Ultimately, Lebow holds his own coun-sel; there is nothing really shared about this event; from start to finish—no matter how passionately involved his assistants become, how much they mirror his own mania—he feels him-self alone in this race. And the accolades that come tonight, as people stop him at every corner, are like salt to the wound; he winces slightly with each one. Doesn't *anybody* have any concept of how perfect this marathon might have been?"

Perfection, of course, is in the eyes of the beholder, and for Fred Lebow one forgotten aide station or momentarily over-crowded chute or misplaced mile marker would ruin the whole thing. Of course Fred Lebow also worries that a draw-bridge along the route will somehow be opened in the middle of the race. The truth is, this is not impossible. In New York, stranger things happen almost every day, despite precautions taken by the likes of the eighteen city agencies with which Lebow deals day in and day out in the weeks and months pri-or to the marathon. The margin for error is so great that every last detail must be accounted for over and over again. All you need is one slipup . . . like the 1978 incident when a couple of wiseguys blue-painted a detour off the course in Queens. Luckily, the prank was discovered in time.

Lebow mothers the New York Marathon with such care that inevitably he finds himself in the thick of no-win arguments over who should take part in the race and who should not. In addition to sparring with opponents over the restrictive lottery system, Lebow takes issue with wheelchair "runners" whom he tries to block from the race despite court decisions to the contrary; with Steve Marek, a.k.a. Superman, for many reasons, not the least of which is Marek's costume, which Lebow claims interferes with other runners; and even with Bill Rodgers, the event's number-one commodity, who once differed with Lebow over what constitutes a fair "expense" allowance for a runner such as himself. As recently as one month before the 1979 race Rodgers was saying he would not run New York and Lebow was saying fine. George Hirsch helped mediate the dispute, and after the race Lebow admitted that his cavalier attitude toward Rodgers's threat had been wrong.

This should serve to remind Lebow that no matter how all-encompassing his control over the New York City Marathon, he can never be as important as the champions. But even Lebow can be kidded. As New York City Parks Commissioner Gordon Davis told a crowded press conference, before the 1979 race, "I am the chairman of the marathon, which means I get to spend twenty-four hours a day for two weeks in October with Fred Lebow, which is not as painful as it sounds."

Then Fred Lebow smiled.

PART FOUR

SUCCESS FORMULAS

11

STARTING FROM SCRATCH

It is 4:30 on a damp spring morning in New York City as Jimmy Behr steps out of the guarded doorway of AT&T's International Operating Center, having changed into running togs and Vaselined his nipples. He hands the guard his company I.D. to hold for him, and the guard, an elderly man named Evans, puts it in the breast pocket of his uniform and warns, "You take care out there."

"Don't worry," Jim tells him. "Short workout. Be back in forty-five minutes."

Evans shakes his head in disbelief, just as he does every morning at this hour, even though he has waved Jimmy off dozens of times by now.

It is officially Sunday, but the Saturday night sounds of Lower Manhattan linger as Jimmy Behr moves into an easy jog and then a run, his carrot-red, shoulder-length hair lifted by the wind, his pencil-lean figure barely intruding on the mosaic of activity at almost every street corner of Sixth Avenue. Sirens are heard in the distance as Jim reaches Canal

Street, where Chinatown overlaps Little Italy. There is virtually no traffic, and Jim runs right down the middle of the street, past a park shared by winos asleep on benches and lobster-shift workers out for a breather on their "lunch" hours.

Jimmy wears a T-shirt marked NEWARK DISTANCE RUN, red nylon shorts, ankle-length socks, and a pair of Tiger Jayhawks. He has no wristwatch, but has folded into his shorts a wad of tissues should he need to wipe the moisture from his glasses. He glides past retail shops that sell groceries, carpeting, records, motorcycles, and lighting fixtures; past a few small, quiet parks; past apartment buildings without doormen to his first landmark, Chelsea High School, and up toward Houston Street.

"It's pretty quiet around here except on the weekends," Jimmy says, breathing easily, wiping his brow. "There are two environments here: weekend and nonweekend. This is the weekend. Once you get to Houston Street the scene changes. You get all the kids and the groupies who come to be cool and hang out in the Village. They're all going down to CBGB's, a punk rock club. You always got kids pointing to me, 'Hey, you know where CBGB's is, man?' "

Jimmy comes almost to a full stop at Houston Street. A group of boys on the next block shout to him in Spanish, but he does not acknowledge them. "As you go by," Jim muses, "you remember and translate things into what they'd be during the day." Just then an ambulance passes by, its siren silent, at a moderate speed. It is 4:45, and the tropical humidity has taken the edge off the chill.

"Now we're getting into the hard-core stuff," Jimmy observes. "You would not want to stop here." Jimmy Behr knows of what he speaks. He has run this route at 4:30 in the morning forty, fifty times or more, and he is now part of it. This is his territory, too, the territory of a man who will not stop running, of a marathoner, just as it is the territory of the Night People out for a buck or a good time. Jimmy Behr is one of the regulars in this part of town. The extraordinary is marginally routine here, so the sight of a man running through Greenwich Village on the tail end of a Saturday night is greeted with bemusement by the street-corner habitués. Jimmy digests it all and anticipates the action like a cop on his beat.

Behr continues along Sixth Avenue, unperturbed even though as he approaches Eighth Street, there is a large crowd milling about. "There must be two hundred people there," he explains. "All well-dressed, all black, no trouble or anything. I've always felt it had religious significance."

Through the darkness the aroma of fresh-baking bread is evident. Jimmy inhales deeply, then launches into a summary of what's to appear shortly.

"Most of the people sitting around here are dead-out stoned. You see them nodding out on various park benches. Fancy cars, Eldorados, and all this other crap. And you see the guy with the big hat on. At this hour, especially on a Saturday night, that's when you get all the hookers and transvestites, male and female. It's kind of scary because it's so obvious. The guys come down, a male pair, with beard and earrings, pocketbooks, heels. These guys are all musclemen, too. Nobody's ever propositioned me; you get the whistle, but I don't mind that."

Jimmy is on the northern fringe of the Village now, past Balducci's splendid food market. "There's a church down there," he continues. "This loudmouth guy who's always trying to talk somebody into something—he must be the preacher—is always saying, 'You shouldn't be drinking like this.' Meanwhile, there's about twenty stoned-out on the church steps."

For some reason, and Jimmy can't readily explain it, the Village is unusually tame this night. There are hookers and pimps, and there are two or three whistles and "Keep-it-up-man" and "Hey-Red," and there are sexual goings-on better suited to private quarters, but that's all there is. The preacher is not preaching, and the con men and hustlers and young kids looking for trouble have either called it a night or taken their games across town.

And it's a good thing because the air is foul and unsettling enough. Block after block is lined with rows of neatly wrapped garbage, waiting for the private carters, who seem never to make their pickups. "The street has a kind of slippery film," says Jim. He quickens the pace and instructs: "You want to run through that really fast. That's usually when you do a little interval run."

Jim dodges between two cabs on Fourteenth Street, passes the all-night Dunkin' Donuts where he once stopped on the run for a snack and was intimidated by a waitress unschooled in the social graces, even for that hour and that place, past more speeding cabs, past junkies who lurk in the alcoves of buildings, past the flower district where early deliveries are being made and a truck driver tells his buddy, "There he goes again," and on to Macy's. There Jimmy Behr stops, turns around, and doubles back at a quicker pace, returning to the AT&T building at 5:15 to conclude his 6-mile run, the first of his two daily workouts. Tomorrow will be the same, and the next day. And the one after that. Precisely.

James Francis Behr has his life figured out, his running life—if the two are different—for the next few years and, really, there is nothing that can bend him. He has worked from 8:00 to 4:00, 4:00 to 12:00, 12:00 to 8:00, he has taken graduate school courses on top of that, he has had a lingering stomach ailment, his wife, Pam, has given birth twice, the weather at its worst has been foul, the fatigue after marathons has left him leaden. But Jimmy keeps on running.

Although Jimmy Behr apparently was blessed with a healthy constitution to begin with, he has not had it easy; he just makes it appear that way. Others would make more of it: of running *every single day* for more than five years now; of running at 4:30 in the morning when he had to; of running when the windchill reached 30 below on the South Shore of Staten Island; of running double workouts despite marathon hangovers; of running 16 miles every Monday, Tuesday, Wednesday, and Thursday, 9 on Friday, 16 on Saturday, and the big one, 23, on Sunday, for a total, now, of 112 miles a week, rarely a mile more or a mile less. Jimmy has become ac-

Jimmy Behr's Development as a Marathon Runner

I: PROGRESS TOWARD HIS FIRST MARATHON (3:48; MARCH 1975)

(a) *Foundation:* in the 12 months prior to the race—4–5 days of running per week, at 8:00-mile pace, for a total of 1,300 miles.

(b) *12-week buildup:* 40 miles a week for 12 weeks, at 7:45-mile pace; longest run—one 15-miler.

(c) *Day-by-day schedule for the last four weeks:*

	Mon.	Tues.	Wed.	Thurs.	Fri.	Sat.	Sun.	
Week 4	5	6	5	0	5	8	10	= 39 miles
Week 3	5	6	5	0	6	8	10	= 40 miles
Week 2	5	6	5	6	0	8	15	= 45 miles
Week 1	5	6	5	6	0	3	Marathon	

II: PROGRESS TOWARD HIS FIRST SUB-3:00 MARATHON (2:55:55; OCTOBER 1976)

(a) *Foundation:* daily running for 19 months now; 4,600 miles in the last 12 months, at 7:15–7:30-mile pace.

(b) *12-week buildup:* 90 miles a week; longest run—21-miler done once a week.

(c) *Day-by-day schedule for the last four weeks:*

	Mon.	Tues.	Wed.	Thurs.	Fri.	Sat.	Sun.	
Week 4	10	10	10	12	9	21	16	= 88 miles
Week 3	10	10	10	12	9	21	16	= 88 miles
Week 2	15	10	10	12	9	21	15	= 92 miles
Week 1	10	10	10	12	7	5	Marathon	

III: PROGRESS TOWARD HIS BEST TIME (2:38:16; APRIL 1979)

(a) *Foundation:* 5,500 miles in last 12 months, at 7:00-mile pace; daily running for 49 months; now does double workouts.

(b) *12-week buildup:* 110 miles a week; longest run—23-miler done once a week.

(c) *Day-by-day schedule for the last four weeks:*

	Mon.	Tues.	Wed.	Thurs.	Fri.	Sat.	Sun.	
Week 4	15*	17	18	17	9	19	23	= 118 miles
Week 3	15	17	17	15	9	10	25†	= 117 miles
Week 2	15	17	17	15	9	17	23	= 122 miles
Week 1	15	17	17	14	9	7	5‡	= 93 miles

*Double workouts Monday–Thursday, and Saturday.
†Includes half-marathon race.
‡Marathon was next day, on a Monday.

customed to the incredulity of others and only when prodded will he explain what pushes him to a life of running that developed by happenstance but is today carefully calculated.

"I feel comfortable doing it. I like to run," Jimmy says, seated in his Archie Bunker easy chair on a Sunday afternoon, sipping a Heineken in the living room of his three-bedroom home. With slight embarrassment he adds: "If you want to make the Olympics—even if you have a hope to make the Olympics—you really have to go out of your way. It's either Ron Hill or Chris Stewart [two outstanding British runners] who said, 'On the day that you don't train, the guy who's going to beat you is training.' When it's snowing, the guy who's going to beat you is out there.

"The Olympic Team itself—who makes that? If you can walk on water, you make the team. Just the fact that I have an outside chance of making the Olympic Trials is enough of a goal. It's conceivable. I've taken off an hour from my marathon time; it's been going down at the rate of 14 minutes a year. How many people do you know who can sit here and say, 'I have a chance to get into the Olympic Trials?'"

Not many. Only the top 200 or so marathoners in the country get invited to compete at the U.S. Olympic Trials, based on the best performances in the twelve months preceding the qualifying run. For the 1980 Trials the cutoff was 2:21:54, and for the 1984 Trials, the one Behr is hopeful of making, look for that standard to dip close to 2:20.

Jimmy Behr's best marathon time is 2:38:16. Although he has knocked off 14 minutes a year for the last 5 years, when your time dips into the 2:30s, further progress becomes more difficult. In 1978 there were at least 1,000 men in the United States with marathon times faster than Behr's. While his chances are remote, making the 1984 Olympic Marathon Trials is one of his announced goals. "You may think this is crazy," he told a Staten Island *Advance* reporter, "but I'm thinking about the Olympics." Thus, the *Advance* headlined an October 1978 story about Jim: BEHR ON OLYMPIC TIMETABLE.

His Olympic fantasy is not the only reason Jimmy runs.

There are, of course, the standard motivations of health, fitness, identity, relaxation. He has rapidly developed, through painstaking dedication, into quite a fine runner, often placing within the top 5 or 10 percent in marathons and other races. Along the way he has retained running's simple pleasures, and when you get right down to it—Olympics or not, marathons or not—an everyday 10-mile workout will always be nirvana for Jimmy Behr.

While I will not wager that Behr will ever find himself at the starting line of an Olympic Trials Marathon, I am willing to bet you, even money, that he will not miss a day of running in his life. From March 19, 1975, through March 19, 1980, Jimmy ran every single day, mostly twice a day, for a total of more than 20,000 miles. During that time, he competed in about 100 races, 23 of them marathons. He ran on every type of terrain, in the most oppressive weather. His shifts at work were changed dramatically and on short notice, forcing him to significantly alter his dietary and sleeping habits. And during this period he conspicuously resisted the two major factors in a runner's downfall—illness and injury.

It is remarkable. Forget about the charts and graphs and data. Those alarming statistics and statements from physicians about the prevalence of low resistance, tendinitis, shin splints, and other malfunctions among heavily trained runners do not apply to Jimmy Behr. "The last time I was sick was before I was married, in March 1971," he recalls. "I had the flu and a fever. It was the kind of fever where if I had it now, I would not run. It's the kind where you get dizzy and very light-headed. It would be too dangerous."

I don't believe him. Dangers notwithstanding, Jimmy would climb out of bed and run. Perhaps he would modify the arbitrary 5-mile minimum he established for purposes of maintaining the Streak. Maybe he would run only one lap, a half-mile, around the egg-shaped street of his community, but run he would. The emotional ordeal of not running would be worse for him than a mere virus.

Still, Behr is not altogether impervious to organic failure.

He has had one weakness—his stomach. "The stomach problem began around Boston of '77," he says. "I got stitches. I never had it before. Stitches like cramps. I knew something was up because at Boston I had to stop in the middle of the race [which he went on to finish]. Yonkers I made it through, very slowly. Until you relieve yourself and take the pressure off, you've had it."

Other runners, when faced with frustrating cramps that would make uninterrupted running an impossibility, would simply knock off for a few days so as to be conveniently indoors when nature called. Not Jimmy, not with a streak of, by this time, more than two years. Jimmy had a contingency plan. "I would take a paper towel, tucked into my shorts. Frequently, I had to pull into the woods and let nature take its course and then resume my workout. No one ever spotted me. Naturally, you'd use a little discretion. You didn't want to be caught with your pants down."

Jimmy consulted two doctors who gave him conflicting advice and finally got some reprieve from a local GP whose office he'd passed on his running route from his home on Staten Island. "He gave me a prescription for two pills. One was a muscle relaxant, the other a sulfur pill. I was told to avoid fried foods, pork, gravies, salads, carbonated beverages, and some milk products." When this restrictive formula started to work for Jimmy, he followed it with rigid discipline. He didn't just "avoid" the taboo foods—he abandoned them. Here, for weeks and weeks, is what Jimmy had to look forward to on a typical day: breakfast—two cups of tea with honey and maybe poached eggs on dry toast; lunch—American cheese sandwich on toast and maybe a bowl of broth; dinner—chicken or fish or meatloaf ("with no onions or stuff like that"); snacks—tea or Hi-C with plain crackers. "I had a passion for doughnuts. I'd get a jelly or chocolate doughnut maybe once a week." The sneak.

While that spartan diet might score points with a nutritionist, it hardly carried the bulk required by a man running off at least 1,500 calories a day. But the worst part was the beer drought. Beer, a carbonated beverage, was a no-no, and Jimmy Behr (pronounced *beer*, not *bear*) is the consummate beer drinker. Not your six-pack-a-day guzzler, no. But two, three cans of Bud or, on a special occasion Beck's or Heineken's, round out an evening for Jimmy who, to this day, has on his mantel next to his trophies empty beer bottles saved from various marathon weekends as testaments to his pre-race preparation. Beer—abstaining from it or relying on it—takes on religious significance where marathon running is concerned.

Taking beer away from a beer-drinking long-distance runner can be as devastating as taking cigarettes away from the sedentary. Behr endured both sentences with Eagle Scout honor, although not, at first, simultaneously. It was Thanksgiving Day 1974, in anticipation of his first race three weeks hence when Jimmy "developed a new cure for smoking: The Beer Cure. Every time I wanted a cigarette I had a beer instead. Had about eight or nine that day. I remember very graphically that I ran 3 miles in the morning, then had one last cigarette, and that was it. I took a shower and didn't tell anyone that I had quit smoking. Pam said I was cranky but I don't remember that."

Pam interrupts: "Oh, you were cranky. And not only that—remember the day we had my family over the first time? What an impression. His drinking one beer after another. My mother was beginning to think the marriage was in trouble."

"Your mother was drinking them with me," Jimmy reminded her.

That was the turning point for Jimmy Behr. When he quit smoking and entered his first race, it marked the beginning of his remarkable ascent from a relatively inactive two-packs-a-day, Sunday softball player to a habitual long-distance runner of some distinction. In a sense, Jimmy Behr's story is the story of so many of today's serious adult long-distance runners: an athletic, albeit nonrunning, youth; military duty or advanced schooling; a career and a family and a settled life-style as observer rather than participant until . . . being introduced to running, taking to it, thriving on it, doing well at it, cultivating it as a valid and necessary element in their lives. The Jimmy Behrs of the world, perhaps even more so than the elite world-class runners, cannot imagine themselves not running in the future and not having run in the past. *Living* without *running*?

The last time Jimmy did so was in 1973. That spring, living in a small apartment on Staten Island near the ferry terminal, he'd go out for an evening walk or run once a week, "just to work off frustration." In December of that year Jimmy and Pam moved to a two-bedroom home in a development of town houses called Village Greens, on the other side of the island. The street that encloses Jim's village within the community measures roughly a half-mile, ideal for him to continue to occasionally alleviate common day-to-day anxieties. He recalls the first bite of what was to shortly become a steady diet. "It was a weekday night, probably a Monday in February. I put on blue sweatpants that I used to play football in. Adidas Superstars, which are basketball shoes. Some kind of sweatshirt and a hat and gloves. And I ran around the village one time. I was pretty tired." Tired, but not discouraged. "Within four or five nights, I started running another lap."

Not a very auspicious debut, but a debut paradoxically abetted by Jimmy's ignorance of the sport of running. Knowing nothing about running enabled him to learn strictly by trial and error and to appreciate every measure of progress. "I might have heard about the Boston Marathon, but I didn't care about it. . . . I used to follow football and baseball and basketball and hockey."

Jimmy's armchair enthusiasm for professional sports would soon wane—although, to this day, not diminish entirely—for he built up to 2 laps, then 3, every other day or so for a weekly output of, oh, 5 miles, at a pace of 8 to 9 minutes per mile. Still small potatoes, but the framework for bigger and better things had been firmly built. He ran next with two neighbors who were more advanced than he, "huffing and puffing" to keep up with them. "After that I went out and bought running shoes—Adidas Countrys, an all-leather model."

A runner's first pair of running shoes—oh, the sentimentality, the nostalgia. Grown men and women care for them, save them, talk to them as others talk to plants, reflect upon them fondly; if they are mocked in retrospect, it is like mocking an early period in one's life when one was young and foolish and naïve. The first pair of running shoes, for many runners, also represents a turning point, the transition from layman's foot-wear and the appellation of jogger to a larger commitment and the status of runner.

Jimmy Behr was no different. Six months after he first put his Adidas Countrys to work, on the first Sunday in December 1974, he found himself at Ninety-seventh Street on the East Drive of Central Park, standing in a steady rain with 200 other runners, awaiting the start of a New York Road Runners Club 6-mile race. The First Race.

"It was a terrible day, about 40 degrees, rain," says Jimmy. "I didn't know from anything. I had to use somebody else's locker. I was thinking what a damn fool I was. I calculated it would be easier to run through the puddles than run outside them. So I did, just to save a few steps here and there. What a mess."

Fool or not, Jimmy smiles and says, "I felt pretty neat be-cause I had run 6 miles. I might have done it in 44, 45 minutes. I don't remember what place—very much near the end. I had no idea of pacing. I just relied on intuition. I was exhausted when I got home." He repeats, emphatically, "Jesus, 6 miles. I felt good."

Road racing struck a responsive chord with Behr. Running a few times a week felt good and made sense, but now an-other world opened up for him: the world of the competitor. The race per se was a challenge, of course; but, hell, a few hundred people, *other* runners with values, interests, experi-ences similar to Jimmy's would gather every weekend in Cen-tral Park and take part in good-natured competition, exchange stories and advice over coffee and doughnuts, and reinforce in one another the hitherto unpopular notion that what has come to be known as the running life-style isn't that bad after all.

It was a positive mixture of constructive athletics and good, clean fun, especially enticing for one as vulnerable as Jimmy

Behr. Happily married, a homeowner, moving up but not sufficiently challenged at work, Jimmy, at 26, was still searching for something meaningful and time-consuming and fulfilling, something he might even share with his wife, something that was not, like other things he'd done, a waste of time. To paraphrase Dr. George Sheehan, Jimmy Behr found it in running.

Jimmy Behr was born on Columbus Day, 1947, in New York City, to James and Josephine Behr. Four years later the Behrs moved to the borough of Queens, to a section called Far Rockaway, whose population multiplied in the summer because of its proximity to the beach. Jimmy attended parochial schools and, like most other New York City kids, spent most of his afternoons and weekends playing ball in the streets. Subject to the indiscretions of his age, Jimmy, at 12, also dabbled in another sport, in the waters of nearby Jamaica Bay.

"From one of my friend's backyards, you could go out in the bay and swim across—about a mile and a half each way," says Jim. "Only two of us were brave enough to do it. I was one." The first evidence of daring and commitment in the future marathoner.

But the desire would take time to blossom. At Power Memorial Academy, which had one of the best track programs in the country, Jimmy played trumpet in the band for exercise. And, if anything, his younger brother Timothy's experiences as a fine runner for Bishop Loughlin High further discouraged Jim from trying the sport. Tim would go up to Van Cortlandt Park in the Bronx to run, come home late at night, and tell Jim: "I ran through hell. I had a lot of fun."

Two years after graduation from Power, in November 1966, Jim was drafted into the army, and the following July he was sent to Vietnam. His battalion specialized in field artillery, and it operated in the Central Highlands, in Pleiku and Phi Nurang, and other places. Jim saw combat duty during the Tet Offensive in 1968—saw "a lot of shit," as he prefers to put it.

Somewhere amid the combat was the sobering influence of the military, which further implanted in Jimmy the seeds of self-discipline, seeds that would later grow with his running.

He draws the connections: "We had the monsoon season where it rained for six months. I guess I had it built into me, and now I run in any kind of weather. People ask me, 'Do you run in the rain?' The weather, who cares?

"The army helps build character. I had discipline in high school, which helped in the army, and the army built more. You're expected to get up at 5:00 in the morning and perform normally. They say, 'What if the VC comes up and attacks you at 5:00 in the morning. Are you going to tell him it's too early—I just got up and haven't had my morning coffee?' So I run at 5:00 if I have to. It's no longer a special thing."

The sense of discipline and sacrifice and single-mindedness that had upholstered the character of Jimmy Behr was finally put to use for his own satisfaction on March 17, 1975, the day Jimmy Behr became a marathoner. He had raced that first 6-miler in December 1974, then 10 and 12, a 25-kilometer and a 30, and finally a 20-miler in mid-February in which he placed far back in the pack, "not knowing the bounds of what I could or could not do." But he would learn. It was the Earth Day Marathon on Long Island, since rescheduled for May and renamed the Long Island Marathon. A field of some 300 runners, many of them intent on running Boston's qualifying time of 3:30, coped with a psychologically debilitating course that had several loops to it and nasty, end-of-winter weather.

Jim reached the halfway point in 1:45, an 8-minute-mile pace and a little too fast, all things considered. "I was tired. I took a rest and walked a little. I met this other guy who was in the same boat. We'd walk 2, then run 4; then walk 4 and run 2."

Jim finished in 3:48, got a T-shirt, a picture of himself he later framed, and the requisite discomforts. "I couldn't move. I was stiff and sore and my head hurt. I drank the whole thing of Gatorade. We went down to Pam's parents' home for dinner and they all wondered what was wrong with me. They knew what I had done, but they didn't know what it was."

He took the next day off and resumed running on Tuesday, March 19, the day the Streak began. He reached 1,000 straight days on December 15, 1977, when he ran 14.5 miles, and 1,500 days on April 28, 1979, 12 days after his PR at Boston. He broke 3 hours for the marathon when he ran 2:56:10 at New York in '76. He ran his first sub-2:50, a 2:48:31, at the Jersey Shore in '77. He has run several 2:40s, twice setting a PR, placing fourth and winning trophies, in the little-known Monmouth (New Jersey) Marathon, a favorite of Jimmy's, run early in March and a good tune-up for Boston.

The next week at work—much like every week at work after a marathon—Jim's colleagues at the International Operating Center of AT&T would press him for details. Not that they know about times or pacing or fluid intake or even Bill Rodgers—but they know about Jimmy Behr, the company's Marathon Man, the runner once the butt of their ridicule and then, after Jimmy was written up in the firm's house organ (the *Skyline*), something of a hero.

Jim started at AT&T as a messenger in 1964 and today, five promotions later and having worked shifts around the clock, he is back on the day tour as scheduling supervisor at the IOC, responsible for assigning tours to 700 international operators on all three shifts.

Behr's personnel scheduling is somewhat of an inflated extension of his personal scheduling. He constantly plots his daily activities, chores, and social engagements several weeks, even months ahead, so as to make sure he will, without a doubt, fit in his prescribed running, in terms of mileage and composition, no matter what the circumstances.

Such meticulous planning, together with mileage calculated to the fraction (on November 15, 1977, his diary notes, he ran 21.4 miles), the Streak, the beer bottles saved (and displayed) from marathon weekends, form, it could be deduced, the composite of a person obsessed with running. Perhaps. But on the other side of the ledger, Jimmy Behr has not allowed his running to interfere with career advancement, education (he'll soon receive his MBA), his photography, his appreciation of well-made cars (like his own BMW), old movies, Sherlock Holmes, and the Marx Brothers. Jimmy's running is a 15-hour-a-week passion—15 hours when other people are playing tennis or racquetball or poker or the horses, watching

Suzanne Somers on the tube, nursing plants, sipping martinis, or patronizing discos.

It has been a trade-off, and the deal could not possibly have been consummated if not for Jimmy's biggest fan, his wife, Pam. She has woven her life around Jimmy's running, and although it has been difficult for her at times, she has enjoyed it. Pam does not run herself ("Once I did a little jogging"), but she has learned a lot about the sport, mainly from attending almost all of Jimmy's races, and she has become, she says with stoic pride, a runner's wife.

There is little that can fill a runner's wife with more apprehension than the thought of giving birth on the day of the Boston Marathon, a Boston Marathon in which her husband is entered and hoping to run well. Before Boston '79, Pam Behr, 8½ months pregnant, had her battle plan mapped out.

"If I give birth up there, my mother will fly up on the shuttle, and pick up Sean [their 5-year-old son], bring him to my house, and Jimmy will stay with me. I'm not afraid of having the baby in Boston. I'm afraid I'll go into labor the Friday or Saturday before Boston and Jimmy'll feel guilty because he'll say, 'How can I leave my wife and newborn and go away for the weekend?' "

Fortunately, Jimmy ran a fine race and Pam did not spoil it by having the nerve to give birth that weekend. Jim's time was 2:40:16, a personal best, and he's rightfully counting it as a 2:38:16 because it took him over 2 minutes to reach the starting line after the gun had sounded. Pam's race began twelve days later. On April 28, she gave birth to Elizabeth Anne, 8 pounds 9 ounces.

It would have gnawed at Jimmy had he missed Boston. Not just because it's BOSTON, but because you have to qualify for it, you have to earn your way into it—in Jimmy's case, by having run under 2:50 in a marathon in the twelve months before the event. Any jogger can *enter* a marathon, get his T-shirt, drop out after 10 miles or maybe even finish, half-walking, in five hours, and call himself—the nerve of it all—a marathoner. Jimmy loathes that and he mocks it: the commercialism of running, the faddish elements in it, the designer sweatsuits, the people who dabble in it without commitment or purpose, the pervasiveness of running as a metaphor for so many things. While society's acceptance of, or even infatuation with, running has paved an accessible path for Jimmy and elevated his status, it has also invaded his precious, preferably self-contained territory and detracted from his identity as *the* runner. His 112 miles a week notwithstanding, Jimmy Behr is now, to others if not to himself, merely *a* runner.

He says with concern, "They should have two races—one for the people that are going to run the whole distance and one for the people who want to say 'I was there.'" Still, Jimmy acknowledges, "There is a place for them, and I think it's great people are exercising. But I think the marathon should be left alone. They should realize that it's the essence of running."

12

AGE IS NO BARRIER

THE KID

I was prepared, initially, to dislike the kid. Boy Scout, church-goer, straight-A student, hotshot athlete, handsome. The type of kid your parents always compared you to when you were young and brought home an embarrassing report card from school or spouted four-letter words or hung out on the street corner doing no good long after dark.

Not only does Eric Davis own two dozen Boy Scout merit badges, exemplary report cards, and an exceptional breast-stroke—he also sets the table for breakfast, helps his younger sister with her homework, and doesn't have a cross word in his vocabulary. Eric Davis is 12 years old and, on top of it all, an extraordinary marathon runner.

On October 8, 1978, Eric Davis of Lynchburg, Virginia, raced the certified 26-mile-385-yard course of the Richmond Newspapers Marathon in 2:48:53. He placed seventeenth in the field of 2,722 starters, and since Eric was 11 at the time, his performance established a U.S. age record for the distance.

Despite his achievement, despite his success and reputation in school, in athletics, in the community, Eric Davis remains humble, grateful, kind, sensitive, sincere, and, for a young man his age, even charming. Indeed, he is everything a parent could hope for in a child, so much so that one is compelled to search for a flaw; there is a sense of investigative failure in not finding one.

If for a time, though, one becomes a bit too accustomed to Eric's endearing demeanor and forgets how crude and clumsy most 12-year-old boys are, one is quickly straightened out by a friend of his from Norfolk. This kid is 13, a runner but not a marathoner, which is not surprising. Marathon running requires commitment and character; this kid *is* a character.

We had driven to Norfolk from Virginia Beach after Eric had run in the 1979 Shamrock Marathon, picked up his friend, and then had gone to dinner in an Italian restaurant. While Eric was mannerly, soft-spoken, and restrained, his buddy, loudly and smugly, boasted of his own running achievements, his Boy Scout merit badges, his parents' wealth; he complained about the service and persisted in needling the waitress. He was clearly spoiled rotten, perhaps not atypical for a fine athlete his age.

It is Eric Davis who is atypical. He seemed embarrassed by his friend's antics at the restaurant but retained his poise, the same poise he had shown in defeat earlier that day (St. Patrick's Day of 1979) when he dropped out of the Shamrock Marathon after 18 miles. His record-breaking run in Richmond had come five months earlier and he was not ready for another one. His training had not been going especially well and a month before, in sub-zero conditions at Beltsville, Maryland, Eric (and many others) had dropped out of the Washington's Birthday Marathon. At Shamrock (where he had run 3:10 in '78 in his first marathon) Eric had hoped just to break 3 hours, to get back in tune with running a sub-7-minute-per-mile pace for 26.2 miles.

It was a glorious day for it. A cool breeze curled in off the beachfront strip at Chesapeake Bay and there was that ideal blend of morning chill plus the muted presence of the sun that facilitates comfortable long-distance running. Perhaps it was just a bit too warm for a marathon. Atlantic Avenue, where the race would begin, was thick with contestants and their families, and there was a festive atmosphere not at all uncommon these days at marathons and other road races.

This resort town, whose kids-on-the-prowl ambience resembles a set for *American Graffiti*, was thoroughly caught up in the Shamrock Marathon this Saturday morning, prompting race director Jack Bocrie to declare: "The weather is perfect— the best in seven years. Traffic is down and out. In ten minutes everything should be super ready."

Eric Davis, however, was not quite super ready. It was a four-hour car ride the night before for his Lynchburg party— Eric, his dad, Eric's friend, two of his Dad's running buddies, and me—and we had arrived in Virginia Beach just in time for the 10:00 P.M. deadline for entry pickups. Eric didn't get to sleep until midnight, was awakened at 2:30 by crank calls from a roomful of teenage girls, was up for good at 6:00 and forced down a token breakfast of toast and jam. Dinner for Eric had been far from the kind of fare recommended by the marathoner's handbook. His father had insisted on economizing at a roadside joint familiar to him, and Eric had downed a double burger, french fries, onion rings, a coke, and an ice cream cone.

"Still," said Eric, massaging his muscles before the race, "I feel rested. I feel okay."

It was a clean start. The runners shot down Atlantic Avenue where several miles later they would make the first of several detours, taking in a nature trail that houses wildlife, and would work their way onto the path adjacent to the beach where most of the spectators would enjoy the event and where it would finish. The course was flat, and it was not an especially strong field as marathons go. Barry Heath was the favorite. The only record-breaker in the bunch was, well, Eric Davis. Eric was also the youngest runner and the only one whose father had brought along an old Schwinn that he planned to ride on the course after meeting his son at the 18-mile point. "It means a lot to me," Eric said. "It keeps me going. Besides that, he breaks the wind."

Bernie Davis, a 42-year-old engineer who had run a 2:54 marathon, entered the 5-mile race (the event's trilogy was completed by a 1-mile beach run) and did fairly well for his current so-so condition: seventy-fifth place in 31:40. The 5-miler started about a half-mile after the marathon, which gave Bernie just the right amount of time to recover, change into dry clothing, lug his Schwinn to the 18-mile point, and wait.

The checkpoint, actually, was 17.8 miles. In his record run in Richmond, Eric's 2:48:53 computed to roughly a 6:30-per-mile pace, the first 18 miles of which were, by necessity, about 15 to 30 seconds faster per mile. But this day he was looking for merely a sub-3:00 which, if on target, should bring him past his anxious father and the beat-up Schwinn in the low 1:50s, or 6:45 per mile.

The motorcycle cops ushered the leaders past the swelling crowds at this critical juncture, the point in a marathon where only the better runners continue to look smooth and strong. The first runner to appear was bearded Ron Martin, like Heath a Briton, wearing an old William & Mary uniform and encouraged by his former college coach, Roy Chernock. Martin had a sizable lead, Tom Fitzpatrick was next, and then came Heath, wearing the uniform of his club, the Tidewater Striders.

Another 35 runners passed and Bernie Davis, getting a bit edgy, was given false security by the appearance of a friend, Frank McFadder of Lynchburg, whose shirt read SIX DOLLAR MAN and who was en route to a mid-2:40s performance. The top runners were now well on their way to the final miles, having passed one by one or in pairs; then the second echelon wove through in clusters, each runner clinging to the security of the other as the strain of the marathon became difficult to manage. Eric was not yet within view, and there was a growing sense that something was wrong. Almost two hours had elapsed.

Bernie strained to get a glimpse of his son, and finally he did. A few hundred yards down the shoreline course, Eric was spotted. Walking. We hurried toward him and, as Eric left the race, Bernie hugged his son and consoled him. After a few moments Eric shook him off and walked unattended to the car, obviously disappointed but mostly expressionless. He changed to warm clothing, sipped a Pepsi, applied ointment to his chafed lips, and soon felt composed enough to talk about it.

"I just don't feel too good. My heel is tied up right behind the bottom. I have stomach problems. I started to fade at 8, got sorer and sorer. At 10 I decided I'd drop out later on. I thought I could have finished, but I'd have to slow down a whole lot. I was dehydrated and cramped up at 12."

These were not excuses. This is a kid who already knows his body and is learning about its limitations, a kid who started out a little too fast for his own good in this one, perhaps buoyed by people "who knew who I was and gave me a lot of encouragement." Pacing is a hard thing to master amid conflicting stimuli. Eric seemed confused but not done-in. "No," he insisted, "I don't feel any pressure. I like to finish a lot better, but it doesn't bother me. I'm looking forward to another marathon."

Yet Eric's setback, and the speculation as to the effect it will have on him, athletically and otherwise, draw attention to a heated issue that has risen from the smoke of the running explosion: Should kids run marathons and other long-distance races? It's a question I had to put to Bernie Davis. "You're talking about when you run so hard when you're younger you probably won't be doing it when you're older. We feel that won't happen. Even if it does, you have the satisfaction of doing it well when you're younger. Of doing it and enjoying it now." Bernie's response seemed rehearsed, and he admitted he'd been asked that before.

And for good reason. Thousands of parents around the country are being asked the same question as long-distance rolls thicken with their children's names, children as young as 4 or 5, whose futures can be imperiled by the physical and emotional stress of doing a lot of competitive running. The concerns center on the *amount* of running, not the notion of running per se, which can be as vital to kids as to adults.

The extremes of the bell curve are most clearly dramatized by the case of one Bucky Cox from Lawrence, Kansas. In the summer of 1978, Bucky, who was then 5, ran a marathon in Junction City, Kansas, in 5:25:09. The temperature was in the 90s, and 33 older entrants dropped out. Bucky's time is listed by the National Running Data Center as a U.S. age-5 record for "men." As precocious as Bucky is, he found that it's a dog-eat-dog world in the 6-year-old bracket. In the fall of '78 he lowered his best time to 4:49:26 in the Mayor Daley Marathon in Chicago, but there was already a 4:22:41 on the books from 6-year-old Clark Minton of Texas. Neither Bucky nor Clark, however, was hasty enough in getting his career going and thus missed a shot at 4-year-old Brent Bogle's record of 6:03:35.

Six hours, 3 minutes, 35 seconds! Think about it. A 4-year-old child concentrating on, and struggling with, a difficult physical task for more than 6 hours. What was that about the short attention span of kindergarteners? Sure it's a snail's pace at 14 minutes per mile, but 6 hours plus is also *twice* as long as many runners spend out on the road during a marathon run. Forget for a moment the medical debate; the complaint is simple— this stuff is downright unnatural.

Bucky Cox's trainer, Ray Foster, works at the University of Kansas as a research associate in its Bureau of Child Research. *Sports Illustrated* said Foster rewards Bucky with "positive reinforcement" in the form of nickels, and quotes Foster as saying: "Some people equate reinforcement with bribery. I would equate it with bribery if we pushed him to do it. But he has said he wants to race."

Bucky's female counterpart is 9-year-old Jennifer Amyx of Woodsboro, Maryland. Jennifer holds "women's" age records in the marathon for 5 (4:56:36), 6 (4:00:36), 7 (3:57:54), and 8 (3:26:29). She runs 70 miles a week, occasionally 100, with her parents' blessings. Her father, Herb, a research scientist, says he's surveyed the literature—limited as it is—on children's running and found no negative data concerning distance running and young children. "Every parent experiments on the child," Amyx told writer Connie Bruck, "and I think if you are deliberate about it, you have a better chance of getting good results."

However, some medical experts contend that these kids will pay for their good results with epiphyseal injuries. Bruck, in her article for *The Runner*, "Children at Play," states: "The epiphyseal, growth plates in joints at the end of a large bone, are largely responsible for growth of the long bones in a growing body and most of these soft epiphyseal plates are closed by age 20. If badly injured, they can stunt growth." But Dr. Gabe Mirkin, co-author of *The Sportsmedicine Book* and past chairman of the Amateur Athletic Union's Age-Group Subcommittee, told Bruck: "As far as we know, there is no increased incidence of epiphyseal injuries in kids who run. What I see in my practice is that they get stress fractures in the same places adults get them, and they heal a lot faster."

Despite the abuses and potential dangers, it is hard for a lot of people to get worked up over the idea of children running marathons. Most parents have all they can handle just keeping their kids out of trouble and would give anything to see their offspring hooked on such good, clean fun as running. Helen and Bernard Davis don't know how lucky they are. Eric could quit running tomorrow and turn to a dozen activities he enjoys and excels in.

When word of Eric's 2:48:53 circulated, he became a celebrity. His picture appeared on *Sports Illustrated*'s "Faces in the Crowd" page with this caption: "In addition to finishing 17th in a field of 2,722 in Richmond, Va. Newspapers Marathon, Eric, 11, set a national age-group record. His time of 2:48:53 was 2:15 faster than the mark set by David Chun of Honolulu in 1975." The local press couldn't resist splashing his picture across the sports page in the week following the race, and for some time after. It was carried as far as Merion County, Oregon, where the Woodbern *Independent* of December 20, 1978, headlined: WORLD'S BEST MARATHONER VISITS. The Davises were spending Christmas with relatives.

A spotlight such as this can be a monkey on the back of a young boy, especially one in so unpredictable a sport as long-distance running. Fortunately for him, Eric's other interests have served to dilute the attention thrust upon him. He is not just Eric Davis, the marathon runner. He is Eric Davis, the star-ranked Boy Scout, the honor-roll student, the medal-winning swimmer, the trackman, the cub reporter on the Sandusky Middle School newspaper. Versatility is a virtue. In Eric's case, it has helped him cope with occasional failures and has cast his accomplishments in a somewhat different light than would be likely had he been *only* a breaststroke champion or *only* a marathon champion.

Eric Davis is, so far, protected. He has helped himself by his versatility and his departure from the midst of two marathons after Richmond—but it is more than that. It is partly his character, which is subdued and appreciative; partly his age, which, at 12 now, is a bit too old for Bucky Cox–like fawning; partly his parents, who are religious and conservative; partly Lynchburg, which is religious and conservative, a place not given to haste or hype.

Eric has at least 250 awards, maybe 20 or 30 for swimming, the rest for running. They are of every color and shape, of every description and inscription. They are all neatly arranged, ordered testaments to his growth as an athlete. It is all there: the Virginia Ten-Milers; the marathons, the Junior Olympics, the Superstars. The scrapbooks and photo albums represent a chronology of almost every race the kid has run and are marked by such yellowing headlines as SHORTAGE OF TRAINING NO BARRIER TO 11-YEAR-OLD, and ERIC DAVIS: 12-YEAR-OLD WONDER, and by autographs from Barry Brown, Marty Liquori, and Jacqueline Hansen. One, in particular, reads: "Eric, I want to wish you luck in your Lynchburg race and your future races. See you in '88. Bill Rodgers."

Eric's potential for this future meeting is further evident later in the day at the daily track team workout at the Sandusky Middle School. The school goes from grade 6 to grade 8. Eric is in the sixth grade, and one of the few sixth-graders on the team. At 2:45 both the boys' and girls' teams gather.

They loosen up and joke, chewing wads of bubble gum, and, after the coaches appear, go through calisthenics together. It is the end of the first week of spring track practice, and although the first meet is only two weeks away, the mood is relaxed and informal.

It is an inspiring sight, indeed—70 or 80 boys and girls, black and white, repeating drills, running, jumping, throwing and hurdling on a clear, cool Friday afternoon, the Blue Ridge Mountains visible in the distance. I have spent the better part of the last fifteen years watching youngsters run track, and one thing is obvious to me at the Sandusky field: All but one of these youngsters is learning *how* to run, jump, throw, and hurdle; the other one knows how to execute his specialty and is merely striding through the session in order to stay loose for his competition the next day. He is, of course, Eric Davis.

Eric is 5 feet tall and weighs 80 pounds. He has the handsome Filipino features of his mother, Helen: big, round eyes, dark complexion, pronounced cheekbones, and lustrous hair, which he parts down the middle in the style of the day. His calf muscles are well defined. Many of the boys are a head taller than Eric, but while they run in bulky, awkward bursts, he runs like a deer. Eric glides. His gait is smooth, his knees lift high, he is efficient. He works at his pace, at leading the distance runners, after a 2-mile warm-up, through an untimed "pyramid" workout of three-quarters, a mile, a half-mile, a quarter, a 220, and a 110. Eric is polished, almost delicate in comparison to his teammates. If he is flawed at all, it is that he seems too tight on top, in his shoulders, arms, and neck, but such muscular tension will ease in time.

Sandusky is a sports school, a winner, but it is a ragtag assembly out there, some kids wearing regulation uniforms and running shoes, others in trousers or with hats, or wearing sneakers or spikes. Eric is the only one who even looks the part, but he is no prima donna. He has not even told the head coach, Bill Hurley, what he will be up to tomorrow for fear that Hurley would frown upon a 5-mile workout, no matter how contained, the day before a marathon.

"I've never seen anyone of his caliber at his age," says Hurley. "Good all-around runner, lotta determination. He's got leadership qualities. He looks like Jim Ryun, good body type. The fact that he's had a lot of attention hasn't showed. You can work with him."

Hurley has also worked with Eric at Heritage High School where he moonlights as cross-country coach. Hurley permitted Eric to practice with the team last fall and compete unofficially in some of the meets. "He was the third or fourth best runner in the group," Hurley says. "These kids were 16, 17; Eric was 11. When he's a ninth-grader, he's gonna be the best cross-country runner in the state. This kid could end up on the Olympic Team."

If not in running, then maybe in some other sport. For two straight years, at 10 and 11, Eric won his age-group division of the citywide Superstars competition, patterned after the NBC program. The ten events: high jump, long jump, 100-yard dash, 880-yard run, 50-yard swim, 880-yard bike race, football throw, basketball free throws, weight lifting, and obstacle course. Too much too soon? Until recently, the school superintendent thought so. It took a lot of politicking to get him to authorize sixth-grade competition in such noncontact sports as track and tennis. Eric was relieved about this and echoed his dad's sentiments: "I don't think it's bad. Even if I do burn out, if I stopped now, there'd be a chance that I wouldn't be any good when I did grow up. So I'd be missing out. If I run now I get the fun out of it now. And I could really be good when I grow up."

GOLDEN OLDIES

In 1978, Marion Epstein and her husband Irving turned 60 years old. To honor the occasion, they wished to exchange special birthday gifts, gifts they could cherish and remember fondly in the years ahead. It went without saying that such gifts would have something to do with running. At a time of life—beyond "middle" age but certainly not "old"—when many couples face an identity crisis and harbor anxieties about what each day will hold for them, Marion and Irving

Epstein live from run to run, race to race, marathon to marathon, in love with the activity that consumes them.

The Epsteins, who live in Brooklyn, New York, symbolize not only the retardation of physical and psychological aging that running has come to mean for older people but also the marital closeness that frequently develops when partners in marriage become partners on the road. Common interests and experiences are the raw materials of any solid relationship, and if a husband and wife can share something as personal and challenging as marathon running, their relationship can be greatly strengthened.

In August 1978, Marion turned 60, in September it was Irv's turn, and in October they exchanged their gifts. They gave one another a Marathon Spree. They agreed to attempt to run a marathon every weekend in October, November, and December. A treat, the Epsteins called it. "We decided we had to do something worthy of people 60 years old," Irv said, "and also to let our kids know that we're not quite ready for baby-sitting or rocking chairs." The Epsteins spent the latter part of September planning their itinerary and the next three months fulfilling it.

Irv reviewed the couple's indulgence. "We ran Hanover [New Hampshire] the first week, the second week of October was Atlantic City, the third week was Philadelphia, the fourth week was New York City. We couldn't find one after that. The week after that was Harrisburg [Pennsylvania]. Then we drew a blank again. The next week was Philadelphia again. Then we drew a blank again—or did we? No—the week after Philly we did Baltimore and then, oh yeah, the week after Baltimore we did Charlotte [North Carolina]."

Drawing a blank meant searching unsuccessfully for a marathon close enough to home to accommodate travel time, budget, and two people who run very, very slowly. The spree ended in Charlotte on December 16, and the next week the Epsteins ran a 30-kilometer (18.6-mile) race in New York's Central Park just to keep themselves honest. "We could have easily done another marathon," said Irv, who finished all 8 in the spree—the fastest a 4:57 in Baltimore, the slowest a 6:06

in Philadelphia. Irv can run considerably faster (his PR is 4:10), but he prefers to run with his wife. Marion completed 6 of the 8 marathons, going only 16 miles in Hanover and 14 miles in the second race at Philly. Her fastest was a 5:06 in Atlantic City, her slowest the 6:06.

Finishing the marathons was the easy part. Getting to them was tricky. The Epsteins don't drive—Marion used to have a license; Irv's never had one. "We'd get there the cheapest, most convenient way," said Irv. "Charlotte you had to go by plane. Baltimore, Philly was by train. Hanover by car—Eddie [the Epsteins' only son; they have three daughters] and his wife and baby went up there. He'd run a few, too. I'm afraid to look up what it all cost."

"Over a thousand dollars," Marion offered.

"The money was well spent," said Irv. "The time of our lives. We look forward to doing it next year and into the future, if at all possible financially."

"To me," says Marion, "running a marathon is like living. I enjoy it so much that it helps me mentally and physically. I enjoy it much more than a 10-mile race, or other races. It's so special because I know I can conquer it. It makes me feel beautiful. I just can't describe it any other way. It's a challenge. Just to be there and know I can do it."

The Epsteins have acquired something of a following among runners in the Greater New York area. This is so because they run together, because they are among the older competitors, because they race frequently, because of some publicity they have received, but mainly because they usually finish last in race after race after race. This does not at all deter them from their appointed rounds. They admit to their slow pace, which seems little faster than a brisk walk, and tell you that they are not much interested in time but merely in completing the distance. And when they do complete it, their efforts rarely pass unappreciated. "They cheer," says Marion, smiling. "What an ovation we get coming in. They get us things to drink and kiss us and hug us and say, 'You did a great job. Well done.' People are very gracious."

Finishing last can have its own rewards. The biggest of the

dozens of awards on display in the Epsteins' home is the huge trophy given to Marion at the 1978 Long Island Marathon— for finishing last. It was presented to her by the East Meadow Chamber of Commerce, which called her "an unforgettable track star." The standard awards were given out two hours before Marion finished (her time was 6:03), and hundreds of entrants waited around in honor of Marion Epstein for the special tribute.

The realization that the Epsteins will most likely finish last dictates that they take certain precautions, however. It seems that there are not *always* gracious people waiting for them at the finish line. Nor are race officials always posted along the tail end of the course to direct stragglers to the proper destination. When they consider running a new race on an unfamiliar course, the Epsteins seek assurances from race directors that they will not be left strictly on their own. In the winter this can, indeed, be important for the couple, what with the dangers of early darkness and menacing motorists.

Their apprehensions are not unfounded. "I was running by myself in the Yonkers Marathon, 1977," Marion recalls. "It was point-to-point, and coming back there was no one to show us the way. So instead of taking that turn by the Ramada Inn, we went on straight for 2 hours and got lost. By this time I was alone."

Irving and Eddie were also in the race, running ahead of Marion this time, and Irv recalls, "The exact same thing happened to us. We asked the policeman and he said to turn off at the Ramada, but the sign is not so big so we went right past it. About a half-mile down the road, someone told us, 'Hey, the cutoff's back there.'"

"We got disgusted," said Marion, "but we finished."

And there was Earth Day, '73. "At 22.5 miles the guy gave me the wrong distance," said Marion. "He says to me I have *6* more miles to go. I kept running and running, and I got lost."

And there was Albany in '77. "They had a figure-8," says Irv. "There was supposed to be a man sitting there at the crossovers. But he didn't see nobody down the road, so he walked away. By the time we got there, we didn't know where to go. So we started running loops in another direction until somebody said, 'What are you doing here? If you're looking for the marathon, go back over there.' "

"We ran a 27-mile marathon," says Marion. "They even had it in the paper."

The Epsteins seem to attract misfortune wherever they race. Several years ago, in their early running days, the sight of the couple, shuffling along as they do, Irving rail-thin and Marion a bit chunky, seemed an alien threat both to their contemporaries and to rowdy teenagers who could not hold back their ridicule or an occasional beer can. In a period of months, Marion got lost in a 15-kilometer (9.3-mile) race in Scarsdale and was disqualified; was smacked by a sunbather when she accidentally splashed him while running on the beach; and was mugged while running in Central Park. Similarly, Irving, while running with (or slightly behind) his oldest daughter, Loraine, was stopped and questioned by police who, he said, "thought I was chasing a girl."

More recently, this comedy of errors has taken a turn for the worse. Three days before the March 1978 Albany Marathon, Marion was hit by a cyclist—and she was not even running at the time. "He knocked me down so hard I was bleeding from the throat," she said. Marion was treated at a hospital and released. But in the race itself, in her eighth mile, "I started spitting blood. I was so frightened I stopped immediately."

Two months later both Marion and Irv were sidelined in the same week for the same reason: dogs. A Great Dane broke away from its leash and took a piece out of Marion's back. A mongrel attacked Irv on his morning run near his place of work, a city-run medical clinic in one of Brooklyn's tougher neighborhoods. Bleeding heavily from the leg bite, Irv, back at work, went to the infirmary and said, "I want a Band-Aid." A medical aide insisted the wound required stitches and Irv countered, "You can't sew it up, it's two weeks before Yonkers." But sew it up they did, twelve stitches worth and, says Irv, "For the next two weeks I couldn't run, so we walked every night. I bet we did 50 miles just walking."

And two weeks later Marion and Irv ran the Yonkers Marathon.

The difficulties, of course, have been worth it. Marathon running for the Epsteins has been one continuous party. Before the party began, in 1970, Irv was a cashier in a factory and Marion managed a dry-cleaning store. Irving, at 5 feet 10 inches and 190 pounds, was overweight and irritable. Ditto for Marion, 5 feet 2 inches and 150. Marion suffered regular bouts of pneumonia, bronchitis, nausea, and low blood pressure. Running was the ideal antidote for both Epsteins. Two years and 2,000 miles later, each had lost 30 pounds and, they say, they have not been sick a single day during that period. The couple took up running encouraged by their son, Edward, who had boasted to them of his conditioning in the army, where he was a boxer and did road work around an aircraft carrier.

Marion recalled their initiation. "It was Good Friday, 1970. Actually, the day after. It was cold and we were freezing, but we went down to the beach and ran, maybe, a quarter of a mile. We ran barefoot. The bones in my legs—I felt like a cripple afterwards. I said, never again. The following week we went down to the beach and did it again. And it felt so good. Then we started running regularly, but only on weekends at the beach. I loved it."

When I visited the couple, the welcome mat in the hallway outside the front door of their walk-up was covered with four pairs of running shoes, neatly arranged. Warm-up jackets and drying T-shirts hung on a coatrack, evidence of the 12-mile workout the couple had finished about an hour before my arrival. We reviewed what was essentially a revolution in their lives—the metamorphosis they'd undergone since starting to run—and while Irv and Marion Epstein are not long-winded disciples of the running-is-a-panacea school of thought, their story is so simple and so satisfying that it makes one wonder if there is any limit to the therapeutic value running can have for older people.

Irv and Marion's recollections of the origins of their marathon running complemented each other's as they reconstructed the humble beginnings of their initiation on the beach at Coney Island.

Marion: "I just kept running on the beach on weekends, the spring of 1970."

Irv: "I'm afraid you're not thinking because the crucial part of the story is that right about that time Loraine came home. She was working in Denver. She was 23, 24, and she saw we were fooling around on the beach, so I said, 'Come and run with us.' So she got into running, and we all started picking up the mileage. We used to count bays [at the beach]. We'd run 40, 45 bays. A few miles over and back—no big deal. We used to figure something like 8, 8½ bays a mile. We had a helluva lot of fun.

"Remember the day we went down together and a thunderstorm broke out? Everybody went home and the three of us in our swimsuits just ran through the thunder, too stupid to realize you could get hurt like that. We ran through the whole storm."

Marion: "After the storm was over, the lifeguards came back and yelled at us."

Irv: "We were a long way from racing, but Loraine was also running with Eddie, picking up her pace, and she started going to races, like the old Cherry Tree Marathon. One day she came home and said, 'Why don't you run a marathon?' That was in '72. Kurt Steiner of the Road Runners Club said that if the four of us ran—Marion, myself, Loraine, and Eddie—we'd be the only family on the East Coast that ran a marathon together. That tickled our egos. We had never run any race before, but we started training for the New York Marathon, putting in heavy mileage. Unfortunately Marion, because of her job, was going to do the marathon on only 35 miles a week. That's why I told her to drop out after 14 miles."

Marion: "And I felt so good, I could have continued. I remember that. Irving said, 'Drop out.' "

Irving: "I've got to tell you something about her. This person is fearless. She didn't worry about herself. I worry about her. I finished it in 4:24, Eddie and Loraine didn't run. There were about 200 in it that year. I didn't know what we were getting into.

"After that first marathon it clicked. Hook, line, and sinker—I swallowed it. She knows how I felt. I could have cried right there. It was the most meaningful experience ever in my sports life."

Until the participatory sports boom of recent years, it was taken for granted that the value of strenuous sport—of setting goals and striving to reach them and, on another plane, of intense conditioning—was beyond the reach of older people and even medically unsound. Sports scientists have proven this assumption to be ridiculous, and they have been supported by legions of marathoners over 40, over 50, over 60, and some over 70 and even 80. This has indeed been one of the delightful outgrowths of marathon running: the resumption of considerable exercise by people over 40, people who, by and large, had previously led mostly sedentary lives.

Fitness After Forty (1977), Hal Higdon's fine book, provides tables that show how age contributes to the "decline" in a person's performance in marathons and other events. Based on statistics from Ken Young of the National Running Data Center, Higdon cites the following theoretical slowdowns: at age 40 (4.5 percent), at 80 (58.1 percent). The table also indicates that the optimal age of marathon performance is 29 and that a 3-hour marathoner at age 29 would be expected to run 3:29:20 at 50 and 3:55:45 at 60, all other things remaining equal.

Higdon himself has done as much as anyone to foster the acceptance of older people as legitimate athletes. He has done this through his public speaking and his writing, most recently as Senior Writer for *The Runner* magazine, but also as an outstanding athlete in his own right. Now 48, he's been running for 30 years and is the only athlete to win National AAU titles on the junior, senior, and masters levels. Twice he has won the gold medal in the 3,000-meter steeplechase at the World Masters Track-and-Field Championships. So fine an athlete is Hal Higdon that his own marathoning defies the slowdown tables in his book. In his prime, at age 33 in 1964, Higdon was the first American finisher in the Boston Marathon, placing fourth in 2:21:55. At 47, in the 1978 New York Marathon, Hal ran 2:30:26, a U.S. age record. A slowdown of roughly 8½ minutes—or about 5 percent in 19 years—is testimony to Higdon's capacity to sustain a high level of fitness. But even Higdon's record is dwarfed by that of Jack Foster, the 46-year-old New Zealand Olympian, who at age 42 ran the marathon in 2:11:19, a world age record. But Higdon and Foster and such immortals as the late Clarence DeMar, the ground-breaking Ted Corbitt, and the ageless Johnny Kelley are very different from the Epsteins, who "found" running later in life.

To some runners, Marion and Irving Epstein are heroes. "One guy sent us a letter," said Irv. "He wanted to know what our training was, what we eat. (We're hyphenated vegetarians; we eat fish but no meat.) I apologized to him. We didn't do nothing unusual. I told him, 'You're a better runner than we are.' "

If "better" means faster, Irv has a point. But what the Epsteins concede to others in speed, they make up for in durability. From their first race, the '72 New York Marathon, through the spring of '80, Irving Epstein had run 162 races and Marion 149, about 25 percent of them marathons. In 1978, Irv ran 2,503 miles, according to his ledgerlike running diary. Marion ran 2,118.

A consistent theme of the Epsteins' is to finish what they start out to do. "Once you decide you must finish," says Irv, "everything else is only along the way of finishing. There are no nonimportant marathons. We like some better than others, but . . ."

A summer vacation in Florida, a winter trip to Puerto Rico, and a once-every-few years sojourn to Wales to see Loraine and her husband, Dave, are the only indulgences the Epsteins allow themselves outside of marathon running. "Friends ask if I have any vices, like drinking or staying out late," says Marion. "I say my vice is marathon running. I don't care for any other form of entertainment."

Irv concurs: "All through our lives we've been family-oriented. We run a race, we visit the children, we don't seem to need anything else. Parties and stuff like that bore us. Thank God I don't have to go out. Social life—to me I don't need it. It don't sell me nothing. We come home, we talk about a run, about the kids, the telephone rings, we watch TV, maybe a sporting event—who needs more? Then Saturday's a race, Sunday's a race or a long run . . ."

Marion listens respectfully, in tacit approval of the doctrine her husband is setting forth. Then Irving says, once more with feeling: "If at this stage of the game, we can't do something we like, what's it all about?"

13

WOMEN:
FULLY EQUIPPED

At exactly 2:30 on the afternoon of September 22, 1979, in the town of Waldniel in West Germany, 262 women from 24 nations on 5 continents poised behind the starting line as Dr. Ernst van Aaken, the patron saint of women's distance running and a resident of Waldniel, looked on from the announcer's platform.

"Fünf . . . vier . . . drei . . . zwei . . . eins," called the blue-blazered starter from the DIV, the West German equivalent of the AAU. In the eerie quiet, he fired his pistol and the women were off, on a run of 26 miles 385 yards in the Avon International Women's Marathon.

Kathrine Switzer, manager of special promotions for Avon, Inc., and the driving force behind the event, was quite in character. She'd pleaded with the enthusiastic crowd to stay behind the barriers, but when her rusty German failed to get results, "I flung myself at them and ended up watching the start from between people's legs."

Switzer, exhausted by this time from weeks of planning

and deadlines, had compulsively ensured that every detail would be taken care of and she did not want a stray amateur photographer, however well-intentioned, to get in the way. The Avon race, in a sense, was the vindication of everything that had happened to Kathrine Switzer since that infamous day a dozen years back when she'd been pushed around, threatened, and nearly ejected as an "illegal" entry in the Boston Marathon.

Kathrine Switzer was a 20-year-old journalism student at Syracuse University at the time. The other 600 official starters in 1967 were men.

While the synopsis of Switzer's celebrity in 1967 has by now become something of a cliché, her life leading up to Boston as a young woman in love with athletics in a disapproving society and her life after Boston as a crusader for athletic parity between the sexes is symbolic of the rejection, acceptance, and promotion of women in marathon running. Her experiences—the good ones and the bad, the lessons and fulfillment and triumphs—represent the experiences of all women marathoners. I asked Kathy to tell me more about them.

"The thought process has just become clear after all these years," she said. "Let's start off with Kathrine Switzer, age 12 and 13. Very skinny, a really ugly little kid, wanting desperately to do something significant. I wanted to make the field-hockey team in high school. This was George Marshall High School in Newport News, Virginia, outside of Washington. We were real second-rate, but we did have uniforms and equipment. Actually, I wanted to be a cheerleader. Or, I *thought* I did because anybody who was anything was a cheerleader. But my father made fun of me and my mother said no, cheerleaders have bad reputations for hanging around boys. I was glad they said no and I had an excuse for my girl friends: My parents won't let me.

"So I went out and did exactly what the hell I wanted to do, which was to dash the hell out of the ball, run up and down the field, team strategy, that sense of team camaraderie. Then I got really smug about the cheerleaders. They didn't even know what was going on. I knew the sport. I was a jock.

"I wanted to make the field-hockey team. I didn't want to be an ass. After all, I was a skinny little kid with glasses, right? My mother was sort of the image of Betty Crocker, but she had a Ph.D. in English. She's a guidance director at Fairfax College. She was voted year after year one of the outstanding educators in the United States. A really brilliant woman who showed me her well-roundedness. She encouraged self-realization through whatever means—artistic or athletic. My father: 6 feet 5 inches, 270, no fat. A big colonel. Kindly and wonderful. If my brother, who was three years older than me, did something, there was no reason I couldn't do it, too, according to my father. In the early sixties—it was unbelievable.

"With the field-hockey thing, I confided in him that I was afraid I wouldn't make the team because a bunch of the other girls were older than me and had experience. If you want to make the team, he told me, it doesn't matter if you have experience, you can make up for it if you're really fit. He told me to run a mile. 'I used to do a mile a day in combat boots,' he told me. 'You can, too. You live on an acre. If you do 7 laps of the acre . . .'

"So I got PF Flyers and started running. I was 13 or 14—a freshman at Marshall. I didn't go fast; I just covered the distance. If there was a difficult part in my running career, it was then. I was trying to do this mile, and the neighborhood was in an uproar. They thought I was a crazy kid. Every morning I did it, and no one else was running then. I went to my mother's ragbag and took out these old shorts she had. I had to tie them with a piece of string around my waist because they were huge and baggy. And an old T-shirt of my brother's. I even got to the point where sweat kept coming down my face—although my body wouldn't sweat—and I had to put something around my head."

K. Switzer, The Runner, was born, but even then she realized that the value of the sport was not just in running per se but in how it enhanced life. "The bane of my existence—and also the joy of my existence—is that I do a lot of things," Switzer says of her life today. "I'm an executive and I have a family and I still go home and make dinner at night. And

I travel around the world." And of her life yesterday: "I was convinced they all worked together—the Greek thing: the scholar-athlete. I swear I started running because of what that meant. I believe you work together as a whole. I have a lot of disdain, even now, for top athletes who are just top jocks."

Switzer made the field-hockey team. "My father was right," she says. "I was so much better than anyone it was unbelievable. I was center halfback and I played offense and defense. Scored. Aggressive as hell. Never got tired." Kathy won a varsity letter in field hockey and played on the team for the rest of her high school days, convinced that her mile a day was a major factor in her success. She used the same system to make the basketball team, so her sophomore, junior, and senior years at Marshall High consisted mainly of field hockey, basketball, and running.

This was 1964. It was the year of the Tokyo Olympics, in which the longest women's running event was the 800 meters, or metric half-mile. K. Switzer was running twice that distance every day in basketball sneakers just as a warm-up. In 1964 cheerleading was still de rigueur for teenage girls with physical dexterity and good looks. And for those with an inclination toward running, the longest distance permitted women by the AAU was 1.5 miles, in cross-country. There was a maverick, here and there. In 1963, according to the defunct *Long Distance Log*, Lyn Carman and Merry Lepper hid on the sidelines and then sneaked into the Western Hemisphere Marathon in Culver City, California, as the race began. A race official tried to push them off the course. Carman punched him, and went on to run 20 miles. Lepper completed the race and was timed by a sympathetic official in 3:37:07. "However," wrote Nina Kuscsik, in the Annals of the New York Academy of Sciences, "even as they were reaping benefits from their training, they were being warned by women physical educators who often held dual roles as AAU officials that running long distance was harmful and they would not be able to bear children if they continued."

Switzer increased her distance to 2 miles, then 3. Every day during the summer of '64, she ran 12 laps around the Marshall

High School track, in Keds ("Running shoes? That's really technical"), and then went off to Lynchburg College. She was a hit in field hockey but not with the ministry students. "They were the biggest makes on a date. I walked out of more cars and walked home. Thank God I could run, too."

When lacrosse was introduced at Lynchburg, Switzer joined that team too—"and ran and ran and ran" as part of the game. She would practice her field hockey and her basketball and her lacrosse, but all that still wasn't enough of a workout for her; so Kathy would also go out to the track and run a mile. Or 2. Or 3. Sometimes she'd even run the cross-country course. She knew nothing of organized track, she says, only that women did run track, in the sprints, because she'd seen that on TV in the Olympics. A sprinter she wasn't, but a runner—that she was. And when it came time to focus on the one thing that meant the most to her, Kathrine Switzer, Lynchburg coed, decided to quit field hockey and basketball and lacrosse and "be a runner."

Switzer told her lacrosse coach she was quitting to run cross-country, having seen the men do it, and her lacrosse coach told her she was out of her mind. Besides, women could not run on a team—those were the rules. Even if they could, the coach implied, how could she let the lacrosse team down like that? "I felt guilty for a while," Switzer says. "But then I thought, 'Hey, wait a minute: I love it and it's my life so I should do what I do best.'"

As a sign of further emancipation, Switzer broke up with her boyfriend, an "archetypal male chauvinist" from the Naval Academy who admitted he thought she was a "freak" because of all the running she did. She was not one to tolerate insensitivity. She knew her rights. Either you worked with her, or she worked by herself.

So she worked by herself for a while, oblivious to the snide comments and incredulity. Then, like an aspiring actress waiting at the Hollywood lunch counter for a director's nod, she was approached one rainy night at the track by the Lynchburg track coach. He had his stopwatch dangling from his neck and he was timing Switzer as she ran her routine laps.

"Can you run a mile?" the coach asked her.

"Sure I can run a mile," replied Switzer.

"We got a track meet coming up Saturday," said the coach. "Eleven lettermen just flunked off the team because the college changed the eligibility requirements. We got a big meet this weekend and I got only one person to run the mile. You're not going to win. You're not even going to place. You're going to finish last. But if you can run the mile, we can enter you. Will ya run?"

"Sure, Coach."

That was 1966, the spring. On April 19, while Kenji Kimihara of Japan raced to victory in the seventieth Boston Marathon, becoming the ninth straight foreigner to win the event, a woman named Roberta Gibb ran undetected in the field of 415 runners. Her identity would not be known until she reached the finish, 3:21:40 after her start, ahead of more than two-thirds of the field. Gibb was an unassuming outlaw, not at all the cunning, PR-minded spokeswoman who would follow her in '67. For this reason she is rarely given credit for her breakthrough. Instead, K. Switzer was splashed across the world's media as the naughty lady who forgot her place. And despite Gibb's performance, Boston and AAU officials, trying to save face, minimized her run and remained steadfast in denying long-distance running opportunities to women.

Gibb, then 23, had been running for three years prior to the race and as calculated preparation for it increased her training distance to 15–20 miles per day in the months before it. Years later, writing in *Runner's World*, she said: "My numbness disappeared as I danced across the finish line. I won! I won! I did it. Where does the music go when the symphony ends?"

Track meets were not very big in Lynchburg, Virginia, in 1966. It was still eight years before the Virginia Ten-Miler, one of America's great road races, would be held for the first time. On this Saturday in April, for the Lynchburg–Potomac dual meet, the college stadium was packed. Even NBC was down there. The local papers had given it advance play during the week. The AP bureau in Richmond picked it up and soon word spread throughout the country. Even the New York *Herald Tribune* used it. Kathrine Switzer was going to run the mile.

The college paper, naturally, took quite an interest in the meet, certain that its sports editor would get the inside scoop. "I was also sports editor of the paper," says Switzer. "Wrote myself up pretty well."

There were 4 runners in the mile, and Switzer finished fourth—"to tumultuous applause. It was like they were embarrassed that I'd finished last, but what do you expect? I didn't run poorly. I didn't stop. I did 5:59."

It was probably the first time in track history that a 5:59 mile had inspired such attention and debate. Kathy did a lot of interviews and received a lot of letters. She recalls: "People who were mature or cosmopolitan thought it was fantastic. Then there were guys on campus who would turn the other way or say something nasty or laugh as I walked by. The women were not as vocal as the men, but they were polarized, too. Some of them were very affronted and thought of me as nonexistent. Completely written off. The polarization was about 50–50. One guy hanging out of his dorm window would see me coming and say, 'Why don't you just run away, little girl?' "

This was good preparation for what would follow after Boston; it also served to harden Kathy, to strengthen her resolve and her nonconformity. Switzer left Lynchburg after two years, as she had planned all along, and enrolled at Syracuse University to study journalism.

There she experienced a kind of liberating culture shock. "It was like walking into heaven. My two roommates were crazy artists. You could do anything you wanted. I could stay out all night. I could stay out on weekends. I could wear blue jeans. The first thing I did was go out and buy one pullover sweater and a pair of jeans."

Switzer continued to run, 3–4 miles a day, but soon pushed it to 6 when she read that a top woman runner named Doris Brown did 6 a day. She joined the cross-country team, courtesy of Coach Bob Grieve. Of course she was the only woman on the team, but no one seemed to mind very much. In practice she was given the role of "rabbit," and her teammates were to try and catch her, which they did. Each day Kathy would run a little farther. "We had a wonderful time. They sort of adopted me. The guys on the team were all skinny little guys, and I was bigger than all of them. I was about 5 feet 6 inches and weighed 135. Hefty. Voluptuous. But it looked good in those days. There was a sister-brother relationship with them."

One little guy she became particularly fond of was Arnie Briggs. "He looked about 106 years old," Kathy jokes. "Thin and gaunt. Gray skin color was the same as his gray hair color. He had on a gray sweatsuit and looked like a monochrome." Briggs was the unofficial assistant coach, which meant he didn't get paid for helping out. He was a pretty good marathon runner in his day, having run 2:32, and he filled Kathy with colorful stories of races past, coming back most of the time to one or more of his 18 Bostons. He would tell Kathy these stories as they ran together on the track, she in running shoes and he in canvas sneakers.

"It annoyed me," Switzer says of Arnie's Boston fixation. "I was always so out of breath I couldn't answer him. It was his Kilimanjaro, Matterhorn. Mythical, super-wonderful. Finally I said, 'Why don't we run on the road?' He said, 'Road running is best, you'll really love it.' "

After that, the two of them began to run at least 9 miles together every night, Arnie as Kathy's confidant and coach and protective partner. Through the harsh Syracuse winter they did it, even one night when the temperature had dropped to 20 below and a blizzard blew in. "It was frightening. We couldn't see. There were no cars out there. He said, 'You must be freezing; let me give you my sweatshirt.' I said, 'Keep your goddamn sweatshirt.' We kept running and he said, 'I've never known a man who could have kept up with me like that.' That was sort of the turning point. He no longer had to 'protect' me. I was becoming more mature."

Kathy used her newfound maturity as fuel for more running, pushing herself to run every day with a 20-miler on

Sundays. Arnie continued to talk about Boston with reverence. Finally, it became too much for her. "Arnie," said K. Switzer, "I'm going to run the Boston Marathon."

"Women can't run the Boston Marathon," Arnie Briggs told her.

"You've been telling me how good I am, how I'm as good as you and I have all this potential—and now, I can't?" exclaimed Kathy.

"A girl can't run the Boston Marathon," Arnie insisted.

"If I can do 20 miles, why not 26?" Kathy asked him.

"Law of diminishing returns."

"If you can do it, why can't I?"

"I don't know. But you just can't do it."

"Roberta Gibb did it. I read it in *Sports Illustrated*."

"No broad ran the Boston Marathon." Arnie wouldn't budge.

The two of them stood out on the road, in the middle of their workout, arguing. "You can help me," Kathy told him. "We can go together, or we can't." They resumed running and said nothing for a while. Finally, Arnie gave in. "If you can prove to me in practice you can run the distance, I'll take you to the Boston Marathon."

"You're on."

Through the winter of 1967, they ran together, keying on the day in early March when a trial run of 26 miles would be attempted. When that day came, Switzer was at her strongest, and just 20 yards from their imaginary finish line she convinced Briggs to continue the run for another 5-mile loop, fearful that their car-measured 26 miles might have been a bit short. "I'd never forgive myself," said Kathy, "if I got to Boston and a quarter of a mile from the finish line dropped dead."

Recalling the last mile of that last loop, Kathy says: "Arnie was not talking. He went from the center of the road to the curb, and back. He swore. Arnie never swore. His eyes were dilated. I put my arm through his arm, held him at the elbow and said we're going to run it in. I came dancing through the finish and Arnie blacked out. But he came to right away and told me, 'You can run the Boston Marathon.' "

The next day Kathrine Switzer entered the 1967 Boston Marathon. She filled out the entry blank Arnie had gotten for her. She took the then required physical at the school's infirmary and mailed it all in. She signed her name as K. V. Switzer, not, she insists, to fool anyone—"I didn't know it was against the rules, just that it was the mores"—but out of habit. In class at Syracuse she would sign her papers that way, she said, to try to diminish the chances of her grade being influenced one way or another by her sex.

Kathy went to Boston with Arnie and two other Syracuse runners and her fiancé, Tom Miller, who told her, "If you can run the Boston Marathon, I can run the Boston Marathon." Miller, already a nationally ranked hammer thrower, had added some more running to his training regimen. The group entered as a team, the Syracuse Harriers.

Switzer was given number 261. It was cold and raw and wintry at first, about 36 degrees as Kathy remembers it, so she wore a tattered sweatsuit she planned to remove and toss away as she and the weather warmed up during the afternoon's run. Will Cloney, the race director, gave her and the other gathering starters a "Move it, let's go" in Hopkinton, and soon enough they were off. Kathy describes the race with enthusiasm that has not ebbed, like this:

"Four miles went by and the press bus came along and everyone on it was saying, 'Yeah, there's a girl in the race!' I talked to them. I was in the middle of the pack, and just wanted to finish, even in over 4 hours. Then I heard another vehicle coming up. Tom was on the left, Arnie on the right, and me in the middle. Then I heard these footsteps out of cadence with the other runners. Sounded like hard shoes. I realized they were getting closer and turning to see who it was, somebody grabbed me. It was Big Jock. I never saw a face more frightening in my life. It was totally contorted with rage and anger. He's screaming at me to get out of his race, to 'Gimme those goddamn numbers.' No reason. Didn't say you're a woman or anything. Just gimme those numbers. And he tried to snatch the number right off my back. The runners in front of us looked frightened and said nothing. The press was on its feet and were yelling in my defense. Arnie is saying, 'Leave her alone, Jock, leave her alone.' It turns out they used to run the Boston together.

"No man I'd ever known at that point had been violent with me or dragged me; nobody had ever really discriminated against me. There were people who socially didn't like the idea of my running, but nobody had suppressed me, put me down, said you can't do it. I became really scared. Like a child, I thought maybe I've done something wrong, terribly wrong. But I jumped back at Jock and said 'Leave me alone!' But he came up to me again and grabbed me again. Will Cloney had jumped off the bus first, but he couldn't catch me. Jock and me and Jock and Arnie were going at it. Tom didn't say a word but was running hard. Then he hit Jock on his left shoulder [pictures show it to be a kind of football body block]—Tom weighed 225—and Jock went four feet off the ground, flying through the air. He landed on his ass and on his side, in front of me, between the road and the grass. I was terrified. What to do? So we took off—the three of us.

"The press is screaming at the truck driver to follow us, and as he accelerated a couple of reporters fell off the back of the truck. It was a riot. Now I was crying and running along as fast as I can. Arnie is screaming, 'Just run fast, run fast!' And Tom is screaming, 'Boy are we in trouble!' He's mad at me. 'I'm in a terrible position. How am I going to make the Olympic Team?'

"Then—beep,beep! Here comes the officials' bus again with Jock hanging on its side and shaking his fist at us and screaming and cursing. Arnie told him to go to hell. It's snowing and raining and I was totally drained. Tom wasn't even talking to me. He tore off his number, complained that he was going to get kicked out of the AAU and that we were running too slowly to suit him, and sprinted ahead. Arnie told me repeatedly just to relax and try to finish. How can I relax? At every corner I was thinking that cops were going to arrest us. The crowd reaction was incredible—again, polarized. A lot of men would say, 'Hey, you stupid broad, why do you have to run the race?' and some woman would be standing there saying, 'Come on, baby, you gotta do it for all of us.'

"About 13 or 14 miles, past Wellesley, I said to myself, 'If you get arrested, what are you going to do?' I decided I was going to resist arrest. All of a sudden, I didn't want to worry about all the trouble I was in. I'll resist arrest and finish the race and deal with it later."

Still, while K. V. Switzer ran she first had to deal with herself, and the conflicting emotions that made her feel guilty, then determined, then confused, then heroic. "Why would anyone want to throw me out? I was trained. Arnie kept telling that to Jock. 'I've trained her, Jock, leave her alone. She's okay. I've trained her.'

"As I got further along I thought maybe it's not that other women don't want to run this race. Because I was sort of smug, I thought I could, but maybe they'd been discriminated against all their lives. This is the first time it had ever happened to me. Then I run along further and I realize, holy shit, it's not just running, it's in all sports. Look how wonderful this is, look how great it makes me feel. I became very philosophical in a hurry. The issue was forced upon me. I realized that there are very few things people can do to change society. But I was resolved to tell other women how good running is, to spread the word, one by one."

Switzer had to finish before she could be given a pulpit. Four hours had passed and there were very few runners left on the course. It was raining and icy and the crowd had left the finish. The officials were gone. One photographer and two writers were left. In the final yards to the finish, Kathy and Arnie and another Syracuse runner, John Winter, held hands until K.V. asked to be alone. She says now: "All the anguish had gone away. We did 4:20, just happy to finish. A reporter gave me a blanket—that was really nice."

The relief of it all. The swaying, soothing, rubbery feeling of finishing a marathon, a first marathon with a lifetime's worth of pressure and conflict—you can live off it for weeks, especially if it didn't hurt and your muscles didn't cramp too severely. Switzer had little time to savor it. She didn't have to look for a pulpit. She was thrown right onto one after the race.

"Why did you do it?" the reporters asked. "What are you trying to prove?" "Are you a suffragette?" "Where did you get the idea?" "Is this for publicity?" "What do you think this is going to lead to?" "What are you trying to prove?"

Kathrine Switzer was tranquilized. "I just like running," she told them.

That night at about 10:00 P.M. Kathy and her cohorts drove back to Syracuse so she could make class the next morning. When they stopped in Albany for coffee, they were given the first indication that K. Switzer had done something that, Cloney and Semple's disclaimers to the contrary, would not be pushed under the rug. They saw the first edition of the Boston *Globe*. "It was all over the headlines," Kathy says. "They covered the whole page. We got much more coverage than the people who won the race."

Twenty-four hours after Kathrine Switzer had reached the Prudential Center, just about everyone in the civilized world knew about the 20-year-old Syracuse University coed who had defied the male establishment and successfully negotiated one of the most famous and challenging events on the annual sports calendar, the Boston Marathon.

It was the Lynchburg Mile revisited, but the excitement was magnified at least 26.2 times. "I got home," says Kathy, "and the radio said, 'Syracuse coed breaks the Boston Marathon, but she failed to finish.' So I called them up and said, 'Oh yeah, well, this is me and I did finish it.'"

Switzer wrote a first-person piece for the college newspaper. The AP and UPI and the local press kept calling. She got 200 letters a week—"about 50–50." Even Johnny Carson wanted to talk with her.

"He wanted to make it a big ha-ha," says Kathrine. "But I got on and was serious. He turned the whole script over. He's a very sensitive guy. He doesn't make jokes when he can see that you don't want to make jokes. Mary Travers and Joyce

Switzer's Training Before Her Best Time of 2:51:37 in April
1975

Background: 80–110 miles per week for a year

Approach: "hard/easy" schedule

Weekly Schedule:
Monday through Saturday:
    A.M.: 6 miles at 7:45 pace
    P.M.: about 4 miles, plus occasional speed,
            then 3-mile cooldown
Sunday: 20-mile run

Nature of speedwork:
Intervals: repeat 440s in 82 seconds or
          repeat 880s in 2:45–2:50 or
          repeat 220s in 37.5 seconds or
          repeat 2 miles in 12:20

Nature of weekly 20-mile run:
first 5 miles at 8:00 pace
second 5 miles at 7:45
third 5 miles at 7:30
final 5 miles at 7:15

Brothers also were on with me. But here's my point: I'm on
the Johnny Carson show and I get this letter from the AAU,
suspending me. I was suspended for : (1) running a race of
more than a mile and a half (that was the longest distance per-
missible for a woman runner); (2) forging an entry; (3) joining
a race with men; and (4) traveling without a chaperone."

Tom Miller and Arnie Briggs were suspended as well for
"aiding and abetting," says Switzer, who had aroused such
curiosity in running circles that promoters throughout the
country invited her to compete in their races. She could not
compete, however, because of the AAU suspension. In the
aftermath of Boston, Switzer became less interested in pro-
moting herself as a cause célèbre and more concerned with
getting married to Tom Miller and with her next semester at
Syracuse, her senior year. Still, there was a job to do, an institutionalized chauvinism to overcome. Even *The New York*

Times, which by 1967 was thought to be a paragon of civil-rights support, wondered: "What is a girl, a former beauty contestant, doing in a marathon?" After Kathy told them what, the *Times*'s major concession to her was, ". . . despite her soft brown hair and winsome look, she can be more than peaches and cream."

The *Times* did not quote Jock Semple, probably because his language was not fit to print in a family newspaper. In his place, it quoted Will Cloney, who said: "Women can't run in the marathon because the rules forbid it. Unless we have rules, society will be in chaos. I don't make the rules, but I try to carry them out. We have no place in the marathon for any unauthorized person, even a man. If that girl were my daughter, I would spank her."

The climate was right, in 1967, for Kathrine Switzer and then others to break through the barriers against women in marathon running. First, there were the spare beginnings of what came to be known as the Running Boom. Second, there was the Women's Movement, which insisted that women belonged in sports, on varsity teams, and in Little League. Third, there was the foundation and framework for radical change—the sixties and its impatient, sometimes amorphous, always courageous, remarkably successful challenge to the way things were but ought not to be, whether they happened in Pleiku, Birmingham, Columbia University, or the White House. By the spring of '67, the proper precedents had been set—indeed blood had been spilled setting them—and the mood was angry: If it's right, do it, whether you do it from Selma to Montgomery, or Hopkinton to Boston.

Later that year the world record for women—which had little significance in view of the small number of women running marathons in the few places around the world that permitted it—was lowered from to 3:18 to 3:15:23 by Maureen Wilton, a 13-year-old Canadian, and then to 3:07:26 by Anni Pede-Erdkamp of West Germany, a disciple of Dr. Ernst van Aaken. By this time Nina Kuscsik, a 28-year-old mother of three from Huntington Station, Long Island, who excelled in other sports, had taken up running after deciding that "marathon running epitomized athletic achievement."

"Being unofficial at Boston had peculiar consequences," Kuscsik has written. "Our times were not recorded, so we were required to do some detective work as we neared the finish line. We looked for the nearest male runner and got his number. Then we searched the race program until we found the name that corresponded to the number. After several months every official finisher's time was listed in *Long Distance Log*. We would search for this runner's name as if it were our own, for their time was the time we took for ourselves."

This scavenger hunt would continue. Sara Mae Berman, Kuscsik, and Switzer were among 5 women bandits at Boston in 1970 and were the only 3 women to run it in '71. Meanwhile, there was scattered women's activity across the country, some approved (by race administrators, not the AAU) and some with the "unofficial" sobriquet. In 1971 the women's world record was lowered four times, twice by Beth Bonner of the United States, who in the second annual New York City Marathon ran 2:55:22 and became the first woman to run a marathon in under 3 hours. The second fastest woman in that race, at 2:56:04, was Nina Kuscsik. Soon afterward, the AAU raised its ceiling on women's distance events to 10 miles but also decided that "selected" women would be permitted to run marathons, subject to the approval of the AAU's national chairman for long-distance running. "Selected women," wrote Nina Kuscsik, "were essentially those who had already run marathons, so in effect they went full circle."

The following year, 1972, also was pivotal. Boston Marathon officials finally allowed women into their treasured arena, and Nina Kuscsik, Sara Mae Berman, and Kathrine Switzer were among 8 women who finished, Kuscsik leading in 3:10:21. That fall the AAU's influence infected the hitherto "liberated" New York Marathon and there was an edict that women entrants would be separate but equal with the men— they would have to start their run 10 minutes before them. At that time the marathon started from the west side of Central

Park, not at the Verrazano Bridge, and at the moment of scheduled departure, the women runners sat down peacefully at the starting line and refused to budge for 10 minutes in a scene reminiscent of a 1960s student demonstration. When the men began, the women did, too. Shortly thereafter, the AAU's divisive system was abolished.

Midway between the Boston and New York marathons of 1972, Kathrine Switzer received her master's degree in public relations from Syracuse University. She took her diploma, left her husband the hammer thrower, and set off for New York City to seek her fortune. She already had the fame. Instead of loitering in the lobbies of PR firms looking for that big break, K. V. Switzer decided to go from New York to Munich for the Summer Olympics and also do Europe on $5.00 a day for a spell. After making the travel arrangements, one day she harnessed all of her PR nerve, strutted into the *Daily News* building, and asked to see the sports editor.

"Hi, I'm Kathrine Switzer. I'm a helluva writer," she told him.

"I've heard about you," said the editor. "You're the kid who ran the Boston Marathon."

"Yeah, but that's only half of it. I'm a great journalist."

"Oh, so you can write, too, huh."

"Yeah, I just got a master's from Syracuse."

"Okay, type this," the editor said, handing her a piece of wire copy.

Switzer worked on the copy, gave it to the editor, and said wouldn't it be just wonderful if he would hire her as a stringer for the Olympics. And he did. "Holy cow!" Switzer said, and off she went to Munich. She was much too late to acquire official Olympic press accreditation, but bigger obstacles had not thwarted K. V. Switzer in the past.

"To get in and out of the press facility, I simply put on a sweatsuit and ran in and out. I told them I was going in for an interview, and they thought I was an athlete. Until the Arabs came I couldn't do anything except write some stories which I sent on an outside wire back to New York. The only thing that really lined up under my byline was the first-person from Munich of that incident. That was sort of like growth of ten years, in those two days. Being there let me know that the bottom line for athletics is really very commercial. The athletes were marionettes. The whole thing was a vast conglomerate of politics and money. It was an awakening experience and also a shattering one. I think I had some very naïve ideas about that—which is surprising because I was the one they tried to throw out of the Boston Marathon. That I still had stars in my eyes was kind of incredible."

After the Olympics, Switzer stayed in Europe for several months rather than return home and face what had become her "disastrous" marriage. She wanted to compete in the many races over there to which she had been invited, "and then think about going home." Switzer raced from Oslo to Istanbul, bunked with families she met en route ("some were very, very humble and some were very, very wealthy"), wrote a few articles about it, came back to the States in the spring of 1973, and got divorced.

"I also knew what I wanted to do," she says. "I wanted to be in public relations. I wanted to keep up my writing. I wanted a job, 9:00 to 5:00. I wanted an apartment. I wanted to work out a training schedule. I wanted a new car, new clothes, and a bath every night."

Switzer wrote sports profiles for *Argosy* magazine and in only two months' time landed a sports PR position with AMF "for $3,000 more than I was asking." She learned a lot about sailboats, motorcycles, skiing, and bowling, resumed her serious training, and met Philip Schaub, whom she would later marry. Philip, who smoked, drank, and liked opera, found Kathy's "possessed" running hard to swallow, which is one reason, she said, she was attracted to him. But after a two-week trip that summer to Moscow for the World University Games, Kathrine found four-packs-a-day Philip had given up smoking and was running 5 miles a day. "He said, 'I just had to do it because I love you, and I've got to understand what you're feeling,'" Kathy recalls. "And he became an authority. The next thing I knew he had a training schedule for me."

This reformed smoker had become quite a taskmaster. "He

was peaking me for Boston," Kathy said. She reluctantly agreed to follow his program, if only to teach him that it would not work so she could be her own runner again after Boston.

They were living on Second Avenue and Twenty-fifth Street, a section of Manhattan about equidistant from Greenwich Village and Midtown. Philip had plotted a 1.2-mile loop for his pupil to negotiate and had her do a fast one and a slow one, 7 or 8 a night, almost every night after work. "It was winter and he'd never say anything like 'It's freezing, hurry up,'" Kathy says. "He'd say, 'Two seconds too fast, slow it down a little,' or 'Get with it,' flogging me just terrible."

Switzer lost 18 pounds and went to Boston looking to improve her PR of 3:20:30, achieved the previous year in Boston '73. Philip was looking for 3:04. Kathy ran 3:01:39, placed fourth among the 20 women finishers. "I was in pain," she says, "but it was heaven."

Miki Gorman, the world record-holder (2:46:36), won the women's race in 2:47:11. She was 39 years old. Six women bettered the winning time run by Jacqueline Hansen in 1973. The growth of the women's field and the quality of its performances at Boston represented a new plateau for women marathoners. That Gorman was pushing 40 also was significant. "She put new hope into all the women runners who felt their careers were about to fade because of age," wrote 35-year-old Nina Kuscsik, third to Gorman in that race.

After that the undefined presence of women marathoners began to take shape. Whether woman should run marathons and undergo such stress was no longer an issue. This was a relief not only because entry denials were obviously discriminatory but also because it allowed the movement to advance at a faster rate and to gain respectability. There was an AAU Marathon Championship for women. There was the first International Marathon Championship for women (the United States and 6 other nations competed in Waldniel, West Germany, 40 women finishing the race). Running shoe manufacturers began designing shoes for women. Bonne Bell and

L'eggs were among the firms that sponsored races for women only; these became enormously popular, and some men, ironically, objected, charging reverse discrimination. Physicians and physiologists studied the effects of marathon running on women and found they could withstand them at least as well as men could. The media treated women's races as athletic events, not as athletic aberrations. What had trickled along since the mid-sixties mushroomed, and soon women marathoners were . . . athletes. Essentially, almost everything that had been part of the growth of men's marathoning in the early seventies became part of women's marathoning in the mid-seventies.

It was also a period of transition for Kathy Switzer. In the 1975 Boston Marathon she was second to Liane Winter of West Germany, clocking 2:51:37, then one of the best times ever run by a woman and a mark destined to be her best ever. (Winter ran 2:42:24 and set a world record.) This encouraged Kathy to train even more vigorously, to run 100 miles a week, which resulted in a series of injuries and brought her to the realization, in 1976, that "it's time to do something other than be an athlete."

Switzer took her sense of responsibility "to make things happen in sports for women," and with her sense of promotion she helped Bonne Bell with its first race, a 7-miler in Cleveland. It was such a rousing success that Jess Bell, president of the company, asked Kathy to leave AMF and work for him. Kathy told him she'd give it some thought while continuing to assist Bonne Bell part-time. "I knew the women's sports movement was going to be one of the great social revolutions of the century. Really. And that a company had to be there. And I knew I could be part of it if I could be at the right place at the right time."

Switzer found herself in this position the following year, at a meeting in New York of the Women's Sports Foundation's board of directors, of which she was a member. An Avon executive told her that the Atlanta Track Club had proposed that Avon sponsor a marathon for women in Atlanta. He asked Kathy if she would examine the proposal and tell him what she thought of it. "That's like asking me to open Christmas presents," she told him.

Switzer's report stated, "The proposal is valid. If you are interested in it, first, you've got to double the budget, and this is what you've got to do . . ."

"Would you do me a big favor," Switzer was asked, "and give me an outline?"

Switzer took a week off from work and spent eight hours a day at the typewriter, turning out a fifty-page proposal for Avon. It was a manifesto—not only for the suggested marathon but for a series of women's races. Charts. Lists. Footnotes. The definitive work of its kind. "What I've been dreaming of for ten years," said Switzer. "It had to be done, whether for Avon or anyone else."

When Kathy dropped the report on the Avon executive's desk, "I could see his face start to drop. He expected two sheets of paper." The executive called Kathy at 9:00 the next morning and said, "I stayed up all night and read the proposal, and it's the best proposal I've ever read. Would you consider working for Avon?"

That August of 1977, two months after a record 2,000 women participated in the L'eggs Mini-Marathon in New York and ten months after the second International Women's Marathon in Waldniel, Kathrine Switzer went to work at Avon. Her title was Manager of Special Promotions, and her responsibilities included managing Avon's tennis tour and what was at the time its only race, the Avon Marathon in Atlanta. She embellished the marathon by bringing in several foreign runners and by inviting Dr. Ernst van Aaken to be the event's special guest, in part "to try and force the Olympic issue" which was—and is—that the longest running event for women in the Olympics is the metric mile, or 1,500 meters.

The Avon Marathon was run on March 19, 1978—Palm Sunday in the Bible Belt. Because of church traffic, the race was started at 1:00 P.M. "The response was overwhelming," says Switzer, and Avon told her, "You mean we got all of that publicity just for one race?" It was a total field of 225, with

17 of the top 20 women marathoners in the world competing, and victory went with great surprise to Martha Cooksey, an unheralded runner from Orange, California, who ran 2:46:16, 5 minutes faster than her previous marathon best.

Midway through the 1979 Avon International Women's Marathon, Joyce Smith and Carol Gould of Great Britain, both mothers of two children and both coached by Joyce's husband, Bryan, held a half-minute lead. Their halfway time was 1:18:04. Their side-by-side strategy soon changed as Smith got stronger while Gould came down with stomach trouble. Smith reached the Waldniel finish line in 2:36:27, a British Commonwealth Games record and a personal improvement of more than 5 minutes. Only 5 women had run the distance faster. Although Smith, who would be 42 a month later, had been a competitive runner for 24 years, this was only her second marathon. Gould, despite two pit stops, was third in 2:40:37, also a large improvement for her.

The event, engineered by Kathrine Switzer and Dr. Ernst van Aaken, was a success, if a qualified one. That 200 women from 25 nations competed, 16 of them running under 2:50 and another 20 under 3:00, was historic. But the acknowledged leaders in women's marathoning did not take part, snipping a bit of credibility away from the race and also emphasizing that women's marathoning had grown so large by the end of the 1970s that there were diverse interests—and opportunities—amid the women's common concerns. Grete Waitz (see chapter 15), who set the world record of 2:32:30 in the 1978 New York City Marathon, was in Lynchburg, Virginia, on September 22, 1979, breaking the world record for 10 miles with a time of 53:05 and making sure she'd be fully rested for her New York Marathon defense four weeks hence (which she was, running another world record of 2:27:33). Joan Benoit, who set an American record (2:35:15) in the 1979 Boston Marathon, passed up Waldniel for Eugene, Oregon, and on September 9 won the women's division of the Nike-Oregon Track Club Marathon in 2:35:41. Christa Vahlensieck of West Germany and Cooksey missed Waldniel because of injuries.

In Waldniel, Dr. van Aaken told the audience at the awards ceremony, "Five years ago Christa Vahlensieck broke 3 hours here for the first time. Today 36 runners did it. I just hope that the small seed planted here five years ago will grow into a big plant and that the gray-haired men of the International Olympic Committee will give women the chance to run the marathon distance soon."

A decade ago women fought for the right to run the marathon. By their achievements they earned that right, and by their politics and courage they received it. Today there are at least 5,000 women marathoners in the United States and another several thousand throughout the world. Hundreds of women have broken 3:00 in competition and more than 50 have bettered 2:46:24—the world record five years ago. But because of the complex rules by which an event can be added to the Olympic program and because of pockets of resistance to it within the IAAF and IOC, an Olympic Marathon for women—bound to happen eventually—was considered unlikely to be approved in time for the 1984 Olympics in Los Angeles. In which case there is almost certain to be an uprising among women and a surrogate women's marathon staged at the time of the 1984 Olympics, possibly right in Los Angeles. I hope K. V. Switzer runs it, just for old times.

14

SHORTER AND RODGERS

"Once I got on the asphalt for the last 6 kilometers, I knew it was the end. At 41 kilometers I think I said to myself, 'My God, I've really done it.' You almost can't believe after all that work, training, worry, and direction that finally there it is.

"From there on in, it was just a victory lap. I ran through the tunnel and around the track. I had already decided early that I wasn't going to sprint in. I was going to run pace to the end. Even after I was in the stadium and saw that I could have gotten the Olympic record by running hard, I didn't want to do that. I figured that's bush league."

—FRANK SHORTER

"I'm feeling so-o-o good as we near the final turn onto Ring Road that I pull a Kip Keino move: I finally take my hat off and wave to the crowd. I know it's flamboyant, but that's how I feel. The next thing I know, I am about 50 yards from home and the clock reads 2:09:22. So I push it. I recall Ron Hill's best of 2:09:28 and try to beat it. Jeez, had I known I was moving that fast with a mile to go I might have pushed it even more.

"The cops grab me real quick. They give me some water and pull me away from the victory stand, thinking I have to lie down or something. But I feel great, except for my stomach.

"It takes a while for everything to sink in. Inside the Pru I talk to reporters, but there's also this podiatrist from the BAA who tries to get me in a picture with him for his business. He did it the last two times as well. He says, 'Lemme take a look at your blisters,' and kneels next to me for the photographer. I tell him I don't have any blisters. So he just picks up my leg and smiles for the camera."

—BILL RODGERS

These accounts by Frank Shorter and Bill Rodgers describe the climax of each runner's most important marathon victory. Shorter, in *Runner's World*, wrote in November 1972 of his Olympic triumph in Munich; Rodgers, in the July 1979 issue of *The Runner*, recounted his third Boston Marathon triumph, in 1979. These brief recollections reveal much about the two men and the times in which they've run. We see Shorter—pragmatic, analytical, restrained, respectful, talking only of the race, not of the atmosphere surrounding it. We see Rodgers—exuberant, responsive to the crowd, somewhat overwhelmed, mindful of opportunists. While these men have much in common, they are essentially different in character, so different that I doubt they could become close friends under any circumstances. They are drawn together in their running—in competition, in celebrity, in their personification of the American Dream, which, for millions of Americans in the 1970s, became the Run, the Race, the Marathon. Frank Shorter and Bill Rodgers—people commonly talk of them together—are the two most important American runners of the decade, indeed two of the most important American athletes of the decade. One recoils at the thought of the 1970s without them, of where running would be without them. Perhaps others would have become what they became. If we say that running produced a Shorter and a Rodgers—that in the forefront of a revolution history provides us with extraordinary people—then we are relieved. If we say no, Frank Shorter and Bill Rodgers to a large extent made running, then we must be apprehensive, concerned about who will succeed them. I suspect the truth lies somewhere in the middle: Running was made by George Sheehan and Joe Henderson and Kenny Moore and Jim Fixx and Hal Higdon and Will Cloney and Fred Lebow and Kathrine Switzer, and Frank Shorter and Bill Rodgers.

FRANK SHORTER'S LONG REIGN

The 1972 Olympics were the Olympics of controversy and terror, hardly an appropriate backdrop for a marathon. On September 10, just five days after the shootout at the Munich Airport, Frank Shorter and 79 others grouped for the start of the marathon.

In 1972 there were about 125 marathons held in the United States, drawing an average field of fewer than 100 starters. Only 406 people ran in the third New York Marathon, and the Nike Waffle Trainer was yet to be born. In the previous Olympics, Americans had finished fourteenth (Kenny Moore), sixteenth (George Young), and twenty-second (Ron Daws) in the marathon, which in Mexico City's high altitude was won by Mamo Wolde, an Ethiopian. To most Americans, running was something you had to do in high school gym class or in boot camp but not something a true-blue American *wanted* to do. Running was primitive, better for people with no football to watch on weekends. Like Ethiopians.

On September 10, 1972, Frank Shorter changed all that. Such is the power of TV. ABC did for the marathon that day what it later did for football with its Monday night telecasts. Instead of Howard Cosell, Erich Segal was in the booth with Keith Jackson to do the color commentary. Erich Segal, in addition to writing *Love Story*, was a marathon runner himself, a veteran of many Bostons and once Frank Shorter's professor at Yale. Segal "knew enough about the event," wrote John Jerome in the April 1978 issue of *Outside* magazine, "to drape plenty of prime-time poetics over it: Pheidippides, carbohydrate-loading, shaving shoe soles to save weight, blood in urine. And The Wall, the excruciating goddamn Wall, that mystical point somewhere after the 20th mile, at which every competitor exhausts his supply of muscle starch and his brain tells his body that he can't go on. Heroic stuff."

And what are Americans if not worshipers of heroes? Here was Frank Shorter to tame the Ethiopians and put the Russians and others out of business before an audience of millions accustomed to seeing American sprinters, and once in a while a miler, do that to the Ethiopians and the Russians and all those hard-to-pronounce people from countries full of peasants and women with broad shoulders. Distance runners? From Ethiopia, Finland, Great Britain? Yes. From America? We know better. Life is a 100-yard dash. Who's got time for a marathon, whatever that is.

At 10,000 meters the tightly bunched leaders were paced by Derek Clayton of Australia, the world record-holder, and Ron Hill of Great Britain. The split was 31:15. Shorter was eighth here, in 31:23, but he ran the next 5,000 in 14:57 and acquired a 5-second lead. He increased the lead with every kilometer to over a minute at 30 kilos and over 2 minutes at 40 kilos, as Erich Segal and a nation suddenly at home with a marathon urged him on to the stadium and the finish. Just before Frank Shorter was to reach the Olympic Stadium to conclude his victorious marathon—surely one of the most emotional moments in televised sport—an unidentified man ran into the stadium and onto the track.

"That's not Frank!" cried Erich Segal. "That's not Frank! It's an impostor! Get him out of there! It's not Frank." Segal was properly shocked and appalled for all America and the world. Olympic authorities grabbed the man, a German, and escorted him out of the stadium.

Then Frank arrived, hair short and mustache trim, running smooth and clean, wearing number 1014 on his ill-fitting USA singlet. Segal saluted him, unabashed in his rooting. When Shorter reached the finish, he closed his eyes and raised his arms symmetrically, straight out. His hands were fisted. Frank Shorter was the first American to win an Olympic Marathon since Johnny Hayes's 1908 triumph. His time was 2:12:20, more than 2 minutes ahead of runner-up Karel Lismont of Belgium. Wolde was third. Kenny Moore and Jack Bachelor,

Shorter's American teammates, were fourth and ninth, respectively, Moore missing the bronze by 31.4 seconds. It was also the best U.S. "team" showing in an Olympic Marathon.

"As our training went on this summer, I could see that the three of us were capable of fine efforts," Shorter told the press after the race. "They are such good friends, and I owe them a great deal of thanks for being here today. Jack and I have trained together for a long time now. Kenny is such a fine human being, and he got me to run this crazy race."

"I kept trying to talk him into the marathon," Moore acknowledged that day in Munich. "The reason was that he was handling me so easily in the 6-mile and on the track that I wanted to get him into my race. Well, now he has handled me in my race."

We can thank Kenny Moore for encouraging Frank Shorter to become, as John Jerome insightfully called him, "The Man Who Invented Running."

"There was something about all those miles, all those minutes of TV coverage through the streets of Munich, something about that silken, light-footed stride and flying hair that lodged forever in our consciousness," wrote Jerome. "Running, somehow it looked ... glorious. *That's* how Frank Shorter invented running: by running on camera, and by glorifying it so."

Shorter was 24 years old then—running in Munich, the place of his birth. His father, an Army doctor at the time, had been stationed there. Shorter grew up in Middletown, New York, with his nine brothers and sisters and attended Mt. Hermon Prep School in Mt. Hermon, Massachusetts, where he began running competitively and became the New England Prep School 2-mile champion. Shorter returned to Mt. Hermon in the fall of 1979 for a commemorative cross-country race which he won in record time. He'd not been back there since the '68 race.

After Mt. Hermon, Yale. And Bob Geigengack, the renowned Olympic coach. Frank Deford recalled the story in *Sports Illustrated*: "Shorter's unremarkable track career was about to die a natural death, unmourned, in the spring of

1969. . . . He approached Geig one day and said, 'Geig, if I really worked at it , how good could I be?'

"Without pausing for breath, the coach shot back, 'Well, I think if you really applied yourself you could be very good. I think you could make the Olympics and even win a gold medal.' "

Shorter took the fantasies of such storybook advice seriously and a month later won the NCAA 6-mile title in 29:00.2 (in the 5,000 he placed fourth in 13:43.4). After that, his first major victory, Shorter excelled in every distance event and became, even before Munich, one of the most successful American distance runners ever.

He won the Springbank Road Race twice. He won the first 2 of 4 straight National AAU cross-country titles. He won the Sao Silvestre New Year's Eve Run. He won the 10,000 against the Russians in Leningrad. He won the Pan-Am Games Marathon. He won 3 more AAU track titles—one, a 13:10.6 indoor 3-miler in '71. I recall vividly, watching Shorter circle the Madison Square Garden track 33 times, not once succumbing to the tedium but picking up his pace toward the end as the crowd cheered him to a new U.S. indoor record.

Even then there was something in Shorter's demeanor and style—a self-assurance, a persistence, a litheness, a creased expression that announced, "This is hurting a little but I don't care"—that suggested to me that here was a man marked to do the things in sport we will not forget.

That June of '71, a year in which marathon running was still considered something akin to racewalking on the popularity scale and a man named William H. Rodgers was working as a hospital orderly and smoking and getting around on his motorcycle, Frank Shorter ran his first marathon. It was the 1971 AAU Marathon in Eugene, Oregon, and Shorter placed second in 2:17:45, losing by about a minute to Kenny Moore. Two months later Shorter won the Pan-Am Games Marathon in 2:22:40. Four months after that came the first of 4 Fukuoka triumphs (in 2:12:51). And then, in '72, victories in the Olympic Trials 10,000 and Marathon (tying intentionally with his good friend Kenny Moore). And finally Munich, where seven days before the marathon Shorter placed fifth in the 10,000 in 27:51.4, then a U.S. record.

Runners like Frank Shorter live in four-year cycles, dictated by the quadrennial Olympics. They say the Olympics are not everything to them, and either they are lying or they can't admit it, even to themselves. The Games are there like an omnipresent reminder that every workout and every race counts for something and that when you're not putting in your miles or your intervals or your hills or getting your international incubation in Europe, someone young and fast from Ethiopia or the Soviet Union is, and they'll be there with you in the Games, assuming you get that far. This is a weighty burden—ask Marty Liquori and Jim Ryun and Gerry Lindgren.

It is a burden Shorter carries well, as Kenny Moore has observed: "Frank does whatever he has to, whatever is needed. Ultimately, he even won a gold medal that way."

Between 1972 and 1976, Shorter was unapproachable as the world's best distance runner. He won several more National AAU titles in track and cross-country and numerous road races and marathons, most significantly Fukuoka, a race not yet well known in America beyond the running grapevine but acknowledged elsewhere as the world's preeminent marathon. Frank Shorter won Fukuoka in 1971, 1972, 1973, and 1974, running 2:12:51, 2:10:30 (a U.S. record), 2:11:45, and 2:11:31. He beat the Finns, the British, the Japanese, the Africans, the Soviets, and the Germans—anyone the world could throw at him. It was like the Yankees winning the World Series four straight years—against an all-star team.

Shorter was then attending law school at the University of Florida and running for the Florida Track Club with his buddy Jack Bachelor. He was running day after day, packing strength and reserve into a frail-looking body noted for its 2.2 percent body fat. Ten miles, 15 miles, 20 miles; 440s over and over again, each in 60 seconds, with short jogs in between. His picture on the cover of *Track & Field News, Sports Illustrated, The New York Times Magazine.* Shorter was the only runner recognized by the American sports establishment. Jim Ryun was gone, an enigma to begin with, an Olympic failure. This Frank

Shorter was relentless. When he had to, he could speak out and make his voice heard. And when growing numbers of recreational runners read of the time Shorter and Bachelor ran up the back of a car and over it without breaking stride, after the motorist had intimidated them, Shorter endeared himself to these runners and became idolized by them as never before. Here was a man with gold feet who still had to worry about errant drivers.

By 1976, Shorter had company in U.S. marathoning's 5-minute-per-mile club—an upstart named Bill Rodgers, who'd broken Shorter's American record at the 1975 Boston Marathon. Shorter, running more comfortably than ever, beat Rodgers by 7 seconds in the Olympic Trials that year, and a consensus of *Track & Field News* experts made him its unanimous favorite to equal Abebe Bikila's feat as a 2-time Olympic Marathon champion.

A marathoner myself by then and a rabid Shorter fan, I remember sitting in Montreal's Stade Olympique listening to my heart pound an hour into the race, seeing only periodic checkpoint splits on the scoreboard. The stadium's TV hookup to the course had malfunctioned and the pro-Shorter crowd—many Americans were in attendance—waited in frustration for news from the front lines. The last split we were given was at 35 kilometers. Waldemar Cierpinski of East Germany, almost totally ignored by the prognosticators, was 13 seconds ahead of Shorter. Lasse Viren, the 5,000 and 10,000 champion, was farther back and could not win. The rest did not matter.

In the stadium there was tremendous pulling for Shorter, from people who had watched him win so often, even if only on TV, and from people who themselves ran and identified with him. Frank Shorter to them was like every other dedicated runner—he just ran a lot faster and looked a lot better doing it. When Cierpinski entered the stadium, alone, there was a collective sigh so great one could almost see it. Viren first might have made sense—here was an immortal. But who was Cierpinski? The 26-year-old former steeplechase and 10,000 specialist had converted to the marathon in 1974, entering the Olympics with a PR of 2:12:22. "A comer," said *Track & Field News.*

Cierpinski crossed the finish line in 2:09:55 for a new Olympic record and, seeing a *1* on the lap indicator, took another lap to be sure, finding Frank Shorter at the finish to congratulate him. Shorter's time was 2:10:46, his second best ever. "I could do no more than I did yesterday," Shorter told the press the next day. "I will just have to accept the fact that I was second best."

Others blamed it on the rain. Shorter runs marathons in the rain like Bill Rodgers runs them in the heat. "I enjoyed the rain," said Cierpinski. "It encouraged me."

Frank Shorter began Part Three of his running career. First there was The Beginning, to Munich; then, The Sustained Preeminence, ending in Montreal; then The Business, The Injury, The AAU and, most recently, The Comeback—subdivisions of a changing Shorter, one more complex and with more responsibilities and more pressures on him. He dances like an acrobat on the edge of his swirling world.

Shorter left Florida with his wife, Louise (whom he married in 1970), and moved to Boulder, Colorado, where he could train at an altitude of 5,000 feet or more. He developed a line of running attire that bears his name. He opened a retail shop and mail-order business to which he has since added two branches, one in Durango, Colorado, and another in East Lansing, Michigan. He became national Run for Your Life spokesman for the Connecticut Mutual Life Insurance Company. He did track-meet commentary for NBC. He signed an unprecedented deal with the AAU and Hilton International that permitted him to do promotional work for the company and appear in its television commercials without losing his amateur status.

Although the changing IAAF rules allowed for such an arrangement, the agreement was controversial because Hilton had to pay the AAU $25,000 for the right to become a national sponsor and to enlist Shorter's services for promotional purposes (for which he is paid). The AAU (since converted into The Athletics Congress), even before this, had been criticized for fighting for amateurism on the one hand while dealing from the bottom of the deck with the other. Shorter was cashing in, people said. He was part of the hypocrisy. Just another opportunist.

There are people in this country who believe football players should make a lot of money but runners should remain poor and pure, as gentlemen (and women) upholding anachronistic ideals of centuries past. Frank Shorter is used to people telling him he can't do something. He was in hot water for a while with the IAAF because he was earning money as an "amateur." He came out of that with his amateur status, and his business, intact, and he didn't have to eat crow to do it.

In April 1979, about two weeks before the Boston Marathon, Frank spent a week in New York arranging the Hilton deal. There was the private dinner party, the press conference, the "Today" show stint, the meetings with executives from Hilton and the AAU, the filming of the first TV commercial, the daily running that could not wait, and Louise, into her ninth month of pregnancy and from the looks of her ready to give birth at any moment. Frank's life seemed particularly strenuous. Not to worry. Frank had it all figured out, including the doctors on alert in New York, Chicago (the connecting point home), and Boulder, just in case.

On the day of the press conference, a Thursday, I chatted briefly with Shorter in his hotel room at the Waldorf (one of 180 hotels in the Hilton chain), where Louise offered Frank the remains of a half-eaten breakfast and spoke to him appeasingly, as though he were the one nine months pregnant. Frank had a luncheon appointment and I would only have a few minutes; I felt guilty taking even that much of his time.

If Frank Shorter were not the athlete he is, one would think of him first as a good businessman. Shorter is tough—his favorite word to describe those he respects. He is extremely quick and intelligent, the lawyer in him (he does not practice) evident now and then. He is articulate. At that AAU press conference, I was embarrassed for my colleagues by the vapid questions being asked, especially in view of the importance of the news, and I threw Shorter a couple of zingers, only to have him deflate them with what writer Eric Olsen calls "that upright regality of his."

Frank Shorter has a rap on everything. Training at altitude. Marathon tactics. The Africans. Sprinters. After the 1979 Boston Marathon, I asked him how he could explain his seventy-eighth place, when prior to the race he'd said he was in 2:13 shape. His reply: "Biomechanically, I wasn't running right. I looked at my shoes afterward and I could tell I was off center somehow." After the 1979 Falmouth Road Race, in which Shorter placed fifth, 1980 Olympic hopefuls Alberto Salazar and Rudy Chapa, there as spectators, pressed Shorter with question after question about altitude training, questions he confidently answered. "That is not an idle mind," says George Hirsch.

At the time, in the summer of '79, Frank Shorter was in the midst of a successful comeback, a comeback surprising even to his fans (they had counted him out after his surgery and amid the rise to greatness of other marathoners, like Bill Rodgers).

Early in 1977 Shorter injured his left foot. He ran on it, as runners will do despite "minor" injuries, and he didn't run poorly either. On the July Fourth weekend, Shorter won the Chicago Distance Classic (20 kilometers), which had 6,500 runners, and the Peachtree Road Race (10 kilometers), which had 5,000 runners. Among the thousands were Lasse Viren and Bill Rodgers. But the injury nagged, and Shorter stopped running a month later after giving in to the growing sense that surgery was the only answer.

On April 26, 1978, nine days after Bill Rodgers won his second Boston Marathon (edging Jeff Wells), Dr. Stan James, an orthopedic surgeon in Eugene, Oregon, operated on Shorter. As Eric Olsen, who visited Shorter in Boulder a year later, explained in *The Runner*: Dr. James "cut into Shorter's left foot and found that a ligament had pulled away from one of the joints, taking with it a piece of bone, and that cysts had formed in the ligament and bone spurs had grown out around the injury. James removed the chips, cysts and spurs." Said Shorter, "I was faced with the choice of having the operation or perhaps never running or jogging again."

Shorter rested, strengthened his legs on a weight machine, rode a stationary cycle, even competed in a bike race. He ran again in July, building up mileage gradually, of course, and then he raced. On September 3, 1978, Shorter entered a 10-kilometer race in Santa Fe, New Mexico, and placed fifth in 32:59. Two weeks after that he ran the Virginia Ten-Miler in 52:16 (placing fourteenth, Bill Rodgers winning), and a month later the New York Marathon in 2:19:32 (placing twelfth, Bill Rodgers again winning) and suddenly, six months after surgery, three months after running his first step, he was once more causing people to wonder if indeed Frank Shorter really would make it back all the way.

It was just about then that *Time* magazine named Shorter one of its "50 Faces for America's Future." Shorter, then 31, was one of the youngest leaders named to the honor roll. "All those on the list," *Time* said, "share one characteristic, the sense of boldness that remains the prime prerequisite for leadership in any era."

"I'm really flattered," said Frank Shorter. "It's nice to be recognized for all the things you've tried to do."

RODGERS INHERITS THE THRONE

While Frank Shorter is the aristocrat—son of a physician, prep school, a fling at med school, Yale, Giegengack protegé, attorney, Boulder, Vail—with a definite if subtle elitism that breeds intolerance for others' flaws or weaknesses, Bill Rodgers came up the hard way.

"I was an escort messenger," Rodgers writes in his autobiography, *Marathoning* (1980), of the time in 1971 when he worked at Peter Bent Brigham Hospital in Boston to fulfill his obligations as a conscientious objector to the Vietnam war. "I carried samples of blood, the mail, various medical supplies. I transported patients from one area to another. I had to take dead bodies to the morgue. All of it added up to an upsetting emotional experience. It may have been work that had to be done by someone, but you couldn't help feeling that you were being dumped upon."

Perhaps that, in part, explains Rodgers's friendliness, the knee-jerk warmth and sincerity he shows to others, even to people he does not know well or at all, like the people who surround him after races, win or lose, and ask him questions about running and would he autograph a shoe or a T-shirt or a race number or a magazine that has his picture in it. Bill Rodgers will talk to them, kid them, get kidded back, ask them how they did in the race. He will do this until no one else is waiting for a turn, which can be a couple of hours, and then he'll talk to reporters who talked to him a few hours before but have a few last questions that cannot wait, and then he'll pose for photographers, even for a kid with an Instamatic, and then if he hasn't yet done so he'll do a radio or TV spot, and then, seeing his wife, Ellen, looking tired and forlorn, he'll finally excuse himself and find a quick shower and a bite to eat.

Bill Rodgers is a nice guy. Forget for a moment that going into 1980 he was the best marathon runner in the world, the winner of 3 Bostons, 4 New Yorks, of other marathons from Waynesboro, Virginia, to Fukuoka, Japan, world record-holder for 25 kilometers on the track, and a dinner guest of Jimmy and Rosalynn Carter. The next time you would like to chew the fat or go out for beer and pizza or for a run or to take in a movie, find someone who is just like Bill Rodgers. Or, better yet, give Bill a call—he just might take you up on it.

Not long ago, before calculating the realities of world-class stewardship, Rodgers was so accommodating and trusting and naïve that he would hardly ever refuse an invitation to compete or make an appearance or take part in a clinic or show up for a press conference. The offers were not magnanimous then, but Bill could not say no. "Marshmallow," Ellen would call him. At Ellen's insistence, Bill has become less apt to hop out to Boston's Logan Airport and head off to any event he's invited to. Nowadays, moreover, the invitations are so numerous that careful selectivity is essential. A man could get tired. Ellen oftentimes intercepts the phone calls just to make sure.

Even with Ellen on sentry duty (if she doesn't watch out for him, who will?), Bill gets totally absorbed in every pre-race encounter with the press, exhibiting the same candor, high spirits, and courtesy he'd show if he were gabbing with running enthusiast Tommy Leonard and the gang over at Boston's Eliot Lounge. It is not that Rodgers has an affinity for reporters or enjoys the publicity they give him—although he does not mind seeing the BR logo of his running attire in print; business is business—but that Bill is a talker, he's always got a point to make, an observation, a question, and it does not occur to him as it does to his counterparts in other sports that he might be misunderstood or misquoted or intentionally disparaged in the next morning's headlines.

Two days before the 1979 Boston Marathon, Rodgers attended a press conference on the Skywalk of the Prudential Building, where blowups of wonderful photos chronicling the history of the race were on display. With Clarence DeMar (one of Bill's idols; the other is Abebe Bikila), Tarzan Brown, Gerard Coté, and others posted behind him, Rodgers gave reporters enough material for a week's worth of copy and revealed a dream, which he would again describe in his July 1979 article for *The Runner*.

Rodgers wrote: "Just a week before the race I have my first race dream. Boston's the only race I ever dream about, and while I seldom remember my dreams, these are unforgettable. This time I'm caught at the start of the race in my training shoes—at the back of the pack. Utter futility. (A few days later Ellen tells me she's dreamed that I've won.)"

Forty-eight hours later, Ellen was proven the better soothsayer, as Bill beat Toshihiko Seko of Japan in the final miles and broke his U.S. record with a mark of 2:09:27.

Just before he rounded the final turn and headed for the finish, Rodgers took off this hat and clutched it in his right hand as a security blanket in the best tradition of Holden Caulfield. With 100 yards to go, he nodded to his audience, already in a frenzy hearing the announcer holler hyperbolically: "Here he comes, the greatest distance runner in the history of the world . . ."

Afterward, relaxing with a Pepsi, Rodgers said, "I've had a streak and I'm into my prime years, but it ain't gonna last forever." Alluding to the Olympics, he added, "There's only one thing missing. If I get that I'll retire. Happily."

Prior to 1976, Bill Rodgers looked to the Olympics with a different kind of anticipation. He was not the favorite but an up-and-comer. With little international experience behind him, he would find the Montreal race a cram course in the dynamics of running 26 miles 385 yards for all the marbles in a field of marathoners whose strengths, weaknesses, and strategies were generally not known to one another. Rodgers hung with the leaders for the first 12 miles on that drizzly Saturday in Montreal but fell back after that and finished fortieth, in 2:25:14. Looking back on it three years later, Rodgers said, "Due to a metatarsal injury on my right foot I was overly cautious and curtailed my speedwork (which had inflamed the injury) in the crucial six weeks or so prior to the Games."

While Rodgers's showing in Montreal was somewhat disillusioning to him, it was only sixteen months earlier, in March 1975, that his running first drew any attention. The occasion was the IAAF World Cross-Country Championship, an annual event that draws an eclectic assortment of runners, from mile record-holders to steeplechasers to marathon specialists, but is of little interest to Americans, coming as it does at the critical juncture between the indoor and outdoor track seasons. Rodgers was not much of a track runner anyway, so the opportunity to run a 12-kilometer race on a horseracing course in Rabat, Morocco, sounded like a good idea.

Bill placed third. Third! In such races, seasoned men with lines on their faces and Olympic medals on their mantels place third, not 27-year-old nobodies from the Boston suburbs who look like they don't need to shave. Rodgers's time was 35:27—only Ian Stewart (Scotland) and Mariano Haro (Spain) finished ahead of him. But since even a good track paper like *The New York Times* couldn't care less about cross-country races in Rabat, even if they are world championships, when Bill Rodgers lined up at the start of the 1975 Boston Marathon just three weeks later, what little status he had was still based on his fourteenth-place 2:19:34 the previous year. (In his first Boston, in '73, Bill dropped out after 21 miles. "I came out of that race with the feeling I would never be a good distance runner," he would write in his autobiography.)

What Frank Shorter did for the marathon in Munich in 1972, Bill Rodgers did for it again in Boston in 1975. He won it, of course, glorifyingly so, wearing those white gloves of his, stopping four times for drinks and once to tie his shoe, setting an American record of 2:09:55. "I didn't stop long," said Rodgers. "Maybe 5 seconds, and swoooosh—I was off again! I even stop when I'm training. It's just a natural thing for me to do."

While Rodgers had no other victories to speak of up to that point, he was well prepared to run a 4:57.3-per-mile marathon and break Frank Shorter's U.S. mark by 35 seconds. He had joined the Greater Boston Track Club, which had a fine coach in Billy Squires. Under Squires, Rodgers was running twice a day, rarely less than 100 miles per week, and doing speed-work. He'd been running 15 or so miles a day since 1972, when he was fired from his hospital job. When Rodgers tried to unionize the orderlies, the administration told him to take a walk.

Instead, having little else to do, he took a run. A long one. Bill had already been running at the Y "as an outlet from that stultifying job," and when his motorcycle was stolen it gave him the impetus to continue getting around more on foot. While Bill Rodgers was starting to make a name for himself in running, he was working at a state institution for the retarded, but he soon left there to devote himself full-time to running and its allied interests.

Like Shorter, Rodgers opened a running shop, Bill Rodgers Running Center, and now has three of them, all in Boston. His line of running attire, even the gloves, is sold in stores throughout the country. He is finally making a good buck, as an athlete of his caliber should, and in January 1980, he and Ellen finally moved from their modest house in Melrose, a

Boston suburb, to a roomier spread in Sherborn, not far from the Framingham checkpoint on the Boston Marathon course. It was a symbolic move in more ways than one, since Framingham, on October 28, 1973, had been the site of Rodgers's first marathon victory. It was the Bay State Marathon, and his time was 2:28:12.

Almost a decade earlier at Newington High in Connecticut, Bill was running a 4:28.8 mile and doing a 2-miler in 9:36. And then at Wesleyan he became the kind of runner even *Track & Field News* barely notices. But, thankfully, he roomed for a period with Ambrose Burfoot, who won the Boston Marathon in 1968 and offered Rodgers a tip or two about distance running. "He was a tremendous influence on me," Rodgers has said. "I recall how Amby trained 'through' the collegiate track competition (most of which he still won), developing a base for the marathon. It was clear, after training for two years with Amby, that his success was based on his moderate but long-term approach to training."

It was a system that would work for Rodgers, too. His training would not be moderate by anyone's standards: an average of 130 miles a week at roughly a 6-minute-per-mile pace. Nor could the amount of racing be called moderate: 35 races, for example, in 1978 alone. But recognizing that even the best runners had in them but a few superlative efforts a year, Rodgers would, as Burfoot did, train "through" most of his races; keying only on a handful, like the marathons and a couple of shorter road events. These he would peak for—increasing his mileage to as much as 175 a week and doing more speedwork in the weeks before a race, then cutting back, getting more sleep and psyching himself for the kill in the final, crucial week or ten days before the showdown.

This formula, which Rodgers watches over with meticulous care, as he must, has rarely failed him. Twice when it failed at the place of his greatest triumphs—Boston—the heat was to blame. In 1976, on a 90-degree day (even 100-plus in spots) dubbed the Boston Broiler, Rodgers was unable to finish, and Jack Fultz won in 2:20:19, the slowest winning time at Boston since Burfoot's 2:22:17, in '68. In 1977, after 20 miles when "the old gut had gone," Rodgers again dropped out, and Jerome Drayton won in 2:14:46. It was sunny and warm then, too, but not nearly as oppressive as the year before.

When Rodgers won his third straight New York City Marathon, in 1978, on a warm and humid day, it seemed as if he'd finally licked his problem with the heat. With moderate heat, maybe, but apparently not with severe heat, the kind that wilted him in the First Montreal International Marathon in August 1979. On that day the temperature was in the 80s by starting time and in the 90s at points along the course, which was virtually shadeless and offered no protection from the bright, piercing sun. Only the hint of a breeze wafted in from the St. Lawrence River.

Midway through the race Rodgers, wearing number 13, began to lose the composure that is evident in his winning races. In his eyes and in his gait, there was a certain insecurity. Ellen Rodgers, riding the press bus with reporters and Tom Fleming's wife, Diane, said after 20 miles, "I wish he'd drop out." But her husband kept on to the finish, where his 2:22:12 put him in fifteenth place. "I knew at 10 I didn't have it. My feet were burning," Rodgers told a throng of reporters, mostly Canadian, who were enjoying their first post-race parry with Rodgers and generally ignoring the two men who had put on a great show—Kebede Balcha of Ethiopia, the surprise winner in 2:11:35, and Dave Chettle of Australia, second in 2:11:41.

Rodgers got a laugh from the press when he said, "I wish the Olympic Marathon was at the Winter Olympics."

15

GRETE WAITZ:
NORTHERN
LIGHTNING

It is warm and humid and overcast on this June morning in
New York City, the kind of a day in New York that reminds
one of those terribly sticky, sweaty summer days that are not
long off. I am in Central Park standing with other reporters
and photographers on the back of a flatbed truck. This truck
has been acquired by the PR people in charge of the L'eggs
Women's Mini-Marathon to carry the press around the
10,000-meter course so that the appropriate observations can
be made and pictures can be taken of the women who assume
the lead. The truck is better suited for the transport of produce, and its driver is better suited for the administration of
torture to prisoners of war. For reasons known to none of us,
at arbitrary points he picks up speed, putting the field beyond
our view. And even when the truck does not desert the field,
we are taken under trees whose branches hang so low they
swipe us periodically, drawing our attention away from the
wonderful running going on right near us. This scene, truck
and all, has happened two years in a row now, as though to

test young journalists on various counts of perseverance and coarse language. In '78 the composition of the race was altogether different. Kathy Mills, the fine Penn State runner, dueled with Martha White, an up-and-coming high school senior from State College, Pennsylvania, home of Penn State. White, now at the University of Virginia, pulled away from Mills in the last mile and won by 150 yards, in an excellent 10,000-meter time for women of 33:29.7.

Today, a year later, it is completely different. Today there is one runner out there, not a high school or college girl but a woman. She is tall and lean and her pigtails bob as with every stride she lengthens her lead over the rest of the record-breaking field of 5,000 runners, some of whom are out there just for the experience or to just finish, others to achieve a fast time and place high among the leaders. This woman is wearing the red-and-white colors of her native Norway. She does not look behind her—"a sign of weakness," she says later—but keeps her eyes fixed on the hilly roadway of the park, rarely glancing at the press truck or the other two race vehicles, or at the cyclists who form a motorcade that will escort her to the finish line where relayed reports have already told the waiting throng that she is a certain winner and possible record-breaker. Her stride is not especially long for one running so fast, but her form shows no defect and her concentration does not lapse for a moment. Her first mile was 5:14, the second 5:03, then 4:55, 5:13, and 4:53. Her 5-mile split is 25:18, a 5:03.6 pace, faster than any woman has ever run for 10,000 meters, on the track or the road. It is clear that this woman will not falter, and as she runs the final mile with the same grace and drive and speed with which she ran the preceding 5, I begin to root for her and to enjoy her performance even more, flushed by the realization that I am privileged to be watching a woman who is destined to be hailed by future generations as one of the great runners of our time.

I am watching Grete Waitz. Grete Waitz is undeniably the best woman distance runner in the world. Grete Waitz (pronounced Whites) is the 1977 World Cup champion at 3,000 meters, the World Cross-Country champion, the world record-holder in the marathon. It is the ultimate triad—track, cross-country, marathon. No man has come close to her in relative versatility, and now, in her first 10,000-meter race, she is adding that distance to her world-class repertoire.

The truck pulls ahead of Waitz and rushes to the finish line to ensure that we will witness the breaking of the tape. It is unusually quiet, almost eerie, at the finish—none of the standard tumult. This is because the informed crowd is focused not on any anticipated one-on-one sprint to the wire but on time, on the digital clock whose reading on the winner will be the qualitative measure of the day. Waitz appears, runs the last 200 yards in about 30 seconds, achieving a total time of 31:16. The place breaks up, aware of what has happened but, surely, not entirely certain of its significance or ramifications.

Grete Waitz has done it again. The previous October she ran her first marathon, the New York City Marathon, and defeated her closest rival by more than 9 minutes, breaking the women's world record by 2:18 with a time of 2:32:30. In bringing the record closer to 2:30, she set new standards for women the world over and, in effect, delivered the message that women could run much faster for 26 miles 385 yards than was generally believed. (Indeed, in the Boston Marathon half a year later, 4 more women led by Joan Benoit of the United States bettered 2:40.) And now, too, the 10,000-meter distance will never be the same for women. Waitz, in her first try at the distance, broke the course record by 2:15 and exceeded by 29 seconds the listed track record of 31:45 set in 1978 by Loa Olafson of Denmark. Road performances cannot count for track records, but Waitz's mark when weighed against Olafson's far tops it. Waitz ran uncontested and on a rugged, hilly course. Olafson ran in a men's track race, amid ideal pacing and competitive conditions. Give Waitz the same conditions and she just might come close to 30 minutes flat for the 10,000! Top male runners often don't run that fast; in fact, on this very same Central Park course, 10,000-meter winners rarely better 30 minutes. (Two months earlier, in an open

10,000-meter race with 5,000 runners, only the victorious Kevin Ryan, a New Zealand Olympian, was under 30 minutes, with a time of 29:49.9. Only 5 other men bettered 31:15.)

Are women distance runners bound to take large chunks out of existing records because of their sheer numbers, or is Grete Waitz playing with an extra advantage, be it spirit, hunger, method, or some other factor that lifts her far above the level of her contemporaries?

I sought to find out. When Grete made her first appearance in New York, in October '78, for the marathon, I was running in the event myself and, therefore, could not meet with her. By the time I'd limped to the end with leg cramps in close to 4 hours, she'd fled Central Park, after explaining to shocked reporters why her name was not listed in the race program (she'd entered only three days before the race), what she thought about running 26.2 miles through the five boroughs of New York City, and how she happened to shatter the world record in her very first marathon. Fred Lebow, president of the New York Road Runners Club, promised that Waitz would return to New York for the L'eggs event, so I made plans to see her then. On the eve of the race, she was scheduled to make an appearance at a pre-race clinic—an ideal time, perhaps, for a brief interview. About an hour before the clinic was to begin, I went to the Mayflower Hotel, where Grete and her husband, Jack, were staying and phoned the Waitzes' room. I expected a brush-off—Grete had met with the media for most of the day, and while she knew of the magazine I edit, *The Runner*, she almost certainly did not know of me.

Grete answered the phone. I gave it my best shot, and she agreed, "But only for fifteen minutes."

"Fine," I said. "When can we meet?"

"Is right now good?"

Some tough customer.

Within five minutes, Grete Waitz was in the lobby. She wore blue jeans and a blue short-sleeved shirt, the kind some people call a rugby shirt. At first glance she looked rather plain, her pigtailed hair giving her the countenance of a teenager. We combed the lobby for a meeting room or at least an alcove in which to talk without distraction, and when it was apparent that such was not to be had, Grete pointed to a corner of the lobby where the top of an air vent would provide the best seating available. It seemed a spot more suitable for little kids bent on mischief than for an interview with a celebrity runner, but there was no alternative.

Close up, Grete is very attractive, unlike almost every photo you've ever seen of her with those pigtails pulled back from her head, making her face look round and her nose more prominent than it is. Her blue eyes are flattered by a pinch of blue eye shadow, she has a gold choker around her neck, and she surprises me by exhibiting the kind of open, engaging personality that makes me think about her long after our talk is over.

First I ask her why she disappointed us by not getting into town for Thursday's press conference, which was well attended by other leading women runners.

"When we were in Copenhagen, they were striking," she says, "so we had to wait six hours in Copenhagen when we were on the plane. We were lucky; we had the only plane which was allowed to leave the airport. We arrived yesterday evening. I hadn't been sleeping for twenty-three hours."

Although the weekend in New York will be hectic for her, Grete is comforted by the fact that schools are closed Monday and Tuesday in Oslo, where she lives and works as a teacher, so she and Jack can fly home leisurely on Monday without the pressure of immediately returning to work. Time is important to Grete; there is not enough of it—not enough for a full-time job, a husband, adequate training and competition, and travel to and from the distant corners of the world for the right race at the right time. This is a recurrent complaint of hers, and she has worked out a solution that causes her to sigh with relief. A sabbatical.

"I asked the chief of schools in Oslo for a year off [which she received] because maybe it's the last year I'm going to run, and I've been training hard for many years. I've got invitations from all over the world and it's very difficult to be a teacher. I have to say no to a lot of invitations. Sometimes I feel in competition we are competing on different levels. *I'm a pure amateur—I have a job. I get up at a quarter to six in the morning to train."*

The inference is clear. Her main rivals in track—and track, she'll soon explain, is her number-one priority—are from Eastern Europe, whose premier athletes are supported by the government in institutionalized arrangements under which a runner can train at will and work for a school of "physical culture." This is not Waitz's last year of running, but in her mind it may be the last year in which she can hope to be the best in the world at 3,000 meters, the longest standard track event for women. Her best at the distance is 8:32.1, second to the world record of 8:27.1 held by Ludmila Bragina of the Soviet Union. I think she is wrong—there are more years at the top still to come in track. But maybe I underestimate the wear nine years as an internationalist has had on her. While her feigned pessimism is a way of taking the pressure off, or holding it at bay, this will be her first chance to be a full-time runner, and maybe for Grete Waitz, in track, this will be her first chance to reach her best possible form.

That thought, however, leads to another contradiction. Grete insists the Olympics are not in her plans because, she says, she is not fast enough to win a medal in the 1,500 meters, the longest Olympic running event for women. So what's the point of running full-time?

There are two points, actually. One is road racing. Free from her teaching job, Grete can now indulge in the lucrative U.S. road-racing circuit. It is not just that Grete loves road racing or wants to see the Grand Canyon. As the world's top woman runner and one likely to repeat her victory and even her record in the New York Marathon year after year, Grete's presence will mean an awful lot to race directors and their sponsoring corporations. She will be given a lot of "expense" money, probably more than she'd earn for a full term of teaching in the Oslo school system.

Second, there is the Olympics. The more Grete insists she will not try for it, the less people in Norway—where there are great pressures on her to succeed—will expect of her in the Games. In life, this is called common sense. In athletics, it is called the safety valve. Here is Grete's explanation:

"I don't think I'll go for the Olympics because 1,500 is the longest distance and I think—the Eastern Europeans, they are very strong—to reach the final you'll have to run 3:55, 3:56. My PB is 4:00.6. That was in the European champs [in '78]. That was a very good race for me because I had a chance to run from behind the front runners. It is not easy for me to go to the front. That's the only way *I* could run that fast—I have to have speed from the start. It's very seldom in the Olympics they run that way. They just 'walk' the first 2 laps and they start sprinting, and I can't run fast that way. So I think 4 flat is the limit for me in the 1,500. People tell me, 'You can run faster, just do speedwork.' But I've been running internationally nine years and I'm not ready to change my training. I was in Munich, I was in Montreal, I've been to the Olympics. It's not such a goal for *me*."

Ironically, the boycott of the Moscow Olympics might have been a blessing in disguise for Waitz, taking away the damned-if-you-do, damned-if-you-don't position she might have found herself in during the summer of 1980. And the session in Moscow proved to be good fortune for Grete because the International Olympic Committee approved the addition of a women's 3,000-meter race for the 1984 games in Los Angeles. If still in top form by then, Waitz would have an excellent chance of winning the gold medal.

Grete Waitz was born in Oslo on October 1, 1953, the only girl among three children. She was active as a youngster and got involved in track at age 12, because of the influence of her neighbor, Terje Pedersen, then the best javelin thrower in the world. "He was the hero of all the children," Grete recalls. "They looked up to him. I had always liked running and being physical, so I joined the same club he was a member of." It was the Vidar Club, and young Grete took up the long jump, high jump, shot put, 60 meters—"everything, just for fun."

When Grete was 14 and 15 she concentrated on running only. At 16 she was a member of the Norwegian team that competed in Canada and spent a bit of time in Seattle—her first visit to the United States. In 1960 she moved up to the 400 meters and won some prizes in competition. "Then," she says, "I started to train for longer distance because I understood that I was not a sprinter, that 400 and 800 was the thing for me. Then the ball started to roll and, some years later, 800 and 1,500; then, 1,500 and 3,000." And now, too, cross-country, 10,000 meters, and the marathon.

Waitz's performances have followed a predictable course. In 1969 at 16, she ran the 800 in 2:17.2 and the next four years had 800 bests of 2:07.3, 2:05.7, 2:06.9, and 2:06. Her 1,500 times during that period were 4:29, 4:17, 4:16, and 4:12.7, respectively. In 1973, in addition, Grete also achieved a 9:34.2 for 3,000. Then the breakthrough: in '74, third in the European championship 1,500 (4:05.3); in '75, unbeaten and a world 3,000 record of 8:46.6 run right before her neighbors in Oslo; in '76, another 3,000 record—8:45.4; in '77, a World Cup 3,000 triumph in 8:43.5 and, in another 3,000, the year's best time of 8:36.8; in '78, a 4:00.6 in the 1,500, a world record of 8:32.1 in the 3,000, the first of 3 straight world cross-country championships, and, of course, her first New York Marathon triumph.

Still, within these impressive numbers is the painful experience of '76, of not making the Olympic 1,500 final. A *Track & Field News* experts consensus pegged her for fifth. In her semi-final round, Grete placed eighth (in the same race in which Jan Merrill set the former U.S. record of 4:02.6). The next day the final was won in 4:05.5—by Tatyana Kazankina of the Soviet Union, who repeated her Olympic victory in 1980.

Waitz's disappointment was compounded by the reaction in Norway. "They thought she would win," said Kirsten Damagaard, head of the Norwegian Track and Field Federation and chairman of the Department of Physical Education at the University of Oslo. "They didn't understand the competition she faced and said some negative things. We are a small nation and everybody knows everybody else, which makes the pressure worse. . . . It's a common idea that once you are on top, you should stay there. We have a slogan which goes, 'A silver medal is a defeat.' "

Grete Waitz was hurt and confused. She was also at a critical time in her life: 22 years old, married for one year, teaching for two years, in her sixth year of international competition. She took some badly needed time off. For several months Grete ran for general conditioning but did not compete. What she did do was a lot of thinking and a little cross-country skiing, after which she came to view herself less as an emissary of Norway and more as an independent runner who could enjoy the glow of international stardom and yet accept the inevitable defeats on her own terms. Grete Waitz had grown up a lot in this time and had become more assertive. When she resumed competition early in 1977, she rejected the Norwegian Track and Field Federation's offer for financial support. Grete didn't want the pressure of owing Norway any more than, deep down, she felt she already did.

In '77, in addition to her track successes, Waitz competed in cross-country events for the first time. It seems that Grete Waitz requires little initiation. She runs the marathon for the first time and sets a world record. She runs 10,000 meters for the first time and sets a world record. She runs cross-country for the first time, and wins. And the second time. And the third time. And so on. She has never lost in cross-country. Her aggregate record is equivalent to a world record in a sport which, because of the disparate distances and terrain, has no world record.

Grete's three biggest cross-country victories have come in the IAAF World Championships, in 1978 in Glasgow, Scotland, in 1979 in Limerick, Ireland, and in Paris in 1980. This event, which has grown in stature in recent years, is for both men and women. Held in late March or early April, it is an appropriate finale to the winter cross-country season in Europe. While all 160 member countries of the IAAF are invited to compete, typically only 20 or 25 do so, but usually these are the nations with the best runners. (U.S. success in these championships has been mixed, as top American runners frequently bypass the event because it comes at the end of their country's hectic indoor track circuit and only two or three weeks before the Boston Marathon.)

Waitz's victories in 1978 and 1979 were remarkably similar. In Glasgow she ran on a muddy course a bit less than 3 miles in length and defeated her closest pursuer, Natalie Marasescu of Rumania, by 30 seconds in 16:19. In Limerick, on a muddy course a bit more than 3 miles in length, she defeated runner-up Raisa Smekhnova of the Soviet Union by 26 seconds in 16:48. Smekhnova's teammate, Giana Romanova, was 11 seconds farther back in fifth place. Waitz's victory over the Russian pair—in which she ran upright and somehow *over* the mud which held others to the ground—was important not only for its decisiveness. Romanova was the 1978 European champion in the 1,500 and was rated number one in the world in her specialty. In the '78 Europeans Waitz had run fifth in the 1,500 and third in the 3,000. The Limerick reversal enabled her to regain worldwide preeminence in *middle*-distance running.

While the significance of Waitz's second straight world cross-country victory is undeniable, it is less revered in Norway than it is in other countries. "In Norway," Waitz says, "road running and cross-country are not so particular. In Norway, track and field is just running on a track. Because of the European champs, the Olympics, the World Cup, when you talk to people about track and field, they are just thinking on the track. I look upon myself as a track runner. If I lived in America, I'd look upon myself as a road runner and marathoner."

Despite the athletic bias in her land, Grete prefers cross-country to other forms of running. "You know," she says, "the changing course, no laps, the ups and downs. I like that much better than running on a track. When you run cross-country the most important thing is to win, but when you're running on a track you have to have a good time because when you're finished they look at the time and . . ." Grete lifts her left arm, looks at her wristwatch, and, mocking the demand for records, says in a sarcastic tone: "Oh, 10 seconds from the world record. People always compare your results with the records."

Then, giving the predicament a final thought, she reveals: "If I had been an American I wouldn't run track at all, but since I run in Norway and Europe, that's the main thing for me."

Jack encouraged her to take a crack at the marathon and she ran her first in New York City in 1978. "I read the American track and running magazines," Jack told writer Leslie Goldberg, "and I thought it was time for Americans to know what an excellent runner she is. To be accepted in America, you have to do it in America. It's not enough to run good races in Europe. One thing we noticed in New York was that Grete was completely unknown, even to the so-called experts."

Consequently, when Grete finished the race—after accelerating past favored Martha Cooksey with 10 miles to go and running the second half 4 minutes faster than the first half—people didn't know what to make of it. Who was this mystery woman? Even those of us familiar with her track and cross-country record were puzzled. You don't get lucky in marathoning—the body's energy system sees to that. And that October 22 was not a day for luck anyway: temperatures in the 70s, humid, the New York air heavy. Successful marathons are calculated efforts, the result of appropriate training, of meeting schedules and mileage quotas. The astonishing fact was repeated a hundred times: *It was her first marathon.* Not since a relative unknown named Bill Rodgers won the 1975 Boston Marathon had a runner so shocked the running establishment.

What is Grete's secret? "I have no peculiarities or secrets," she tells me. "I'll run 11 or 12 sessions in a week. In the summer I'll try to train on a track 2 or 3 times a week. Other times I'll run in the woods, sometimes long and steady, sometimes short and faster. I'll try to have training which is changing because it is boring to run the same place and the same distance. I do 80 or 90 miles a week. In the track season it's difficult to run that long because I have to do a lot of speedwork. I would like to do [high] mileage because that's easier than running intervals on the track. That's hard work; that's painful. But I have to do it."

And for her maiden marathon? "I didn't make any special preparation, and I don't think I'll make any special preparations this year. Last year ['78] I succeeded with my way of doing it." (Her formula worked again in '79, as she broke her record with a sensational 2:27:33. See chapter 10.)

Grete Waitz is probably the only world-class marathoner who does not think of herself as a distance runner, much less a marathoner. She is so disciplined, so intense, so used to her own way of doing things after all these years of running that she considers the marathon an intrusion, no matter how good she is at it. "When you have run a marathon," she says, "it is very difficult to train for 2 or 3 weeks after that." After New York, Grete was in pain for a week and a half—a rare problem for her—but was helped by electrode treatments and massage.

But isn't a world record worth the sacrifice? What does Grete Waitz want from running?

The question is not what she wants from running but what she wants from life, and the answer, despite her aforementioned snub at overzealous nationalism, is to be accepted and lionized by the people of Norway. And that will come, as she repeats over and over again, when Grete Waitz is the best track runner in the world. After that, she might permit herself the luxury of competing, for example, in the Avon International Women's Marathon, probably the most important women's distance race in the world. But she could not do that in 1979 or 1980 because the Avon races, on September 22 and August 3, respectively, conflicted with Grete's late-season track appointments in Europe. Just as Waitz will not run the premier women's marathon, she will not run the premier open marathon: Boston. "I'm not interested in running Boston because it comes just before the track season, at a time when I'm doing a lot of speedwork. Running the marathon and doing speedwork—you can easily get injured. Maybe next year or in two years, when I've said to myself, 'I just want to run road races and marathons,' I may run a marathon earlier in the season."

Training in Oslo, with its cold climate, is difficult for Waitz. During the winter of '79, she says, the temperature was −20° C. almost every day for two straight months. It's hard to keep your speed sharp when you're wearing two pairs of trousers, gloves, hat, scarf, "and a lot of other clothing," Grete laments. "It's dark in the morning, dark in the evening. I have to run in the streets—there is 1½ meters [about 5 feet] of snow on the wooded trails. That's the reason I have to train so early in the morning. I have to train before the morning rush starts. If I go out at 7, I have to run out and in, out and in. It's hard. You have to fight against the weather, against yourself, and against the cars. You have to be motivated to be real good. I want to be good, to get good results. But running for so many years I don't have that. You need to have it."

Grete Waitz is awfully rough on herself. Too rough? Perhaps not. Perhaps this is just part of, as she says, "my way." By relentlessly demanding of herself, by setting standards beyond her reach, she sustains the will and strength she admits she has. "My body is strong. I'm big, 172 centimeters [5 feet 7 inches]. Look at my shoulders." To demonstrate, Grete grasps her shoulders with her arms. "I'm broad, yes? I think I'm very strong, not just from training. I've developed a strong will. That is very important. If you want to be a good runner, you have to sacrifice a lot of things."

To escape to a more conducive training locale, Waitz spent time in the winter of '79 in California, Australia, and New Zealand. Her odyssey was highlighted by a series of successful races, including a New Year's Eve 5-mile road race in Los Altos, California, in which Grete ran 25:28 to defeat Julie Brown by 51 seconds and Martha Cooksey by almost 2 minutes. She also ran a 3,000-meter race in New Zealand in 8:36.3, setting a New Zealand "all-comers" record.

Waitz hoped to have more time for such pampering in 1980, when she'd be on leave from her duties as a teacher of Norwegian and physical education at the Bjölsen School in Oslo.

She has taught there for four years, youngsters from 12 to 16, the rough equivalent of American high school. Like teachers everywhere, especially of that age group, Grete is ambivalent in her attitude toward her job. "I can teach younger children, but even though you don't have the discipline problems with small children, it's like play. That's not really teaching. I like to talk to them and discuss things, and you can't do that with small children."

Just then Grete gestures and imitates the "peep-peep" noises she associates with small children. "Sometimes when I reach school and get out of the car, I say to myself, 'Oh, I'm gonna stay here five hours with those noisy children.'"

Still, Waitz takes great pride in claiming, "I don't have any discipline problems, mainly, I think, because I am the person that I am." By this, she does not mean her athletic celebrity but her self-confidence, firmness, and high classroom standards. Her example has not produced a budding Grete Waitz among her students, who, she says, are frightened by the hard work Waitz tells them is required for this sport. Classes begin at 8—which means Grete must do her morning workout at 5:45—and her drowsy students ask her in half-awake voices, "Have you been running *today*, too?"

"Yes, I've been running 8 or 9 miles," Grete tells them.

The community in which the school is located, 15 minutes by car from the Waitzes' home on the outskirts of Oslo, is mad about ice hockey and football. "Some of them are interested in running," Waitz says, "but when they hear I run twice a day and all the training I do, they are a bit scared. They ask me, 'How much did you train when you were my age?' And I tell them I trained 5 or 6 times a week. They train 1 or 2 and think that is very much."

In the aftermath of the Mini-Marathon, the outdoor garden at Tavern on the Green is crowded with early diners sipping warm-weather cocktails. But this demure setting is ruffled when Fred Lebow of the New York Road Runners Club and the L'eggs PR people rush Grete Waitz into a corner of the café, followed by other race dignitaries, the press, and New

York City Mayor Ed Koch. Waitz barely has a chance to grab a drink of water before the shotgun questions are triggered. She answers them politely, still dripping sweat from her record-smashing victory.

The early pace set by Patti Lyons—the "rabbit"? "I knew she was going to take the lead because Fred Lebow told me. I picked her up after 1½ miles. I don't think she followed me."

The record of 31:16? "I didn't think I could run so fast; it's very difficult to say because I hadn't run 10 kilometers before. I think I could've run faster, not by much. When you're running alone, it's very easy just to slow down. When you're running together, the feeling of tiredness doesn't come so soon."

Grete is asked if she said anything to her husband Jack when he joined her briefly with a mile to go.

"No, I don't think that was my husband."

Jack, standing behind her now, pulls at her pigtail and says, "Yes it was."

Everyone laughs.

"She didn't hear me," Jack said later. "She never hears me."

The competition? "I wonder what Julie Brown could have run today, maybe Martha Cooksey, Jan Merrill, too; I wonder why she didn't run. This is good training for the track season."

The boisterous New York crowds? "I like it. It helps me near the finish line. You go into the 'basement' and get that strength you didn't even know you had left."

New York? "It is just entertaining for me to walk in the streets and look at all the people. The Americans are open and friendly. The Norwegians are more reserved; maybe it's because of the culture. I could just sit on a bench in Central Park for hours and look at all the people."

An hour later the awards are given out, from a makeshift podium in the sprawling Sheep Meadow. A few thousand people sit and watch and applaud respectfully as scores of trophies are presented to women in various age groups. It is a tease: Grete Waitz is saved for last. While she waits her turn,

Waitz is surrounded by about a hundred people, mostly young girls, who ask her to autograph their race programs, their T-shirts, their running shoes.

One of the autograph seekers is Berit Rekau, a 17-year-old Norwegian exchange student completing a year of school at Syosset High School, on Long Island. She is from the town of Steinkjer, a ten-hour drive from Oslo, but because of her father's business her family was to move to Oslo in the fall. Berit had seen Grete run track in Norway and said of her idol, "She's some hero. Best track star we've ever had. Today I realized my goal: to be the second best Norwegian in the race."

When Grete Waitz is announced as "the greatest woman runner in the world today," she receives a standing ovation that lasts a minute or more and a bouquet of red roses. She says to the assemblage, "This is the first time I had the opportunity to run with 5,000 women"—shrieks of cheers greet this remark—"and I look forward to run together with you next year." She raises her bouquet and is cheered again.

It is indeed a moment to behold, but I can't help but think it is partly a façade, this posture of glory that Grete Waitz emits. I remember her words to me the night before. "I've been running for so many years now, I'm tired. It is always the same: traveling, competing. It's difficult to have a holiday, to have what people mean as a holiday. We go to other places, but that's just for training and competition—that's not a holiday."

Roger Bannister called it the "burden of expectation." It can make or break an athlete, and right now Grete Waitz is somewhere in the middle, fighting to stay on top and yet trying to preserve the small freedoms so dear to her. That Grete is so cognizant of this fragile balance in her life is both refreshing and frightening. She says, dreamily: "Sometimes I really feel the pressure. It is too much for me. Sometimes I wish I could throw the whole thing away and ..." Grete pauses and laughs, "... and be a common girl."

APPENDIXES
BIBLIOGRAPHY
INDEX

HOW TO FIND
A MARATHON

There are almost 400 marathons held annually in the United States. The major running magazines periodically publish lists of marathons, and national running organizations can also be helpful in obtaining such information. Consult:

The Runner, One Park Avenue, New York, N.Y. 10016.

Runner's World, Box 366, Mountain View, Calif. 94042.

Running Times, 12808 Occoquan Road, Woodbridge, Va. 22192.

National Jogging Association, 2420 K Street NW, Washington, D.C. 20037.

Road Runners Clubs of America: Jerry Kokesh (President), 1226 Orchard Village Lane, Manchester, Mo. 63011; Ellen Wessel (VP-East), 1111 Army-Navy Drive, Arlington, Va. 22202; Harold Tinsley (VP-South), 8811 Edgehill Drive, Huntsville, Ala. 35802; Robert Fitts (VP-North), 6830 Maple Terrace, Wauwatosa, Wisc. 53213; Buzz Yancey (VP-Central), 926 Washington, No. 5, Denver, Colo. 80203; Len Wallach (VP-West), 1060 Continental, No. 104, Belmont, Cal. 94002.

OLYMPIC MARATHON MEDALISTS

1896, Athens, 40,000 meters
1. Spiridon Loues (Gr.) 2:58:50
2. Charilaos Vasilakos (Gr.) 3:06:03
3. Gyula Kellner (Hung.) 3:06:35

1900, Paris, 40,260 meters
1. Michael Theato (Fr.) 2:59:45
2. Emile Champion (Fr.) 3:04:17
3. Ernst Fast (Swed.) 3:37:14

1904, St. Louis, 42,195 meters
1. Thomas Hicks (U.S.) 3:28:53
2. Albert Corey (U.S.) 3:34:52
3. Arthur Newton (U.S.) 3:47:33

1908, London, 42,195 meters
1. Johnny Hayes (U.S.) 2:55:19 OR
2. Charles Hefferson (S. Afr.) 2:56:06
3. Joseph Forshaw (U.S.) 2:57:11

1912, Stockholm, 40,200 meters
1. Kenneth McArthur (S. Afr.) 2:36:55
2. Christian Gitsham (S. Afr.) 2:37:52
3. Gaston Strobino (U.S.) 2:38:43

1920, Antwerp, 42,750 meters
1. Hannes Kolehmainen (Fin.) 2:32:36 OR
2. Juri Lossman (Estonia) 2:32:49
3. Valerio Arri (Italy) 2:36:33

1924, Paris, 42,195 meters
1. Albin Stenroos (Fin.) 2:41:23
2. Romeo Bertini (Italy) 2:47:20
3. Clarence DeMar (U.S.) 2:48:14

1928, Amsterdam, 42,195 meters
1. Boughera El Ouafi (Fr.) 2:32:57
2. Miguel Plaza (Chile) 2:33:23
3. Martti Marttelin (Fin.) 2:35:02

1932, Los Angeles, 42,195 meters
1. Juan Carlos Zabala (Arg.) 2:31:36 OR
2. Sam Ferris (U.K.) 2:31:55
3. Armas Toivonen (Fin.) 2:32:12

1936, Berlin, 42,195 meters
1. Kitei Son (Japan) 2:29:20 OR
2. Ernest Harper (U.K.) 2:31:24
3. Shoryu Nan (Japan) 2:31:42

1948, London, 42,195 meters
1. Delfo Cabrera (Arg.) 2:34:52
2. Tom Richards (U.K.) 2:35:08
3. Etienne Gailly (Belg.) 2:35:34

1952, Helsinki, 42,195 meters
1. Emil Zatopek (Czech.) 2:23:04 OR
2. Reinaoldo Gorno (Arg.) 2:25:35
3. Gustaf Jansson (Swed.) 2:26:07

1956, Melbourne, 42,195 meters
1. Alain Mimoun (Fr.) 2:25:20
2. Franjo Mihalic (Yugo.) 2:26:32
3. Veikko Karvonen (Fin.) 2:27:47

1960, Rome, 42,195 meters
1. Abebe Bikila (Eth.) 2:15:17 OR
2. Rhadi Ben Abdesselem (Mor.) 2:15:42
3. Barry Magee (N.Z.) 2:17:19

1964, Tokyo, 42,195 meters
1. Abebe Bikila (Eth.) 2:12:12 WR
2. Basil Heatley (U.K.) 2:16:20
3. Kokichi Tsuburaya (Japan) 2:16:23

1968, Mexico City, 42,195 meters
1. Mamo Wolde (Eth.) 2:20:27
2. Kenji Kimihara (Japan) 2:23:31
3. Mike Ryan (N.Z.) 2:23:45

1972, Munich, 42,195 meters
1. Frank Shorter (U.S.) 2:12:20
2. Karel Lismont (Belg.) 2:14:32
3. Mamo Wolde (Eth.) 2:15:09

1976, Montreal, 42,195 meters
1. Waldemar Cierpinski (E. Ger.) 2:09:55 OR
2. Frank Shorter (U.S.) 2:10:46
3. Karel Lismont (Belg.) 2:11:13

1980, Moscow, 42,195 meters
1. Waldemar Cierpinski (E. Ger.) 2:11:03
2. Gerard Nijboer (Hol.) 2:11:20
3. Setymkul Dzhumanazarov (U.S.S.R.) 2:11:35

BOSTON MARATHON CHAMPIONS

Men

*1897	John McDermott (U.S.)	2:55:10
1898	Ronald McDonald (U.S.)	2:42:00
1899	Lawrence Brignolia (U.S.)	2:54:38
1900	James Caffrey (Can.)	2:39:44
1901	James Caffrey (Can.)	2:24:23
1902	Samuel Mellor (U.S.)	2:43:12
1903	John Lorden (U.S.)	2:41:29
1904	Michael Spring (U.S.)	2:38:04
1905	Fred Lorz (U.S.)	2:38:25
1906	Timothy Ford (U.S.)	2:45:45
1907	Tom Longboat (Can.)	2:24:24
1908	Thomas Morrissey (U.S.)	2:25:43
1909	Henri Renaud (U.S.)	2:53:36
1910	Fred Cameron (Can.)	2:28:52
1911	Clarence DeMar (U.S.)	2:21:39
1912	Mike Ryan (U.S.)	2:21:18
1913	Fritz Carlson (U.S.)	2:25:14
1914	James Duffy (Can.)	2:25:01
1915	Edouard Fabre (Can.)	2:31:41

1916	Arthur Roth (U.S.)	2:27:16
1917	Bill Kennedy (U.S.)	2:28:37
1918	Cancelled because of World War I	
1919	Carl Linder (U.S.)	2:29:13
1920	Peter Trivoulidas (Gr.)	2:29:31
1921	Frank Zuna (U.S.)	2:18:57
1922	Clarence DeMar (U.S.)	2:18:10
1923	Clarence DeMar (U.S.)	2:23:37
†1924	Clarence DeMar (U.S.)	2:29:40
1925	Charles Mellor (U.S.)	2:33:00
1926	John Miles (Can.)	2:25:40
‡1927	Clarence DeMar (U.S.)	2:40:22
1928	Clarence DeMar (U.S.)	2:37:07
1929	John Miles (Can.)	2:33:08
1930	Clarence DeMar (U.S.)	2:34:48
1931	James Henigan (U.S.)	2:46:45
1932	Paul deBruyn (Ger.)	2:33:36
1933	Leslie Pawson (U.S.)	2:31:01
1934	Dave Komonen (Can.)	2:32:53
1935	John A. Kelley (U.S.)	2:32:07
1936	Ellison Brown (U.S.)	2:33:40
1937	Walter Young (Can.)	2:33:20
1938	Leslie Pawson (U.S.)	2:35:34
1939	Ellison Brown (U.S.)	2:28:51
1940	Gerard Coté (Can.)	2:28:28
1941	Leslie Pawson (U.S.)	2:30:38
1942	Bernard Smith (U.S.)	2:26:51
1943	Gerard Coté (Can.)	2:28:25
1944	Gerard Coté (Can.)	2:31:50
1945	John A. Kelley (U.S.)	2:30:40
1946	Sylianos Kyriakides (Gr.)	2:29:27
1947	Yun Bok Suh (Korea)	2:25:39
1948	Gerard Coté (Can.)	2:31:02
1949	Karl Leandersson (Swed.)	2:31:50
1950	Kee Yong Ham (Korea)	2:27:45
1951	Shigeki Tanaka (Japan)	2:27:45
1952	Doroteo Flores (Guat.)	2:31:53
1953	Keizo Yamada (Japan)	2:18:51
1954	Veikko Karvonen (Fin.)	2:20:39
1955	Hideo Hamamura (Japan)	2:18:22
1956	Antti Viskari (Fin.)	2:22:42
1957	John A. Kelley (U.S.)	2:20:05

1958	Franjo Mihalic (Yugo.)	2:25:54
1959	Eino Oksanen (Fin.)	2:22:42
1960	Paavo Kotila (Fin.)	2:20:54
1961	Eino Oksanen (Fin.)	2:20:54
1962	Eino Oksanen (Fin.)	2:23:48
1963	Aurele Vandendriessche (Belg.)	2:18:58
1964	Aurele Vandendriessche (Belg.)	2:19:59
1965	Morio Shigematsu (Japan)	2:16:33
1966	Kenji Kimihara (Japan)	2:17:11
1967	David McKenzie (N.Z.)	2:15:45
1968	Ambrose Burfoot (U.S.)	2:22:17
1969	Yoshiaki Unetani (Japan)	2:13:49
1970	Ron Hill (U.K.)	2:10:30
1971	Alvaro Mejia (Col.)	2:18:45
1972	Olavi Suomalainen (Fin.)	2:15:39
1973	Jon Anderson (U.S.)	2:16:03
1974	Neil Cusack (Ire.)	2:13:49
1975	Bill Rodgers (U.S.)	2:09:55
1976	Jack Fultz (U.S.)	2:20:19
1977	Jerome Drayton (Can.)	2:14:46
1978	Bill Rodgers (U.S.)	2:10:13
1979	Bill Rodgers (U.S.)	2:09:27
1980	Bill Rodgers (U.S.)	2:12:11

*1897–1923 distance: 24.5 miles.
†1924–1926 distance: 26 miles 209 yards.
‡1927–present distance: 26 miles 385 yards.

Women

1972	Nina Kuscsik (U.S.)	3:10:26
1973	Jacqueline Hansen (U.S.)	3:05:59
1974	Miki Gorman (U.S.)	2:47:11
1975	Liane Winter (W. Ger.)	2:42:24
1976	Kim Merritt (U.S.)	2:47:10
1977	Miki Gorman (U.S.)	2:48:33
1978	Gayle Barron (U.S.)	2:44:52
1979	Joan Benoit (U.S.)	2:35:15
1980	Jacqueline Gareau (Can.)	2:34:28

NEW YORK CITY MARATHON CHAMPIONS

Men

1970	Gary Muhrcke (U.S.)	2:31:39
1971	Norm Higgins (U.S.)	2:22:55
1972	Sheldon Karlin (U.S.)	2:27:53
1973	Tom Fleming (U.S.)	2:21:55
1974	Norbert Sander (U.S.)	2:26:31
1975	Tom Fleming (U.S.)	2:19:27
1976	Bill Rodgers (U.S.)	2:10:10
1977	Bill Rodgers (U.S.)	2:11:29
1978	Bill Rodgers (U.S.)	2:12:12
1979	Bill Rodgers (U.S.)	2:11:42
1980	Alberto Salazar (U.S.)	2:09:41

Women

1971	Beth Bonner (U.S.)	2:55:22
1972	Nina Kuscsik (U.S.)	3:18:42
1973	Nina Kuscsik (U.S.)	2:57:08
1974	Kathrine Switzer (U.S.)	3:07:29
1975	Kim Merritt (U.S.)	2:46:15

1976	Miki Gorman (U.S.)	2:39:11
1977	Miki Gorman (U.S.)	2:43:10
1978	Grete Waitz (Nor.)	2:32:30
1979	Grete Waitz (Nor.)	2:27:33
1980	Grete Waitz (Nor.)	2:25:42

ALL-TIME
50 BEST PERFORMANCES,
AS OF NOVEMBER 1, 1980

Men

1.	Derek Clayton (Aust.)	2:08:34*	1969
2.	Gerard Nijboer (Hol.)	2:09:01	1980
3.	Shigeru Sou (Japan)	2:09:06	1978
4.	Ian Thompson (U.K.)	2:09:12	1974
5.	Bill Rodgers (U.S.)	2:09:27	1979
6.	Ron Hill (U.K.)	2:09:28	1970
7.	Derek Clayton (Aust.)	2:09:37	1967
8.	Alberto Salazar (U.S.)	2:09:41	1980
9.	Bill Rodgers (U.S.)	2:09:55	1975
10.	Waldemar Cierpinski (E. Ger.)	2:09:55	1976
11.	Mark Smet (Belg.)	2:10:00	1979
12.	Jerome Drayton (Can.)	2:10:09	1975
13.	Bill Rodgers (U.S.)	2:10:10	1976
14.	Toshihiko Seko (Japan)	2:10:12	1979
15.	Bill Rodgers (U.S.)	2:10:13	1978
16.	Rodolfo Gomez (Mex.)	2:10:14	1980
17.	Jeff Wells (U.S.)	2:10:15	1978
18.	Tony Sandoval (U.S.)	2:10:19	1980
19.	David Chettle (Aust.)	2:10:20	1975
20.	Jeff Wells (U.S.)	2:10:20	1979

21. Tony Sandoval (U.S.)	2:10:20	1979
22. Garry Bjorklund (U.S.)	2:10:20	1980
23. Toshihiko Seko (Japan)	2:10:21	1978
24. Ron Hill (U.K.)	2:10:30	1970
25. Frank Shorter (U.S.)	2:10:30	1972
26. Toshihiko Seko (Japan)	2:10:35	1979
27. Shigeru Sou (Japan)	2:10:37	1979
28. Akio Usami (Japan)	2:10:38	1970
29. Takeshi Sou (Japan)	2:10:40	1979
30. Benji Durden (U.S.)	2:10:41	1980
31. Frank Shorter (U.S.)	2:10:46	1976
32. Dick Quax (N.Z.)	2:10:47	1980
33. William Adcocks (U.K.)	2:10:48	1968
34. Bernie Ford (U.K.)	2:10:51	1979
35. Chun Son Goe (N. Korea)	2:10:52	1980
36. Vladimir Kotov (USSR)	2:10:52	1980
37. John Lodwick (U.S.)	2:10:54	1979
38. Kyle Heffner (U.S.)	2:10:55	1980
39. Bill Rodgers (U.S.)	2:10:56	1977
40. Bob Hodge (U.S.)	2:10:59	1980
41. Ron Tabb (U.S.)	2:11:00	1980
42. Waldemar Cierpinski (E. Ger.)	2:11:03	1980
43. Hideki Kita (Japan)	2:11:05	1978
44. William Adcocks (U.K.)	2:11:08	1969
45. Derek Clayton (Aust.)	2:11:09	1971
46. Dave Smith (U.S.)	2:11:09	1980
47. Eamon O'Reilly (U.S.)	2:11:12	1970
48. John Farrington (Aust.)	2:11:13	1973
49. Karel Lismont (Belg.)	2:11:13	1976
50. Jerome Drayton (Can.)	2:11:13	1969

*Where performances were clocked in tenths of a second, such as Clayton's 2:08:33.6, they have been rounded "up" to the next highest second in accordance with current international rules.

Women

1. Grete Waitz (Nor.)	2:25:42	1980
2. Grete Waitz (Nor.)	2:27:33	1979
3. Patti Lyons-Catalano (U.S.)	2:29:34	1980
4. Patti Lyons-Catalano (U.S.)	2:30:57	1980
5. Joan Benoit (U.S.)	2:31:23	1980
6. Lorraine Moller (N.Z.)	2:31:40	1980
7. Jacqueline Gareau (Can.)	2:31:41	1980
8. Marja Wokke (Hol.)	2:32:29	1980

9.	Grete Waitz (Nor.)	2:32:30	1978
10.	Joyce Smith (U.K.)	2:33:32	1980
11.	Ingrid Christensen (Nor.)	2:34:25	1980
12.	Jacqueline Gareau (Can.)	2:34:26	1980
13.	Allison Roe (N.Z.)	2:34:29	1980
14.	Christa Vahlensieck (W. Ger.)	2:34:48	1977
15.	Carol Gould (U.K.)	2:35:06	1980
16.	Patti Lyons (U.S.)	2:35:08	1980
17.	Lorraine Moller (N.Z.)	2:35:11	1980
18.	Gayle Olinek (Can.)	2:35:12	1980
19.	Joan Benoit (U.S.)	2:35:15	1979
20.	Chantal Langlace (Fr.)	2:35:16	1977
21.	Joan Benoit (U.S.)	2:35:41	1979
22.	Vreni Forster (Swit.)	2:35:57	1980
23.	Nancy Conz (U.S.)	2:36:02	1980
24.	Gayle Olinek (Can.)	2:36:12	1979
25.	Julie Brown (U.S.)	2:36:24	1978
26.	Joyce Smith (U.K.)	2:36:27	1979
27.	Christa Vahlensieck (W. Ger.)	2:36:47	1980
28.	Lorraine Moller (N.Z.)	2:37:36	1979
29.	Linda Staudt (Can.)	2:37:39	1980
30.	Joyce Smith (U.K.)	2:37:48	1979
31.	Gillian Adams (U.K.)	2:37:56	1980
32.	Kim Merritt (U.S.)	2:37:57	1977
33.	Charlotte Teske (W. Ger.)	2:38:04	1980
34.	Manuela Angenvoorth (W. Ger.)	2:38:10	1977
35.	Laurie Binder (U.S.)	2:38:10	1980
36.	Jacqueline Hansen (U.S.)	2:38:19	1975
37.	Patti Lyons (U.S.)	2:38:22	1979
38.	Christa Vahlensieck (W. Ger.)	2:38:33	1978
39.	Gillian Adams (U.K.)	2:38:33	1979
40.	Lorraine Moller (N.Z.)	2:38:35	1980
41.	Joan Benoit (U.S.)	2:38:42	1980
42.	Ingrid Christiansen (Nor.)	2:38:45	1980
43.	Sue Krenn (U.S.)	2:38:50	1979
44.	Vreni Forster (Swit.)	2:38:58	1980
45.	Jacqueline Gareau (Can.)	2:39:06	1979
46.	Miki Gorman (U.S.)	2:39:11	1976
47.	Gillian Adams (U.K.)	2:39:17	1980
48.	Laurie Binder (U.S.)	2:39:22	1980
49.	Gillian Adams (U.K.)	2:39:28	1979
50.	Sissel Grottenberg (Nor.)	2:39:37	1979

PROGRESSION OF THE WORLD RECORD, AS OF NOVEMBER 1, 1980

Men

Johnny Hayes (U.S.)	Shepherd's Bush, N.Y.	7/24/08	2:55:19
Robert Fowler (U.S.)	Yonkers, N.Y.	1/1/09	2:52:46
James Clark (U.S.)	New York, N.Y.	2/12/09	2:46:53
Albert Raines (U.S.)	New York, N.Y.	5/8/09	2:46:05
Frederick Barrett (U.K.)	Shepherd's Bush, N.Y.	5/26/09	2:42:31
Harry Green (U.K.)	Shepherd's Bush, N.Y.	5/12/13	2:38:17
Alexis Ahlgren (Swed.)	Shepherd's Bush, N.Y.	5/31/13	2:36:07
Hannes Kohlehmainen (Fin.)	Antwerp, Belg.	8/22/20	2:32:36
Al "Whitey" Michelson (U.S.)	Port Chester, N.Y.	10/12/25	2:29:02
Fusashige Suzuki (Japan)	Tokyo, Japan	3/31/35	2:27:49

Yasuo Ikenaka (Japan)	Tokyo, Japan	4/3/35	2:26:44
Kieti Son (Japan)	Tokyo, Japan	11/3/35	2:26:42
Yun Bok Suh (Korea)	Boston, Mass.	4/19/47	2:25:39
Jim Peters (U.K.)	Chiswick, Eng.	6/14/52	2:20:43
Jim Peters (U.K.)	Chiswick, Eng.	6/13/53	2:18:41
Jim Peters (U.K.)	Turku, Fin.	10/4/53	2:18:35
Jim Peters (U.K.)	Chiswick, Eng.	6/26/54	2:17:40
Sergey Popov (USSR)	Stockholm, Swed.	8/24/58	2:15:17
Abebe Bikila (Eth.)	Rome, Italy	9/10/60	2:15:17
Toru Terasawa (Japan)	Beppu, Japan	2/17/63	2:15:16
Leonard "Buddy" Edelen (U.S.)	Chiswick, Eng.	6/15/63	2:14:28
Basil Heatley (U.K.)	Chiswick, Eng.	6/13/64	2:13:55
Abebe Bikila (Eth.)	Tokyo, Japan	10/21/64	2:12:12
Mario Chigematsu (Japan)	Chiswick, Eng.	6/12/65	2:12:00
Derek Clayton (Aust.)	Fukuoka, Japan	12/3/67	2:09:37
Derek Clayton (Aust.)	Antwerp, Belg.	5/30/69	2:08:34

Women

Dale Greig (U.K.)	Ryde, Eng.	5/23/64	3:27:45
Mildred Simpson (N.Z.)	Auckland, N.Z.	7/21/64	3:19:33
Maureen Wilton (Can.)	Toronto, Can.	5/6/67	3:15:22
Anni Pede-Erdkamp (W. Ger.)	Waldniel, W. Ger.	9/16/67	3:07:26
Caroline Walker (U.S.)	Seaside, Ore.	2/28/70	3:02:53
Elizabeth Bonner (U.S.)	Philadelphia, Pa.	5/9/71	3:01:42
Andrienne Beames (Aust.)	Werribee, Aust.	8/31/71	2:46:30
Chantal Langlace (Fr.)	Neuf Brisach, Fr.	10/27/74	2:46:24
Jacqueline Hansen (U.S.)	Culver City, Cal.	12/1/74	2:43:55
Liane Winter (W. Ger.)	Boston, Mass.	4/21/75	2:42:24
Christa Vahlensieck (W. Ger.)	Dulmen, W. Ger.	5/3/75	2:40:16
Jacqueline Hansen (U.S.)	Eugene, Ore.	10/12/75	2:38:19
Chantal Langlace (Fr.)	San Sebastian, Sp.	5/1/77	2:35:16
Christa Vahlensieck (W. Ger.)	West Britain, W. Ger.	9/10/77	2:34:48
Grete Waitz (Nor.)	New York, N.Y.	10/22/78	2:32:30
Grete Waitz (Nor.)	New York, N.Y.	10/21/79	2:27:33
Grete Waitz (Nor.)	New York, N.Y.	10/26/80	2:25:42

THE GREATEST MARATHONERS OF ALL TIME

Men

1. *Abebe Bikila   Ethiopia*

Olympic Marathon champion in 1960 and 1964, both in world record time. Also triumphed in Kosice, Czechoslovakia, and Mainichi, Japan (twice), and Marathon-to-Athens events. Fifth at Boston Marathon in '63. Paralyzed from the waist down in a car accident in 1969 and died four years later after suffering a stroke.

2. *Clarence DeMar   United States*

A 7-time winner of the Boston Marathon. (No one else has won it more than 4 times.) First Boston victory in 1911; last in 1930 at age 41, making him the oldest Boston champion ever. Ran Boston 33 times in a 43-year span. Died in 1958 at age 70.

3. *Frank Shorter   United States*

Olympic champion in 1972 and runner-up in 1976. Won the Fukuoka Marathon in Japan 4 times in a row. Excelled at many other distances. Pan-Am Games victor in '71.

4. *Waldemar Cierpinski   East Germany*

Defeated Frank Shorter at the '76 Olympics with an Olympic record of 2:09:55, and repeated as Olympic champion in 1980, winning in 2:11:03. Only the second man, after Bikila, to win successive Olympic Marathon titles.

5. *Emil Zatopek*   *Czechoslovakia*
Ran only 2 marathons. In 1952, in one of the most remarkable ever, he ran his first—the Olympic Marathon. And he won it with ease, after winning the 5,000 and 10,000 in the same Olympics. Sixth in the '56 Olympic Marathon near the end of a brilliant career.

6. *Ron Hill*   *Great Britain*
European champion in 1969; second at Fukuoka that year. In '70 he won Boston (2:10:30) and Commonwealth Games (2:09:28) titles with very fast times, the latter still the sixth fastest ever. A 2-time British champion. Sixth in the '72 Olympic Marathon. Has run more sub-2:20 times (27) than anyone.

7. *Bill Rodgers*   *United States*
Has won New York City Marathon 4 times and Boston 4 times. U.S. record-holder at 2:09:27. Won Fukuoka in '77. Has run sub-2:11 marathon 5 times. Only fortieth in '76 Olympics. Lost a great chance for an Olympic medal in 1980 because of the U.S. boycott.

8. *Derek Clayton*   *Australia*
First man to run under 2:10—indeed under 2:12—winning the '67 Fukuoka with his record-breaking 2:09:37. On May 30, 1969, he ran 2:08:34 (on an Antwerp course which some say was short but has never been proven so), still the world record. Seventh in the '68 Olympics and only thirteenth in '72.

9. *Jim Peters*   *Great Britain*
First man to run under 2:20 with a 2:18:41 in '53. From '52 to '54, he broke the world record 4 times. A 4-time British champion. Suffered painful defeats in '52 Olympics and '54 Commonwealth Games.

10. *John A. Kelley*   *United States*
Will run his fiftieth Boston Marathon at age 73 in 1981. Won Boston in '35 and '45. Competed in Olympic marathons of '36 and '48. The Grand Old Man of the marathon.

Women

1. *Grete Waitz*   *Norway*
Has run 3 marathons—New York City in 1978, '79, and '80—and each time smashed the world record, finishing in 2:32:30, 2:27:33, and 2:25:42, respectively. Excels at many other distances.

2. *Joan Benoit*   *United States*
Has run 4 marathons, and won 3 of them. Second at Bermuda in her debut early in '79, she followed with a U.S. record win at Boston that year, a near-record win at Nike-OTC that fall, and in February

1980 lowered her U.S. mark to 2:31:23 on a hot day in Auckland, N.Z.

3. *Christa Vahlensieck   West Germany*
Broke the world record twice, the second time in '77 with a 2:34:48 that stood till the Waitz assault. In a 2-year span, from fall '75 to fall '77, she had 6 victories in the 2:40s plus her second record.

4. *Kim Merritt   United States*
The only runner to have won the New York (in '75), Boston ('76), and Honolulu ('76) marathons. Also won Nike-OTC (in her PR of 2:37:57) and was second in New York in '77, second at the Avon International in '76 and '79.

5. *Miki Gorman   United States*
Won New York in '76 (2:39:11) and '77 and Boston in '77 (2:48:33). Had other major titles and several marks in the 2:40s.

6. *Patti Lyons-Catalano   United States*
First American woman to break the 2:30 barrier, in New York '80 (2:29:34). Second at Boston in '79 (2:38:22) and '80 (2:35:08). Won Honolulu Marathon title in '78 and '79, and Montreal Marathon in '80.

BIBLIOGRAPHY

Acheyer, William J. "Tab Before, Water During, Beer Later." *Running*, Winter 1979, pp. 31–34.

Andrews, Valerie. "Women Marathoners Locked Out." *The Runner*, August 1979, pp. 46–51.

Astrand, Per-Olaf, and Rodahl, Kaare. *Textbook of Work Physiology*. New York: McGraw-Hill, 1970.

Bassler, Thomas J. "Marathon Running and Immunity to Heart Disease." *The Physician & Sportsmedicine*, April 1975, pp. 77–80.

Benyo, Richard. "Derek Clayton, the World's Fastest Marathoner." *Runner's World*, May 1979, pp. 66–73.

Black, Jonathan. "The Private Obsession of Ted Corbitt." *The Runner*, December 1978, pp. 27–33.

Bloom, Marc. "Africans' Cup Runneth Over." *The Runner*, November 1979, pp. 74–79.

———. "Boston Marathon 1979." *The Runner*, July 1979, p. 26.

———. "Boston's OTB: Rodgers 7–5, Benoit 8–1." *The Runner*, July 1979, p. 51.

———. *Cross Country Running*. Mountain View, Calif.: World Publications, 1978.

———. "Faster Than a Speeding Bullet." *The Runner*, February 1979, p. 10.

————. "The Glory That Was New York." *The Runner*, January 1980, pp. 22–23.

————. "Hats Off to Rodgers." *The Runner*, July 1979, pp. 30–34.

————. "Making Runners Better." *The Runner*, April 1980, p. 64.

————. "The Marathon." *The Runner*, January 1980, p. 21.

————. "Reflections on a Marathon." *The New York Times*, April 15, 1979, "View of Sports" section, p. 2.

Bruck, Connie. "Caution: Children at Play." *The Runner*, July 1979, pp. 60–67.

————. "The Man Behind the Marathon." *The Runner*, January 1979, pp. 50–51.

Chodes, John. *Corbitt*. Los Altos, Calif.: Tafnews Press, 1974.

Conniff, James C. G. "Heat: The Runner's Worst Enemy." *The Runner*, June 1979, p. 71.

Costill, David L. *A Scientific Approach to Distance Running*. Los Altos, Calif.: Tafnews Press, 1979.

Crossen, David. "Marathon's Benefit to Heart Is Debated." *The New York Times*, Oct. 16, 1979, Section 3, p. 1.

Daniels, Jack; Fitts, Robert; and Sheehan, George. *Conditioning for Distance Running: The Scientific Aspects*. New York: John Wiley & Sons, 1978.

Dayton, O. William; Jokl, Peter; and Mangi, Richard. *The Runner's Complete Medical Guide*. New York: Summit Books, 1979.

Deford, Frank. "In the Long Run, It's Shorter." *Sports Illustrated*, May 24, 1976, pp. 76–78.

Falls, Joe. *The Boston Marathon*. New York: Collier, 1977.

Fixx, James F. *The Complete Book of Running*. New York: Random House, 1977.

————. "On the Run in Search of a Greek Ghost." *Sports Illustrated*, Dec. 25, 1978, pp. 60–66.

————. "What Running Can't Do for You." *Newsweek*, December 18, 1978, p. 21.

Fleischer, Lenore. *Running*. New York: Jove, 1979.

Gardiner, Norman E. *Athletics of the Ancient World*. London: Oxford University Press, 1930.

Geselman, Claire. "Should You Try It?" *Running*, Fall 1978.

Gibb, Roberta. "The First Woman to Run Boston." *Runner's World*, June 1978, p. 42.

Giguere, Paul. "Boston Marathon—Beating the Heat with Common Sense and Hot Water." *The Physician & Sportsmedicine*, June 1976, pp. 31–32.

Glasser, William. *Positive Addiction*. New York: Harper & Row, 1976.

Goldberg, Leslie. "Grete Waitz: Northern Lightning." *The Runner*, April 1979, pp. 44–51.

Gynn, Roger. "Shorter Away Early to Clear Win." *Track & Field News*, September 1972, pp. 38–39.

Harris, Dorothy V. *Involvement in Sport: A Somatopsychic Rationale for Physical Activity*. Philadelphia: Lea & Febiger, 1973.

Harris, H. A. *Greek Athletes and Athletics*. London: Hutchinson, 1964.

Henderson, Joe, ed. *The Boston Marathon*. Mountain View, Calif.: World Publications, 1978.

———. *The Complete Marathoner*. Mountain View, Calif.: World Publications, 1978.

———. "He Made Marathons Look Easy." *Runner's World*, December 1973, p. 32.

———. "The Making of a Marathoner." *New York City Marathon Program*, 1977, pp. 80–85.

———. *Marathon Handbook*. Mountain View, Calif.: World Publications, 1973.

———. "Third Gold for Ethiopia." *Track & Field News*, Oct./Nov. 1968, pp. 18–19.

Hersh, Bob. "The Experts Pick the Marathoners." *The Runner*, August 1979, pp. 66–67.

Higdon, Hal. *Fitness After Forty*. Mountain View, Calif.: World Publications, 1977.

———. "The Runner's Marathon Training Guide." *The Runner*, January 1980, pp. 85–92.

Hill, Garry et al. "Moseyev in an Upset." *Track & Field News*, January 1979, p. 35.

Hirsch, George. "See Frank Run, See Bill Run." *New York City Marathon Program*, 1977, pp. 26–37.

———. "The Inside Track." *The Runner*, July 1979, p. 4.

———. "The Inside Track." *The Runner*, January 1980, p. 4.

Hopkins, John. *The Marathon*. London: Stanley Paul, 1966.

Huizinga, Johan. *Homo Ludens: A Study of the Play Element in Culture*. Boston: Beacon Press, 1950.

Jerome, John. "Frank Shorter, the Man Who Invented Running." *Outside*, April 1978, pp. 33–37.

Kaplan, Janice. *Women and Sports*. New York: Viking Press, 1979.

Kleinfield, Sonny. "The Good Foot Doctor." *The Runner*, September 1979, pp. 72–77.

Kozik, Frantisek. *Zatopek the Marathon Victor*. Prague: Artia, 1954.

Lucus, John A. "A History of the Marathon Race, 490 B.C.–1975." *Journal of Sport History*, Summer 1976, pp. 120–27.

McCarthy, Colman. "The Full Distance." *The New Yorker*, May 29, 1978, pp. 94–101.

――――. "Run for the Money," *The Runner*, August 1979, p. 106.

Martin, David E., and Gynn, Roger W. H. *The Marathon Footrace: Performers and Performances.* Springfield, Ill.: Charles C. Thomas, 1979.

Melzack, Ronald. *The Puzzle of Pain.* New York: Basic Books, 1973.

Merrill, Sam. "Diary of an Obsession." *New York City Marathon Program*, 1977, pp. 50–57.

――――. "Ruiz: Anatomy of a Fraud." *The Runner*, July 1980, pp. 34–39.

――――. "Three-hour Fever: The Nemesis." *The Runner*, January 1979, pp. 92–93.

Milvy, Paul, ed. *The Marathon: Physiological, Medical, Epidemiological and Psychological Studies.* New York: Annals of the New York Academy of Sciences, 1977.

Mirkin, Gabe, and Hoffman, Marshall. *The Sportsmedicine Book.* Boston: Little, Brown, 1978.

Moore, Kenny. "A Gentle Radical Who Runs Scared." *Sports Illustrated*, October 24, 1977, pp. 32–37.

――――. "Taking Part: You Ain't Seen Nothin' Yet." *Sports Illustrated*, January 1, 1979, pp. 38–40.

――――. "Watching Their Steps." *Sports Illustrated*, May 3, 1976, pp. 80–90.

Morgan, William P. "The Mind of the Marathoner." *Psychology Today*, April 1978, pp. 38–49.

――――. "Running into Addiction." *The Runner*, March 1979, pp. 73–76.

Murphy, Michael, and White, Rhea. *The Psychic Side of Sports.* Reading, Mass.: Addison-Wesley, 1978.

Nason, Jerry. "King of Heartbreak Hill." *The Runner*, May 1979, pp. 64–69.

Nelson, Bert, et al., eds. *Olympic Track & Field.* Los Altos, Calif.: Tafnews Press, 1980.

Nelson, Cordner. "Bikila by Fantastic 4:07." *Track & Field News*, October 1964, p. 36.

Nelson, Ralph A. "What Should Athletes Eat? Unmixing Folly and Fact." *The Physician & Sportsmedicine*, November 1975, pp. 67–72.

Olsen, Eric. "Frank Shorter's Comeback: Still a Question." *The Runner*, August 1979, pp. 38–45.

――――. "A Handy Man to Have Around." *The Runner*, April 1980, pp. 59–67.

Osmun, Mark. *The Honolulu Marathon.* New York: Lippincott, 1979.

———. "Inner Vision." *The Runner*, November 1978, pp. 30–35.

———. "Keeping Cool in Hawaii." *The Runner*, April 1979, pp. 52–64.

Parker, John. *The Frank Shorter Story*. Mountain View, Calif.: World Publications, 1972.

Peters, J. H., with Edmundson, Joseph. *In the Long Run*. London: Cassell & Co., 1955.

Price, Jay. "Behr on Olympic Timetable." Staten Island *Advance*, October 20, 1977, p. 29.

Quercetani, Roberto. *A World History of Track and Field Athletics, 1864–1964*. London: Oxford University Press, 1964.

Range, Peter Ross. "Bill Rodgers." *Boston Magazine*, April 1979, pp. 53–72.

———. "Going for the Gold." *Playboy*, May 1980, pp. 106–08, 114, 177–79.

Robinson, Malcolm, and Thaler, Paul. "The Runner's 1980 Marathon Calendar." *The Runner*, January 1980, pp. 97–117.

Rodgers, Bill. "Give Me an Inch and I'll Take a Mile." *The Runner*, July 1979, pp. 28–29.

———, with Concannon, Joe. *Marathoning*. New York: Simon & Schuster, 1980.

———. "Road Racing Strategy." *The Runner*, May 1979, p. 15.

———. "Visiting the President." *The Runner*, August 1979, p. 12.

Segal, Erich. "Oh, Pheidippides." *New York City Marathon Program*, 1977, pp. 87–89.

Shainberg, Lawrence. "The Obsessiveness of the Long-Distance Runner." *The New York Times Magazine*, February 25, 1973, pp. 28–34.

Sheehan, George. *Running & Being*. New York: Simon & Schuster, 1978.

Shorter, Frank, with John Parker. "Olympic Forum." *Runner's World*, November 1972, p. 12.

Smith, Lafayette. "2 Africans Whip Field." *Track & Field News*, September 1960, p. 12.

Steffny, Manfred. *Marathoning*. Mountain View, Calif.: World Publications, 1979.

Sullivan, James E., ed. *Marathon Running*. New York: American Sports Publishing, 1909.

Temple, Cliff. "Cierpinski Pulls Big Shock." *Track & Field News*, September 1976, pp. 25–26.

———. "The Women's Showcase at Avon." *The Runner*, December 1979, pp. 76–80.

Virgin, Craig. "Olympic Signals from Fukuoka." *The Runner*, February 1980, pp. 44–45, 49.

Wacaser, Steve. "Quite a Display by the U.S. Trio." *Track & Field News*, September 1972, p. 39.

Webster, F. A. M. *Athletics of To-day: History, Development and Training*. London and New York: Frederick Warne, 1929.

———. *Great Moments in Athletics*. London: Country Life, 1947.

Weiss, Paul. *Sport: A Philosophic Inquiry*. Carbondale and Edwardsville, Ill.: Southern Illinois University Press, 1969.

INDEX

Dangers of running, 31–32
  children and, 32
  compulsiveness, 31–32
  heat, 32
  menstrual changes, 32
  older runners, 32
Daniels, Jack, 105
Darius, 14
Davis, Bernie, 180, 181
Davis, Eric, 177–86
Davis, Gordon, 157
Davis, Helen, 185
Daws, Ron, 35
"Daydreams of a Night Jogger," 12
Dayton, O. William, 116
Decker, Mary, 115
Deford, Frank, 223
DeMar, Clarence, 17, 125, 127, 130–
  33, 139, 232
"Diary of an Obsession" (Merrill),
  54
Diet, principles of, 31, 90–92
  beer, 31
  carbohydrate-loading, 31, 90–92
  complex carbohydrates, 31
  vitamins, 31
Double workouts, 25
Douglas, Michael, 4, 7
Drayton, Jerome, 236
Durden, Benji, 146

Epstein, Eddie, 188, 189, 193
Epstein, Irving, 186–95
Epstein, Marion, 186–95
ERG (electrolyte replacement drink),
  17
Eucles (Athenian runner), 15

Falls, Joe, 134
"False positives," 44
Fink, Bill, 40
Fitness, principles of, 21–23
  age and, 22–23
  benefits of, 22
  extra running, 21–22
  maximal oxygen uptake and, 22

smoking and, 22
weight and, 22
Fitness After Forty (Higdon), 193
Fitts, Robert, 106
Fitzpatrick, Tom, 180
Fixx, James, 6, 7, 13–14, 15, 16–17,
  154, 221
Fleming, Diane, 236
Fleming, Tom, 150, 153, 236
Floto, Steve, 146–47
Fluid replacement, 30, 104, 106
Ford, Bernie, 104
Forde, Lorna, 115
Foster, Ray, 182
Frederick, Larry, 149–50
Fukuoka Marathon, 104
Fultz, Jack, 235

Galloway, Jeff, 41
Gardiner, Norman E., 14
Gareau, Jacqueline, 137, 153
Geigengack, Bob, 223–24, 230
Gesalman, Claire, 87
Gibb, Roberta Louise, 136, 201, 204
Glasser, Dr. William, 52
Goals, 27–28
Goldberg, Leslie, 247
Goldstein, Dr. Seymour Mac, 102,
  110–11, 113, 114–16
Goodall, Ellison, 115
Gorman, Miki, 137, 154, 214
Gould, Carol, 217
Gould, Dr. Warren R., 105
Grand Valley Marathon, 10
Greek Athletics and Athletes (Harris), 15
Grieve, Bob, 202
Guinness Book of World Records, 105, 116

Hall, Art, 150
Hall, Bob, 9
Handicapped runners, 9–11
Hansen, Jacquelyn, 137, 184
Haro, Mariano, 233
Harris, Dorothy V., 60
Harris, H. A., 15
Harris, Louis, and Associates, 8–9

ABOUT THE AUTHOR

Before joining *The Runner* at its inception three years ago, Marc Bloom was editor of *The Harrier*, a magazine on cross-country running. He is the author of *Cross Country Running* and has written numerous articles about running, mostly for *The New York Times*. He lives with his wife and two daughters, age 8 and 2, in New York City. A runner since 1972, he has competed in about 100 races, including 5 marathons.